THE GOSPEL ACCORDING TO

ST MATTHEW

T0382357

St Matthew

THE REVISED VERSION

EDITED WITH NOTES
FOR THE USE OF SCHOOLS

BY

ARTHUR CARR, M.A.

VICAR OF ADDINGTON, SURREY
FORMERLY FELLOW OF ORIEL COLLEGE, OXFORD

CAMBRIDGE
AT THE UNIVERSITY PRESS
1902

CAMBRIDGE
UNIVERSITY PRESS

University Printing House, Cambridge CB2 8BS, United Kingdom

Published in the United States of America by Cambridge University Press, New York

Cambridge University Press is part of the University of Cambridge.

It furthers the University's mission by disseminating knowledge in the pursuit of
education, learning and research at the highest international levels of excellence.

www.cambridge.org
Information on this title: www.cambridge.org/9781107647978

© Cambridge University Press 1902

First published 1902
First paperback edition 2014

A catalogue record for this publication is available from the British Library

ISBN 978-1-107-64797-8 Paperback

PREFACE BY THE GENERAL EDITOR FOR THE GOSPELS AND ACTS.

THE Revised Version has to some extent super-
seded the need of annotation on the Gospels
and Acts, so far as the meaning of words and phrases
is concerned. But the present Edition will, it is hoped,
serve a good purpose in drawing the attention of young
scholars to the importance of some of the changes
made in that Version.

Another aim is to present in a clear and intelligible
form the best and most approved results of recent
theological work on these books.

The General Editor takes this opportunity of noting
that, as in *The Cambridge Bible for Schools*, each writer
is responsible for the interpretation of particular passages, or for the opinion expressed on any point of
doctrine. His own part is that of careful supervision
and occasional suggestion.

ARTHUR CARR.

CONTENTS.

INTRODUCTION.

I. *The Origin of the Synoptic Gospels.*

THE Synoptic Gospels are related to one another in a way which is unique in literature. A considerable portion of subject matter is common to the three. In this common portion however the differences are as marked and interesting as the points of resemblance. Sometimes a single remarkable word forms a link of connexion in the midst of variety, sometimes the same incident is narrated with such differences of language and observed points that a separate source is unquestionable. Although no undisputed theory has been formed to account for these phenomena, some of the facts which must determine the solution may be stated. For some approach to a solution of the problem has been made in recent discussion.

In Acts ii. 42 we read that the disciples "continued stedfastly in the apostles' teaching." A great part of this teaching must have corresponded in substance to what we find in the Synoptic Gospels. We have examples of the form in which the Gospel was delivered in the addresses of St Peter (Acts ii. 22–36, x. 34–43) and of St Paul (Acts xiii. 16–39, xvii. 3), with which may be compared, as indicating the same acknowledged form, the summary of the Gospel, Rom. i. 3, 4; 1 Cor. xv. 3, 4, and warning against false Gospels founded on different models, 2 Cor. xi. 4; Gal. i. 6, 7 and 1 Tim. vi. 20. But the first and by

far the most important example of an oral Gospel is that
contained in Luke xxiv. 25–27 and 46–48 (comp. Matthew
xi. 4–6). Here Jesus Christ himself preaches the Gospel
of the Resurrection, confirmed by an appeal to prophetic
teaching, in words that have prescribed the form not only
of the Synoptic Gospels, but also of the oral Gospels preserved in the Acts.

From these examples it may be inferred that apostolical teaching in Jerusalem would from the first assume
a definite shape and become the model of catechetical
instruction elsewhere. In this apostolical cycle of instruction the great facts of the Nativity, the Passion, the
Death and Resurrection and Ascension of Jesus Christ
would find a place, and also those words and works
which were of special and typical importance. The first
disciples of the Apostles dispersed throughout the civilised
world would convey the form and substance of the apostolic
teaching to all the Churches.

At a very early date written Gospels would be published
for the instruction of catechumens (Luke i. 4 περὶ ὧν
κατηχήθης) and for use in the services of the Church (Matt.
xxiv. 15). Of these written Gospels the three Synoptics
are the preeminent surviving examples.

It is probable that St Mark's Gospel is nearest in form
and language to the original or catechumens' Gospel of
Jerusalem. For it is reasonable to suppose that the first
Gospel would be moulded on the discourses of St Peter:
(1) who took the lead in the first delivery of the Gospel
after Pentecost; (2) whose Gospel to the Gentiles (Acts
x. 34–43) is on the lines of St Mark's Gospel; (3) under
whose guidance, according to ancient tradition, St Mark
composed his Gospel.

It is held by an increasing number of scholars that
St Matthew and St Luke had this Gospel before them
when they wrote. But it is certain that they used other
sources of information both oral and written. And

St Matthew was of course an eye and ear witness of much that he records.

The first supposed trace of a Gospel according to St Matthew is to be found in the words of Papias quoted by Eusebius (*H. E.* III. 39). As Papias seems to have conversed with those who had seen the Lord, or at least with those who had known Apostles, his testimony is very important. He says: "So then Matthew composed the discourses (or 'oracles' or sayings, τὰ λόγια) in Hebrew, and every one interpreted them as he could." One question that arises out of these words is, whether by the *logia* or 'discourses' we are to understand the present Gospel according to St Matthew, or whether the *logia* are the discourses only, afterwards translated and imbedded in the Greek Gospel as we now have it. The best modern scholarship inclines to the latter opinion. If this is the correct view, the composition of St Matthew's Gospel may be traced as follows. In the first instance he would put on record the discourses of the Lord in accordance with the apostolic cycle of teaching in Jerusalem. At first the discourses would be published, as they were delivered, in the Aramaic vernacular or 'Hebrew' as it is termed in the New Testament. This would be the form or edition of the *logia* alluded to by Papias. Before long a demand would arise for a Greek version of the discourses. This version would be made either by St Matthew himself or by a scribe under the Apostle's guidance. The next step would be to add to the discourses a complete narrative of the work and life of Jesus and of His death and resurrection. In compiling this narrative it is clear that St Matthew availed himself of a document which was known also to St Mark and St Luke. In other words it is now generally agreed either that the three Synoptic Gospels had a common source or else that one of the three formed the common source for the others. The latter alternative accords best with the facts of the case, and it is thought probable that St Mark's Gospel furnished the common matter for the other two. The grounds on which this opinion rests could only be exhibited by a careful comparison between the parallel passages of the three Synoptic Gospels. Such a comparison would shew that whereas the whole of St Mark's narrative is appropriated either by St Matthew or St Luke, this could not be affirmed either of St Matthew or of St Luke in regard to the other two Gospels.

If this view be correct the sources of St Matthew's Gospel are traceable : (1) to the *logia* or discourses mentioned by Papias ; (2) to the narrative furnished by St Mark ; and (3) to the personal recollections of the Evangelist himself.

The existence of the Gospel according to St Matthew is attested by quotation or by references made to it from a very early date. Traces of this book are perhaps discernible in the Epistles of St Paul (1 Thess., 1 Cor., Romans) and of St James and in the Apocalypse. It is cited or referred to by Clement of Rome, c. 95 A.D. ; in the Didaché, placed by some c. 100 A.D. ; by Ignatius, c. 107–115 A.D.; by Polycarp, c. 110 A.D.; by Papias, c. 120 A.D., whose important testimony is noted above; by Basilides, c. 125 A.D., the first to apply the word εὐαγγέλια to the Gospels ; by Justin Martyr, c. 140 A.D.; and Tatian, his pupil, who composed a harmony of the four Canonical Gospels, the Diatessaron, c. 170 A.D. Irenæus, 185 A.D., gives important evidence (*Hær.* III. i. 1). "Matthew," he says, "published his Gospel writing among the Hebrews in their own language, while Peter and Paul were preaching the Gospel in Rome, and founding the Church." Origen c. 230 A.D. confirms the statement that St Matthew wrote his Gospel in the Hebrew or Aramaic tongue (Eus. *H. E.* VI. 25) and according to Eusebius (*H. E.* III. 24) he did so in order to leave to those whom he was quitting a recompense for his absence.

This original Aramaic or Hebrew Gospel of St Matthew
has perished, being as we have seen probably incorporated
in the Greek edition which we possess. Jerome indeed
c. 400 A.D. claims to have had in his hands a copy of the
original Aramaic Gospel of St Matthew. But if this
document is to be identified with 'the Gospel according
to the Hebrews' of which fragments have come down to
us, it was a work which widely differed from the Canonical
St Matthew.

II. *Life of St Matthew.*

Levi the son of Alphæus[1] was a tax-gatherer at
Capernaum. His special duty would be to collect tolls
from the fisheries on the Lake and perhaps from the
merchants travelling southward from Damascus. One
day Jesus coming up from the Lake side passed near the
custom-house where Levi was seated in Oriental fashion,
and He saith unto him, Follow me, and he arose and
followed Him (ch. ix. 9). That Jesus ever addressed
Levi before, we are not told ; but it is reasonable to
suppose that he was expecting the summons, that he was
already a disciple of Jesus, and prepared as soon as
Christ gave the word to leave all for His sake. At any
rate, Levi must have heard of the great Rabbi and of
His preaching, and have already resolved to adopt the
view of the kingdom of God which Jesus taught.

It is probable that Levi changed his name to Matthew
on becoming a follower of Jesus. This would give significance to the meaning of the name 'Gift of God,'
equivalent to the Greek name Theodore.

The same day Matthew made a feast—perhaps a

[1] Alphæus being also the name of the father of James the
Apostle it has been conjectured that James and Matthew were
brethren. This is of course possible, but can hardly be called
probable.

farewell feast to his old associates—to which he invited Jesus and His disciples.

After this Matthew is not once named in the Gospel history, except in the list of the Twelve ; in the other Gospels he appears seventh on the list, in his own Gospel eighth—the last in the second division. In his own Gospel again—a further mark of humility—he designates himself as "Matthew the publican." His nearest companion seems to have been Thomas (whose surname Didymus has led to the belief that he was Matthew's twin-brother), and in the same group or division were Philip and Bartholomew. Such are the scanty details which the Gospels record of St Matthew.

Since Capernaum was in the tetrarchy of Herod Antipas, it may be inferred that Levi was a tax-gatherer in the service of that prince, and not in the service of the Roman government, as is sometimes tacitly assumed. This is not unimportant in estimating the call and conversion of St Matthew.

No special mention is made of this Evangelist in the Acts of the Apostles, or in the Epistles, but some light is thrown upon his after-life by fragmentary notices of early Christian writers.

We gather that he remained in Palestine longer than the rest of the Apostles, and that he made his fellow-countrymen familiar with the words and works of Jesus. The Church historian Eusebius relates that being about to depart for distant lands to preach to others also, St Matthew left as a memorial to his Palestinian converts the story of the New Covenant committed to writing in their own tongue, the Aramaic or Hebrew dialect which they used.

Of St Matthew's after-life, of his missionary work or of his death, nothing certain is known. Ecclesiastical history is almost as silent as the Gospels in regard to this great Apostle's words and acts.

III.   *Authorship, purpose and characteristics of the Gospel.*

1.   The authorship of the first Gospel has been ascribed by an unbroken tradition to the Apostle Matthew.

2.   Though the date is uncertain it may be fixed with great probability within a few years of the Ascension. Irenæus, as we have seen, states that St Matthew wrote his Gospel when St Peter and St Paul were preaching the Gospel in Rome, and founding the Church.

3.   St Matthew's Gospel was primarily intended for the use of the Jewish converts in Palestine.   It is this fact that gives its special character to this Gospel, in which the quotations from Hebrew prophecy and the allusions to the history of Israel as fulfilled in Christ are more frequent than in the other Gospels.   For the same reason St Matthew traces our Lord's genealogy from Abraham and David rather than from Adam.   In the Sermon on the Mount, he records those special references to the Mosaic Law which are absent in St Luke, and in the same special way he narrates our Lord's strictures on Pharisaic hypocrisy.   To this cause also may be assigned the prominence given by St Matthew to the Jewish thought of a Kingdom of Heaven.

4.   St Matthew does not appear to have arranged the events which he records in chronological order, but in such a way as to illustrate different aspects of our Lord's life and teaching.   A careful examination of the sequence of events and discourses as given in St Matthew's Gospel will exhibit an orderly arrangement of this kind.

It is a Gospel of the kingdom of heaven.   The following analysis is intended to indicate the progress and signs of the kingdom as described by St Matthew. Part I.   The Birth and Childhood of the King, i.–ii. 23.

(*a*) Jesus is the promised King of the house of David;
(*b*) who fulfils the words of prophecy; (*c*) whose kingdom
is recognised by the Gentiles; (*d*) who is the representative of His nation, and fulfils their history. II. The
Beginning of the Kingdom, iii.–iv. 11. The herald of
the Kingdom; the Baptism; the Temptation; rejection
of false ideals. III. The laws of the Kingdom; its
ministers; its signs and the works of the King, iv. 12–
xvi. 12. This part includes the Sermon on the Mount,
the choice and mission of the Twelve, Parables ex-
plaining the nature of the Kingdom and Miracles fore-
casting its operation. IV. The Predictions of the Passion,
by express words, and by Parables, and by significant
incidents, xvi. 13–xx. 34. This section opens out a fresh
revelation of the Kingdom, the condition of suffering, and
the promise of glory in the Transfiguration. V. The
Triumph of the King, xxi–xxv. The royal entry into
Jerusalem; the rejection of the Jewish people; the
Advent of the King in power at the siege of Jerusalem
and at the end of the world. VI. The Passion, xxvi–
xxvii. The Betrayal; the Last Supper; the Trials; the
Crucifixion and Burial. VII. The Resurrection of Jesus
Christ: the Victory of the King, xxviii.

Parables and Miracles peculiar to St Matthew.

Parables. (1) The tares, xiii. 24–30. (2) The hid
treasure, xiii. 44. (3) The pearl of great price, xiii. 45,
46. (4) The draw net, xiii. 47–50. (5) The unmerciful
servant, xviii. 23–35. (6) The labourers in the vineyard,
xx. 1–16. (7) The two sons, xxi. 28–32. (8) The marriage
of the king's son, xxii. 1–14. (9) The ten virgins, xxv.
1–13. (10) The talents, xxv. 14–30.

Miracles. (1) The cure of two blind men, ix. 27–31.
(2) The stater in the fish's mouth, xvii. 24–27.

IV. *Jewish Sects—Scribes, Pharisees, Sadducees, Essenes, Zealots.*

The joint work of Ezra and Nehemiah had been to complete the Torah, or Law, and to enforce obedience to it. Historically, that work followed the lines of Josiah's reform, like that its whole force was directed against idolatry, and like that it tended to centralization of worship at Jerusalem.

The result was the foundation of Judaism. The Law was set forth as a complete system by which men should live. By the Law was understood in a special sense the Pentateuch, every word of which was regarded as inspired, and an immediate revelation to Moses. The Prophets (including the historical books) held a secondary place in the Canon.

From the first the Law needed explanation and development. This need called into existence a body of interpreters who were termed Sopherim or **Scribes**. Ezra had collected and edited all that survived of the sacred writings of the Jewish people. The Scribes explained and applied the rules of the Torah to special cases as they arose. Hence came that development or 'hedging round' of the Law which resulted in the body of minute Rabbinical rules of conduct. Eventually, though not at first, the decisions of the Scribes had the force of law. They *bound* men with burdens. In this way the Scribes were recognised as the legislators and the judges of Israel.

The first Scribes were priests. That the priest's lips should keep knowledge was a rule of the order. Soon, however, the study of the Law spread outside the circle of the priesthood, and a separate, even an antagonistic, body of Sopherim began to teach. And when in the Hellenistic period many of the priests addicted themselves to heathen culture, the Scribes, who were not included in the priestly order more than any others, attracted the respect and reverence of the people. The Scribes were designated by various names, Sopherim, or literary men, lawyers, learned in the Torah or Law, teachers of the Law. Their learning had a wide range ; mathematics, natural science, astronomy, geography, the history and the languages of the surrounding nations, were all required for a full exposition of the Law in its wider sense, and came within the limits of a Scribe's study. The estimation of the Scribes, and of the learning they professed, was high among the Jews. 'Study is more meritorious than sacrifice'; 'A scholar is greater than a prophet'; 'You should revere the teacher even more than your father,' were among the sayings which illustrate this enthusiasm for the teaching of the Law. Titles of honour, such as lord, and master, and Rabbi, came into vogue in the generation preceding the Christian era.

The Scribes were not confined to any one party in the Jewish Church. There were Scribes of the Sadducees as well as of the Pharisees, though the latter were probably the more numerous.

The Synagogue was, in its original intention, more a house of instruction than a house of prayer. It was the chief means by which the teaching and influence of the Scribes were extended, and by which the enactments of the Law were interpreted and enforced. The Synagogue was, in fact, a church, a school, and a court of justice.

Among the enthusiasts for the Law there was an inner circle, whose exact obedience and purity of life distinguished them above all others as specially representative of the national impulse towards zeal for the Law and separateness. To these the name of **Chasidim**, 'the pious,' was given. The Chasidim seem to have given rise, more or less directly, to two schools, sects, or orders—the Pharisees or 'separatists,' and the Essenes.

Although these sects, together with the rival faction of the Sadducees, do not appear under those appellations until the reign of John Hyrcanus (135–106 B.C.), it is not to be supposed that their origin dates from that late period. The different tendencies which afterwards took shape under familiar names originated at the time of the Return, or even earlier.

The fraternity of the **Pharisees** (*Perushim*, 'separated ones') were the popular or nationalist party. They represented and led the enthusiasm for the observance of the Levitical law, especially in regard to avoidance of ceremonial pollution, now characteristic of the whole Jewish people. Their belief included the doctrine of immortality and the resurrection of the body, and the existence of angels and spirits; in the question of the freedom of the will, they inclined to fatalism; as religious teachers, they upheld the authority of oral tradition as of equal validity with the written law.

The name of **Sadducees** has been traced either to Zadok the high priest in Solomon's time, or to Zadok a disciple of Antigonus of Socho, whose teaching, derived from Simon the Just, was wrested into a denial of future rewards and punishments. But a more probable view connects the name with the Hebrew word for 'righteous' (*tsaddiqim*) notwithstanding a slight linguistic difficulty. They were rather a caste than a sect. Admission to the Pharisaic party was not only open but eagerly welcomed; whereas the priestly and aristocratic Sadducees were rigidly exclusive, and insignificant in point of numbers.

In their treatment of religious questions the Sadducean scribes held to the letter of the Mosaic revelation, and denied the authority of the oral tradition as interpreted by the Pharisees : they taught complete freedom of the will in moral action : they were opposed to the Pharisees

as to the belief in angels and spirits; they refused also
to accept the doctrine of immortality as a deduction from
the Pentateuch. The two parties also differed, and
differed bitterly, on many small questions of ritual, and
of legal enactment. Politically, the Sadducees were as
a party open to foreign influences, and it was through
them that Hellenic culture spread in Israel. Such a
policy could have little weight of resistance against the
overwhelming tide of patriotic enthusiasm stirred and
ruled by Pharisaic guidance. Eventually the party of
the Synagogue and of the new learning prevailed over
the party of the Temple and of ancient custom.

Less conspicuous in public life, and dwelling princi-
pally in secluded settlements on the shores of the Dead
Sea, the **Essenes** nevertheless exercised a considerable
influence, and represented, though in an extreme fashion,
one tendency of the post-exilic reform. Although the
name, like that of the Pharisees and Sadducees, appears
late in history, the type of asceticism practised by the
Essenes may be regarded as part of the same movement
from which Pharisaism originated. The Essenes are not
mentioned in the New Testament, nor is it probable that
there is any trace of their influence on Christian life and
teaching at that early period, many of the practices which
the Essenes followed, celibacy, isolation, silence, ceremonial ablutions, abstinence from animal food, being
common to most forms of asceticism. Some tenets which
the Essenes professed were derived from Persian influence, such as a dualistic theory of good and evil, the
symbolism of light, the adoration of the sun, and the
worship of angels. But it was in regard to the sacrificial
system that the Essenes separated most widely from the
ordinary religious life of the Jews. The Essenes abstained
from sacrifices, and from the Temple worship, and refusing
to acknowledge the Aaronic priesthood or the Levitical
order, they had priests and ministers of their own.

The **Zealots** can hardly be reckoned as a separate party, at any rate at this epoch. They represented one extreme side of the Pharisaic movement as the Essenes represented another. At first the points of difference may have been small. It required the stimulus of the Maccabean struggle to ripen their 'zeal' into the fanaticism of later times.

V. *Members of the Family of Herod connected with New Testament History.*

Antipater, the Idumæan (Jos. *Ant.* xiv. i. 3)

Antipater (Jos. *Ant.* xiv. vii. 3)

Herod, the king (Matt. ii. 3)

By Mariamne the Maccabæan princess	By Mariamne daughter of Simon the High Priest	By Malthacé, a Samaritan		By Cleopatra
Aristobulus	Herod Philip (Matt. xiv. 3; Mk vi. 17)	Herod Antipas the tetrarch (Matt. xiv. 1; Lk. ix. 7; Mk vi. 14, king Herod)	Archelaus (Matt. ii. 22)	Philip, tetrarch of Ituræa (Lk. iii. 1)

Herodias (Matt. xiv. 3; Mk vi. 17)

Herod Agrippa I. (Acts xii. 1–23)

Herod Agrippa II. (Acts xxv. 13)

Bernice (Acts xxv. 13)

Drusilla, wife of Felix (Acts xxiv. 24)

THE GOSPEL ACCORDING TO
ST MATTHEW.

1 1–17. The Genealogy of Jesus Christ. Luke iii. 23–38.

THE book of the generation of Jesus Christ, the son of 1
David, the son of Abraham.

Abraham begat Isaac ; and Isaac begat Jacob ; and 2
Jacob begat Judah and his brethren ; and Judah begat 3
Perez and Zerah of Tamar ; and Perez begat Hezron ;
and Hezron begat Ram ; and Ram begat Amminadab ; 4
and Amminadab begat Nahshon ; and Nahshon begat
Salmon ; and Salmon begat Boaz of Rahab ; and Boaz 5
begat Obed of Ruth ; and Obed begat Jesse ; and Jesse 6
begat David the king.

---

1. The book of the generation, i.e. the pedigree extracted
from the public archives which were carefully preserved and
placed under the special care of the Sanhedrin. The expression
recalls, perhaps designedly, Gen. v. 1 'The book of the generations of Adam.' (1) The genealogy is an answer to the question
which would be asked by every Jew of any one who claimed to
be the Messiah, 'Is he of the house of David?' for by no name
was the Messiah more frequently spoken of by Jews and by
foreigners (see ch. xv. 22) than by that of the Son of David.
(2) Both this genealogy and that in St Luke's Gospel trace
Joseph's descent. But see below, *v.* 16. (3) St Matthew traces
the pedigree from Abraham, the Father of the Chosen Race,
through David, from whose house the Messiah was expected ;
St Luke, writing for the Gentiles, traces it from the common
Father of Jew and Gentile. (4) St Matthew gives the *royal
succession*; St Luke, the *family lineage*. This accounts for many
variations in names. (5) This genealogy *descends* from father to
son, and is therefore probably the more exact transcript of the
original document. St Luke's *ascends* from son to father.

C.   1

And David begat Solomon of her *that had been the*
7 *wife* of Uriah ; and Solomon begat Rehoboam ; and
8 Rehoboam begat Abijah ; and Abijah begat Asa ; and
Asa begat Jehoshaphat ; and Jehoshaphat begat Joram ;
9 and Joram begat Uzziah ; and Uzziah begat Jotham ; and
10 Jotham begat Ahaz ; and Ahaz begat Hezekiah ; and
Hezekiah begat Manasseh ; and Manasseh begat Amon ;
11 and Amon begat Josiah ; and Josiah begat Jechoniah
and his brethren, at the time of the carrying away
to Babylon.

12 And after the carrying away to Babylon, Jechoniah
13 begat Shealtiel ; and Shealtiel begat Zerubbabel ; and
Zerubbabel begat Abiud ; and Abiud begat Eliakim ;
14 and Eliakim begat Azor ; and Azor begat Sadoc ; and
15 Sadoc begat Achim ; and Achim begat Eliud ; and Eliud
begat Eleazar ; and Eleazar begat Matthan ; and Matthan
16 begat Jacob ; and Jacob begat Joseph the husband
of Mary, of whom was born Jesus, who is called
Christ.

17 So all the generations from Abraham unto David are
fourteen generations ; and from David unto the carrying
away to Babylon fourteen generations ; and from the
carrying away to Babylon unto the Christ fourteen
generations.

---

16. Jacob begat Joseph. 'Joseph which was the son of Heli'
(Luke), see last note (4); probably Joseph was the son of Heli and
the heir to Jacob. It is conjectured with much probability that
Jacob was Mary's father. In that case, although both genealogies
show Joseph's descent, they are in fact equally genealogies of
Mary's family.

Matthan or Matthat

(According to Matthew) Jacob   Heli (according to Luke)

Mary (?)   Joseph

17. This division into three sets, each containing fourteen
steps of descent, is an instance of a practice familiar to readers
of Jewish antiquities. Such a system necessitates the omission
of steps in descent.

18–25. **The Birth of Jesus Christ.** Luke i. 26–56 and ii. 4–7. St Mark and St John give no account of the birth of Jesus, St Luke narrates several particulars not recorded by St Matthew, (1) the annunciation, (2) Mary's salutation of Elisabeth in a city of Juda (or Juttah), and (3) the journey from Galilee to Bethlehem.

Now the birth of Jesus Christ was on this wise : When 18 his mother Mary had been betrothed to Joseph, before they came together she was found with child of the Holy Ghost. And Joseph her husband, being a righteous 19 man, and not willing to make her a public example, was minded to put her away privily. But when he thought on 20 these things, behold, an angel of the Lord appeared unto him in a dream, saying, Joseph, thou son of David, fear not to take unto thee Mary thy wife : for that which is conceived in her is of the Holy Ghost. And she shall 21 bring forth a son ; and thou shalt call his name JESUS ; for it is he that shall save his people from their sins.

---

18. Jesus. See *v.* 21. **Christ** (anointed). The *title* of Jesus as Prophet, Priest, and King. **Mary.** The Hebrew form is Miriam. **betrothed.** Among the Jews the betrothal took place a year before marriage, and during the interval the betrothed maiden remained with her own family. But from the day of betrothal the pair were regarded as man and wife.

19. being a righteous man, i.e. one who observed the law, and, therefore, felt bound to divorce Mary. But two courses were open to him. He could either summon her before the law-courts to be judicially condemned and punished, or he could put her away by a bill of divorcement before witnesses, but without assigning cause. This is what is meant by *putting her away privily,* the more merciful course which Joseph resolved to adopt.

21. Jesus = Jehovah (Lord), Saviour. *Jesus* represents the Greek form, while *Joshua* represents the Hebrew form of the same name. The same Hebrew root occurs in the salutation *Hosanna* : see note, ch. xxi. 9. Joshua who led the Israelites into the Promised Land, and Joshua or Jeshua, who was high priest at the time of the return from the Babylonish Captivity, are types of Jesus Christ in respect both of work and name. **save his people from their sins.** An announcement of a spiritual Kingdom. Contrary to the thought of many Jews, the salvation

22 Now all this is come to pass, that it might be fulfilled which was spoken by the Lord through the prophet, saying,

23 Behold, the virgin shall be with child, and shall bring forth a son,

And they shall call his name Immanuel ;

24 which is, being interpreted, God with us. And Joseph arose from his sleep, and did as the angel of the Lord

25 commanded him, and took unto him his wife ; and knew her not till she had brought forth a son : and he called his name JESUS.

> **2** 1-12. The Visit of the Magi. Recorded by St Matthew only. The insertion of this and the following incidents (13, 14) by St Matthew again connects the N.T. with O.T. prophecy (see Numb. xxiv. 17 ; Hosea xi. 1 ; Jeremiah xxxi. 15).

2 Now when Jesus was born in Bethlehem of Judæa in the days of Herod the king, behold, wise men from the

---

which Jesus brought was not to be a saving from the Roman or Herodian rule, but a life protected from sin.

22. is come to pass. The Evangelist speaks as a contemporary. The tense is a note of the early date of this Gospel.

23. the virgin shall be with child. See Is. vii. 14. At the time of Isaiah's prophecy Ahaz is alarmed by the threatened invasion of Pekah and Rezin—the confederate kings of Samaria and Damascus. Isaiah reassures Ahaz, who hypocritically refuses to ask for a sign. Yet a sign is given. The virgin, as yet unmarried, shall bear a son, probably a scion of the royal house of David ; he shall be called Immanuel, and before he arrives at years of discretion the deliverance shall come, though a heavier distress is at hand.

1. Jesus was born. The birth of Jesus Christ is now placed at least 4 years, and by some authorities even 6 or 7 years, before the commonly received date. **in Bethlehem.** St Matthew omits the circumstances which brought Mary to Bethlehem. **Bethlehem** (*The House of Bread*, cp. John vi. 51), the city of David, situate on a limestone ridge a few miles S. of Jerusalem. The old name of Bethlehem was Ephrath or Ephratah ; it is now called Beit-lahm. It is worthy of remark that no visit of Jesus or of His disciples to Bethlehem, His birthplace and the cradle of His race, is recorded. **Herod.**

east came to Jerusalem, saying, Where is he that is born 2
King of the Jews? for we saw his star in the east, and are
come to worship him. And when Herod the king heard 3
it, he was troubled, and all Jerusalem with him. And 4
gathering together all the chief priests and scribes of the
people, he inquired of them where the Christ should be

Called afterwards, but not in his lifetime, Herod the Great; he
was an Idumæan (Edomite) who, chiefly through the friendship
of M. Antony, became king of Judæa. The title of King
distinguishes him from the other Herods named in the Gospels.
Antipas, who tried in vain to obtain the title, is called king by
courtesy, Mark vi. 14. Herod was not an absolute monarch,
but subject to the Roman empire, much in the same way as
some of the Indian princes are subject to the British government, or as Servia was till recently subject to the Porte. He
died B.C. 3 or possibly B.C. 4. **wise men.** Marg. **Magi,**
originally the name of a Median tribe, who were said to possess
the power of interpreting dreams. Their religion consisted in
the worship of the heavenly bodies and of the elements. At
this date the name implied a religious caste—the followers of
Zoroaster, who were the astrologers of the East. The tenets
had spread widely; and as the East is a vague term, it is
difficult to determine from what country these Magi came. The
common belief that the Magi were three in number is a mere
tradition, which has been perpetuated by great painters. It
was probably an inference from *v.* 11. An equally groundless
tradition has designated the Magi as kings, and has assigned
names to them, Caspar, Balthasar, and Melchior.

2. his star. The simplest explanation of this is that a star
or meteor appeared in the sky to guide the Magi on their way,
first to Jerusalem, then to Bethlehem. It is, however, quite
possible that the Magi were divinely led to connect some
calculated astronomical occurrence with the birth of the 'King
of the Jews.' **in the east,** or possibly, as the words might be
translated, *at its rising.*

3. was troubled. Herod, with the instincts of a tyrant,
would be alarmed for his throne. His subjects (i.e. 'all Jerusalem') had learnt to dread his outbreaks of passion.

**4. gathering together all the chief priests and scribes of the
people,** or Chief Council. For an account of the Sanhedrin see
note ch. xxvi. 3; for scribes see Introduction IV. and notes on
ch. vii. 29; and for chief-priests, note ch. xxi. 15. **where
the Christ should be born.** Lit. *where the Christ or Messiah
is born.* Where do your sacred writings represent Him to be
born?

5 born. And they said unto him, In Bethlehem of Judæa :
for thus it is written by the prophet,

6   And thou Bethlehem, land of Judah,
      Art in no wise least among the princes of Judah :
      For out of thee shall come forth a governor,
      Which shall be shepherd of my people Israel.

7 Then Herod privily called the wise men, and learned of
8 them carefully what time the star appeared. And he sent
them to Bethlehem, and said, Go and search out carefully
concerning the young child ; and when ye have found
him, bring me word, that I also may come and worship
9 him. And they, having heard the king, went their way ;
and lo, the star, which they saw in the east, went before
them, till it came and stood over where the young child
10 was. And when they saw the star, they rejoiced with
11 exceeding great joy. And they came into the house and
saw the young child with Mary his mother ; and they fell
down and worshipped him ; and opening their treasures
they offered unto him gifts, gold and frankincense and
12 myrrh. And being warned *of God* in a dream that they
should not return to Herod, they departed into their own
country another way.

---

5. Bethlehem of Judæa. To distinguish this Bethlehem from
the Bethlehem in the tribe of Zebulun (Josh. xix. 15).

6. And thou Bethlehem &c. Micah v. 2. The quotation
(as usually in passages cited by St Matthew alone) nearly
corresponds with the Hebrew text.

11. the house. St Matthew gives no hint that 'the house'
was an inn, or that the babe was lying in a manger. The
holy family had by this time moved from the inn to a private
house. **their treasures.** '*Caskets*' or '*chests*' in which
treasures were placed. Such offerings to kings were quite in
accordance with Eastern usage; Seneca says : 'No one may
approach a Parthian king without bringing a gift.' Cp. Ps.
lxviii. 29, lxxii. 10. **frankincense and myrrh.** These were
products of Arabia, and, according to Herodotus, of that country
only. They were both used for medicinal purposes and for
embalming; cp. John xix. 39.

13-15.　The Flight into Egypt.　Narrated by St Matthew
　　alone.

Now when they were departed, behold, an angel of the 13
Lord appeareth to Joseph in a dream, saying, Arise and
take the young child and his mother, and flee into Egypt,
and be thou there until I tell thee : for Herod will seek
the young child to destroy him.　And he arose and took 14
the young child and his mother by night, and departed
into Egypt; and was there until the death of Herod : that 15
it might be fulfilled which was spoken by the Lord through
the prophet, saying, Out of Egypt did I call my son.

16-18.　The slaughter of Infants at Bethlehem.　Narrated by
　　St Matthew alone.

Then Herod, when he saw that he was mocked of the 16
wise men, was exceeding wroth, and sent forth, and slew
all the male children that were in Bethlehem, and in all

13.　the young child. Named first as the most precious charge
and the most exposed to danger.　　**Egypt.** Egypt was at all
times the readiest place of refuge for Israelites, whether from
famine or from political oppression.　It had sheltered many
thousands of Jews from the tyranny of the Syrian kings.　Con-
sequently large settlements of Jews were to be found in various
cities of Egypt and Africa.　In Alexandria the Jews numbered
a fifth of the population.　Wherever therefore the infant Saviour's
home was in Egypt, it would be in the midst of His brethren
according to the flesh.　At this time Egypt was a Roman
province.

15.　until the death of Herod. According to the chronology
adopted above this would be for a space of less than two
years.　　**Out of Egypt did I call my son.** Hosea xi. 1.
The history of Israel is regarded as typical of the Messiah's
life.　He alone gives significance to that history.　He is the
true seed of Abraham.　In Him the blessing promised to
Abraham finds its highest fulfilment.　Even particular incidents
in the Gospel narrative have their counterpart in the O.T.
history.　Accordingly St Matthew who, as writing specially
for the Jews, naturally reverts to this thought more constantly
than the other Evangelists, recognizes in this incident an analogy
to the call of Israel from Egypt.

16.　all the male children. Profane history passes over this
atrocity in silence.　But Josephus may well have found his

the borders thereof, from two years old and under, according to the time which he had carefully learned of the wise
17 men.   Then was fulfilled that which was spoken by
Jeremiah the prophet, saying,

18   A voice was heard in Ramah,
         Weeping and great mourning,
         Rachel weeping for her children ;
         And she would not be comforted, because they
         are not.

19-23.   The return from Egypt to dwell at Nazareth, comp.
      Luke ii. 39, 40.

19   But when Herod was dead, behold, an angel of the
20 Lord appeareth in a dream to Joseph in Egypt, saying,
Arise and take the young child and his mother, and go
into the land of Israel : for they are dead that sought the
21 young child's life.   And he arose and took the young
child and his mother, and came into the land of Israel.
22 But when he heard that Archelaus was reigning over

---

pages unequal to contain a complete record of all the cruel
deeds of a tyrant like Herod.   Besides, the crime was executed
with secrecy, and the number of children slain was probably
not large.

18.   Jer. xxxi. 15, in LXX. xxxviii. 15.   In a singularly
touching passage, Rachel, the mother of the tribe of Benjamin
(whose tomb was close to Bethlehem ; Gen. xxxv. 19), is
conceived of as weeping for her captive sons at Ramah—some
of whom were possibly doomed to die; cp. Jer. xl. 1.   The
Evangelist pictures Rachel's grief re-awakened by the slaughter
of the infants at Bethlehem.   The Ramah alluded to by Jeremiah,
generally identified with the modern Er-Rama, was about five
miles N. of Jerusalem, and in the tribe of Benjamin.

22.   Archelaus.   A son of Herod the Great.   His mother
was Malthaké, a Samaritan.   After a cruel and disturbed reign
(under the title of Ethnarch) of about eight years he was
banished to Vienna in Gaul—the modern Vienne.   His dominions, including Samaria, Judæa, and Idumæa, then passed
into the direct government of Rome.   See note, ch. xiv. 1, and
Introduction v.   **the parts of Galilee.**   Now under the
government of Herod Antipas, full brother of Archelaus.

Judæa in the room of his father Herod, he was afraid to go thither; and being warned *of God* in a dream, he withdrew into the parts of Galilee, and came and dwelt in a 23 city called Nazareth: that it might be fulfilled which was spoken by the prophets, that he should be called a Nazarene.

3 1–12. John the Baptist preaches in the Wilderness of Judæa. Mark i. 2–8; Luke iii. 1–18; John i. 15–34. St Matthew alone names the coming of the Pharisees and Sadducees. St Mark's brief account contains no additional particulars. St Luke adds the special directions to the various classes— people—publicans and soldiers. The fourth Gospel reports more fully the Baptist's disclaimer of Messiahship; he recognizes the Messiah by the descent of the Holy Spirit, he points Him out as the Lamb of God. Again (ch. iii. 25 –36) John shows his own disciples the true relation between Christ and himself—Christ is the Bridegroom, John is the friend of the Bridegroom.

And in those days cometh John the Baptist, preaching 3

---

23. Nazareth. St Matthew gives no intimation of any previous residence of Mary and Joseph at Nazareth. If the Son of David, full of wisdom and grace, had continued to live on at Bethlehem, the home of His ancestors, hopes and schemes, and therefore dangers, might have gathered round Him, rendering impossible such a quiet life as He led at Nazareth. **Nazareth,** said to signify **the Protectress** (Hebr. *natsar*), is a small town of central Galilee, beautifully situated in a sheltered valley among the hills which bound the plain of Esdraelon on the north. **should be called a Nazarene.** The meaning of this passage was probably as clear to the contemporaries of St Matthew, as the other references to prophecy *vv.* 15, 17; for us it is involved in doubt. An explanation may be found in the fact that 'Nazareth' resembles in form and sound two Hebrew words, one meaning *a branch*, the other meaning *to protect*. 'The Branch' was a recognized prophetic title of the Messiah, and to save and protect was the Work and Office of Jesus. In any case Nazarene cannot be the same as Nazirite. The words are quite distinct and in no sense was Jesus a Nazirite.

1. in those days. See Luke iii. 1, where the time is defined. **John the Baptist.** So named by the other Synoptists and by Josephus: in the fourth Gospel he is called simply John, a note of the authenticity of St John's Gospel.   **preaching,** lit. *heralding,* a word appropriate to the thought of the proclamation

2 in the wilderness of Judæa, saying, Repent ye; for the
3 kingdom of heaven is at hand. For this is he that was
spoken of by Isaiah the prophet, saying,

> The voice of one crying in the wilderness,
> Make ye ready the way of the Lord,
> Make his paths straight.

---

of a king.   **the wilderness of Judæa**, i.e. the uncultivated
Eastern frontier of Judah.   The term also includes the cliffs and
Western shore of the Dead Sea.   In this wild and nearly treeless
district there were formerly a few cities, and there are still some
luxuriant spots.   See Tristram's *Topog. of H. L.* Ch. IV.   The
wilderness has a threefold significance, (*a*) as the desolate scene
of John's ascetic life, (*b*) as the battle-field of the Temptation
(see notes ch. iv.), (*c*) as the pathway of the royal Advent.   In
this last aspect John fitly appears in the wilderness as the herald
of a promised deliverance foreshadowed by two great prophetic
types—the deliverance from Egypt (Numb. xxiii. 21, 22; Ps.
lxviii. 4-7), and the deliverance from Babylon, each associated
with a march through the desert.

2.   **Repent ye.** More than 'feel sorrow or regret for sin.' It is
rather, 'change the life, the heart, the *motive* for action.' It
was a call to self-examination and reality of life.   **the kingdom
of heaven.** St Matthew alone uses this expression, but he also
employs the equivalent phrase, *the kingdom of God*, in common
with the other N.T. writers.   In itself the expression was not
new.   It connected itself in Jewish thought with the theocracy—
the direct rule of God—of which the earthly Kingdom was a
shadow.   It implied the reign of the Messiah (cp. Dan. vii. 14).
It became the watchword of the Zealots, 'No king but God.'
Jesus took up the word and gave it a new, deep and varied
spiritual significance, which is rather illustrated than defined.
The principal meanings of the Kingdom of Heaven in N.T. are
(1) The presence of Christ on earth. (2) His Second Advent.
(3) The inner life of righteousness. (4) Christianity, (*a*) as a
Church, (*b*) as a faith. (5) The life eternal.

3.   **by Isaiah the prophet.** The reference in Is. xl. 3 is to the
promised return from Babylon. A herald shall proclaim the
joyous news on mountains and in the desert through which the
return should be.   This incident in the national history is transferred to the more glorious deliverance from bondage and to the
coming of the true King.   **The voice.** The message is more
than the messenger, the prophet's personality is lost in the
prophetic voice.   **Make his paths straight.** The image would
be familiar to Eastern thought; a Semiramis or a Xerxes orders

Now John himself had his raiment of camel's hair, and a 4
leathern girdle about his loins ; and his food was locusts
and wild honey. Then went out unto him Jerusalem, and 5
all Judæa, and all the region round about Jordan ; and 6
they were baptized of him in the river Jordan, confessing
their sins. But when he saw many of the Pharisees and 7

---

the mountains to be levelled or cut through, and causeways to
be raised in the valleys.

4. raiment of camel's hair. A kind of tunic or shirt coarsely
woven of camel's hair, ' one of the most admirable materials for
clothing, it keeps out the heat, cold and rain.' *Recovery of
Jerusalem*, p. 445. **locusts and wild honey.** Thomson, *Land
and Book*, pp. 419, 420, states that though tolerated, as an
article of food, only by the very poorest people, locusts are still
eaten by the Bedawin. Burckhardt mentions having seen locust
shops at Medina and Tayf. After being dried in the sun the
locusts are eaten with butter and honey. Sometimes they are
sprinkled with salt and either boiled or roasted. Locusts were
eaten by the people besieged in Mafeking in the Boer War of
1900. Thomson adds that wild honey is still gathered from trees
in the wilderness and from rocks in the Wadies. The clothing
and dress of John were in fact those of the poorest of his fellow-
countrymen. The description would recall—is probably intended to recall—that of Elijah, 2 Kings i. 8.

6. were baptized, or *immersed.* In baptizing John introduced no new custom, for ceremonial ablution or baptism was
practised in all ancient religions. Among the Jews proselytes
were baptized, besides being circumcised and offering a sacrifice,
on admission to the Mosaic covenant. John's baptism was the
outward sign of the purification and ' life-giving change,' and
contained the promise of forgiveness of sins. Christ too adopted
the ancient custom and enriched it with a new significance, and
a still mightier efficacy. From the history of the word it is clear
that the primitive idea of baptism was immersion. This was for
long the only recognized usage in the Christian Church, and
much of the figurative force was lost when sprinkling was
substituted for immersion. The convert who entered the clear
rushing stream, soiled, weary, and scorched by the hot Eastern
sun, and then after being hidden from the sight for a few
moments ' buried in baptism ' reappeared, fresh, vigorous, and
cleansed, having put off ' the filth of the flesh,' seemed indeed
to have risen to a new and purified life in Christ. Rom. vi. 4.

7. Pharisees. The name signifies ' Separatists '; the party
dates from the revival of the national life, and observances of

Sadducees coming to his baptism, he said unto them, Ye
offspring of vipers, who warned you to flee from the wrath
8 to come? Bring forth therefore fruit worthy of repentance:
9 and think not to say within yourselves, We have Abraham
to our father: for I say unto you, that God is able of
10 these stones to raise up children unto Abraham.   And
even now is the axe laid unto the root of the trees: every
tree therefore that bringeth not forth good fruit is hewn
11 down, and cast into the fire.   I indeed baptize you with
water unto repentance: but he that cometh after me is
mightier than I, whose shoes I am not worthy to bear:

---

the Mosaic Law, under the Maccabees. Their ruling principle
was a literal obedience to the written law and to an unwritten
tradition.   Originally they were leaders of a genuine reform.
But in the hands of less spiritual successors their system had
become little else than a formal observance of carefully prescribed rules.   The 'hypocrisy' of the Pharisees, which stifled
conscience and made them '*incapable of repentance*,' is the
special sin of the day rebuked more than any other by the
Saviour. The **Sadducees** were the aristocratic and priestly party,
they acquiesced in foreign rule and foreign civilisation.   They
refused to give the same weight as the Pharisees to unwritten
tradition, but adhered strictly to the written law of Moses.
Their religious creed excluded belief in a future life, or
in angels and spirits (Acts xxiii. 8).   See also Introd. IV.
offspring, or *brood*, of vipers.   **wrath to come.** That is, the
divine judgment on sin (Rom. ii. 5).   'Fleeing from the wrath
to come' therefore implies feeling God's hatred of sin, which
leads to repentance, that change of heart and life which the
Pharisees needed.

9. We have Abraham to our father.   The Jewish doctors
taught that no son of Abraham would enter Gehenna.   'Shall
the born Israelite stand upon earth, and the proselyte be in
heaven?' (Talmud).   **of these stones to raise up children.**
Stones are regarded as the most insensate, the furthest removed
from life, of created things.   The Hebrew or Aramaic words for
children (*banim*) and stones (*abanim*) are similar in sound; there
is therefore probably a play on the words.

10.   fruit.   The Oriental values trees only as productive of
fruit, all others are cut down as cumberers of the ground.   He
lays his axe literally at the root. *Land and Book*, p. 341.

11.   whose shoes I am not worthy to bear. The work of the
meanest slaves.   John, great prophet as he was, with influence

he shall baptize you with the Holy Ghost and *with* fire :
whose fan is in his hand, and he will throughly cleanse 12
his threshing-floor ; and he will gather his wheat into the
garner, but the chaff he will burn up with unquenchable
fire.

13-17. Jesus comes to be baptized of John. Mark i. 9-11;
Luke iii. 21, 22; John i. 32-34. St Luke adds two particulars: that the Holy Spirit descended on Jesus (1) 'in a
bodily shape,' and (2) 'while He was praying.' In the
fourth Gospel, where John Baptist's own words are quoted,
the act of baptism is not named; a touch of the Baptist's
characteristic humility.

Then cometh Jesus from Galilee to the Jordan unto 13
John, to be baptized of him. But John would have 14

sufficient to make even Herod tremble for his throne, is unworthy to be the meanest slave of the Stronger One—the Son of
God.   **with the Holy Ghost**, lit. *in the Holy Ghost.* Not
only is the Holy Ghost the Person by whom and through whom
the grace of baptism comes, but He is also regarded as the
element in which the act takes place.   The original words, both
Hebrew and Greek, translated Spirit or Ghost have an interesting
and suggestive history; see note on this passage in Cambridge
Greek Testament for Schools.   **with fire.**   This metaphor
implies: (1) Purification, (2) Fiery zeal or enthusiasm, (3) En-
lightenment, (4) Love; all which are gifts of the Holy Ghost.

12. fan, Lat. *vannus*, was the instrument by which the
corn after being threshed was thrown up against the wind to
clear it of chaff.   The **threshing-floor** was a broad flat place,
usually on a rocky hill-top exposed to the breeze, or in a wind-
swept valley.   Here the threshing-floor is put for the mingled
grain and chaff lying heaped upon it.   The separation by Christ's
winnowing fan is sometimes a separation between individuals,
sometimes a separation between the good and evil in the heart
of a man or in a society or nation.

13. to the Jordan.   Probably at 'Ænon near to Salim'
(John iii. 23), a day's journey from Nazareth, 'close to the passage
of the Jordan near Succoth and far away from that near Jericho.'
Sinai and Palestine, p. 311.   Cp. also John i. 28, where the
correct reading is: 'These things were done in Bethany beyond
Jordan, where John was baptizing.'   **to be baptized.**   Jesus who
is the pattern of the new life submits to the baptism which is a
symbol of the new life.   He who has power to forgive sins
seems to seek through baptism forgiveness of sins.   But in truth
by submitting to baptism Jesus shows the true efficacy of the

hindered him, saying, I have need to be baptized of thee,
15 and comest thou to me? But Jesus answering said unto
him, Suffer *it* now: for thus it becometh us to fulfil all
16 righteousness. Then he suffereth him. And Jesus, when
he was baptized, went up straightway from the water: and
lo, the heavens were opened unto him, and he saw the
Spirit of God descending as a dove, and coming upon
17 him; and lo, a voice out of the heavens, saying, This
is my beloved Son, in whom I am well pleased.

> **4** 1–11. The Temptation of Jesus. Mark i. 12, 13; Luke
> iv. 1–13. St Mark's account is short; the various tempta-
> tions are not specified; he adds the striking expression
> 'was with the wild beasts.' St Luke places the temptation
> of the Kingdoms of the World before that of the Pinnacle
> of the Temple. Generally it may be remarked that the
> account can have come from no other than Jesus Himself.
> The words of the Evangelist describe an actual scene—not
> a dream. The devil *really* came to Jesus, but in what
> manner he came is not stated. These were not isolated
> temptations in the life of Jesus. Cp. Luke xxii. 28, 'Ye
> are they which have continued with me in my *temptations*.'
> They were in a special way Messianic temptations, i.e. the
> acts were such as the Jews would expect from the Messiah.

rite. He who is most truly man declares what man may become
through baptism—clothed and endued with the Holy Spirit, and
touched by the fire of zeal and purity.

14. would have hindered him. A much better rendering of
the imperfect tense of the original Greek than 'forbade him' of
the A.V.

15. righteousness, as revealed in the law and the prophets.

16. the heavens. A literal translation of the Hebrew word,
which is a plural form. **he** (*Jesus*) **saw.** We should infer
from the text that the vision was to Jesus alone, but the Baptist
also was a witness, as we learn from John i. 32, 'And John
bare record, I saw the Spirit descending from heaven like a
dove, and it abode upon him.' This was to John the sign by
which the Messiah should be recognized.

17. a voice out of the heavens. Thrice during our Lord's
ministry it is recorded that a voice from heaven came to Him.
The two other occasions were at the Transfiguration and in the
week of the Passion (John xii. 28). **beloved.** In the Gospels
always in reference to Christ the beloved Son of God (Mark xii.
6 and Luke xx. 13 cannot be regarded as exceptions).

They would be powerful temptations for a false Messiah, for a pretender to Messiahship; but 'the Messiah of Judaism is the anti-Christ of the Gospels' (Edersheim). Again, they are typical temptations, representative of the various forms of temptation by which human nature can be assailed. For, as has often been said, the three temptations cover the same ground as 'the lust of the flesh, the lust of the eyes, and the pride of life' (1 John ii. 16) in which St John sums up the evil of the world. The lesson of each and all of the temptations is trust in God and submission to God's will— the result in us of the new life.

Then was Jesus led up of the Spirit into the wilderness **4** to be tempted of the devil. And when he had fasted 2 forty days and forty nights, he afterward hungered. And 3 the tempter came and said unto him, If thou art the Son of God, command that these stones become bread. But 4

---

1. led up of the Spirit. The agency of the Spirit of God is named in each of the Synoptists. St Mark uses the strong expression 'the Spirit driveth him forth.' **the wilderness.** See note on ch. iii. 1, but the locality of the temptation is not known. The desert as the scene of the temptation has a peculiar significance. It was the waste and waterless tract (*dry places*, ch. xii. 43) which unpeopled by men was thought to be the abode of demons. So Jesus meets the evil spirit in his own domains, the Stronger One coming upon the strong man who keepeth his palace (Luke xi. 21, 22). The retirement preparatory to the great work may be compared with that of Elijah and St Paul.

the devil. This is the English form of the Greek word *diabolos*, a rendering of the Hebrew *satan*, which means 'one who meets or opposes,' 'an adversary.' The Greek word conveys the additional ideas of (1) deceiving, (2) calumniating, (3) accusing.

2. he afterward hungered. The words imply that the particular temptations named were offered at the end of forty days during which He had fasted. But the parallel accounts represent the temptation as enduring throughout the whole period.

3. that these stones become bread. The temptation is addressed to the appetite, Use Thy divine power to satisfy the desire of the flesh. The very discipline by which He fortified His human soul against temptation is sought to be made an inlet to temptation—a frequent incident in religious experience. Note also that this manifestation of powers entered into the popular belief about the Messiah. Like Moses he would give them bread from heaven. Comp. John vi. 14, 15.

he answered and said, It is written, Man shall not live by
bread alone, but by every word that proceedeth out of the
5 mouth of God. Then the devil taketh him into the holy
6 city; and he set him on the pinnacle of the temple, and
saith unto him, If thou art the Son of God, cast thyself
down: for it is written,

> He shall give his angels charge concerning thee:
>
> And on their hands they shall bear thee up,
>
> Lest haply thou dash thy foot against a stone.

7 Jesus said unto him, Again it is written, Thou shalt not
8 tempt the Lord thy God. Again, the devil taketh him

---

4. Jesus answers by a quotation from Deut. viii. 3. The
chapter sets forth the teaching of the wilderness. The forty
years were to the Jews what the forty days are to Jesus. Christ's
test of sonship is obedience and entire trust in God, who alone
is the giver of every good gift. The devil's test of sonship is
supply of bodily wants, external prosperity, &c.

5. the holy city. This designation used of the actual Jerusalem
by St Matthew alone is transferred to the heavenly Jerusalem,
Rev. xi. 2, xxi. 2, xxii. 19. **the pinnacle,** or winglike pro-
jection, i.e. some well-known pinnacle of the Temple, probably
on one of the lofty porticoes overlooking the deep Valley of
Kidron. It was a Rabbinical tradition that when the Messiah
came he would 'stand upon the roof of the Sanctuary' and
proclaim redemption to Israel.

6. cast thyself down. The depth was immense: Josephus
speaking of the 'Royal Porch' says, 'if anyone looked down
from the top of the battlements he would be giddy, while his
sight could not reach to such an immense depth.' *Antiq.* xv.
11. 5. **it is written.** Ps. xci. [xc. LXX.] 11, 12. The
quotation follows the LXX. version, but the words 'to guard
thee in all thy ways' are omitted in the text. The omission
distorts the meaning of the original, which is simply that God
will keep the righteous on their journeys.

7. Thou shalt not tempt the Lord thy God. Deut. vi. 16.
The verse ends 'as ye tempted him in Massah.' The reference
to Massah (Numb. xx. 7-12) shows the true meaning of the
Saviour's answer. Moses and Aaron displayed presumption
when they tried to draw to themselves the glory of the miracle
instead of 'sanctifying the Lord.' Jesus will not glorify Himself
in the eyes of the Jews by a conspicuous miracle. His work
as the Son of Man is to glorify the Father's name through
obedience. Cp. John xii. 28.

unto an exceeding high mountain, and sheweth him all
the kingdoms of the world, and the glory of them ; and 9
he said unto him, All these things will I give thee, if thou
wilt fall down and worship me. Then saith Jesus unto 10
him, Get thee hence, Satan : for it is written, Thou shalt
worship the Lord thy God, and him only shalt thou serve.
Then the devil leaveth him ; and behold, angels came 11
and ministered unto him.

12-17. Jesus returns into Galilee, and preaches there. Mark
i. 14; Luke iv. 14, who assigns no reason ; John iv. 1-3.
St John gives a further reason 'when the Lord knew how
the Pharisees had heard that Jesus made and baptized more
disciples than John, he left Judæa,' &c.

Now when he heard that John was delivered up, he 12

---

8. an exceeding high mountain. It is idle to ask what this
mountain was, or in what sense Jesus saw the kingdoms of the
world. It is enough that the thought and the temptation of
earthly despotism and glory were present to the mind of Jesus.
The Galilæans put the same temptation to Jesus when they
wished to make Him a king (John vi. 15), and even the disciples
shared the hope of an earthly Messianic kingdom.

9. All these things will I give thee. Satan, the 'prince of
this world' (John xii. 31), claims the disposal of earthly thrones.
This is more clearly brought out by St Luke (ch. iv. 6), 'All
this power will I give thee and the glory of them, for that is
delivered unto me, and to whomsoever I will I give it.' The
arrogance, selfishness and cruelty of contemporary rulers would
give force to such an assumption. A Tiberius or a Herod
Antipas might indeed be thought to have worshipped Satan.

if thou wilt fall down and worship me, i.e. acknowledge as
sovereign, as the lesser kings acknowledged Cæsar.

10. Get thee hence, Satan. It is instructive to find these
words addressed to Peter (ch. xvi. 23) when he put himself as it
were in the place of the tempter. See note *ad loc.*   **him only
shalt thou serve,** Deut. vi. 10-13. Idolatry, multiplicity of
aims, and forgetfulness of God are the dangers of prosperity and
ambition. See context of passage in Deut.

12. when he heard, probably also *because* He heard. It
was a needful precaution against the cruel treachery of Herod
Antipas. At Capernaum He would be close to the dominions
of Herod Philip. The place of imprisonment was Machærus.
The cause of John's imprisonment is stated at length ch. xiv. 3,

13 withdrew into Galilee ; and leaving Nazareth, he came
and dwelt in Capernaum, which is by the sea, in the
14 borders of Zebulun and Naphtali : that it might be
fulfilled which was spoken by Isaiah the prophet, saying,

15 The land of Zebulun and the land of Naphtali,

Toward the sea, beyond Jordan,

Galilee of the Gentiles,

16 The people which sat in darkness

Saw a great light,

And to them which sat in the region and shadow
of death,

To them did light spring up.

---

4 (where see note) and Luke iii. 19, 20. On hearing of the
death of John the Baptist Jesus retired into the wilderness. See
ch. xiv. 13.

withdrew into Galilee. By the shortest route through Samaria.
Galilee = *a circle* or *circuit*, originally confined to a 'circle' of
20 cities given by Solomon to Hiram, 1 Kings ix. 11. Cp.
Josh. xx. 7 and Josh. viii. 2. From this small beginning the
name spread to a larger district. The Jews were in a minority
in those parts. The population mainly consisted of Phœnicians,
Arabs, and Greeks.

13. leaving Nazareth. Partly because of the unbelief of the
Nazarenes, partly (we may infer) in order to be in a frontier
town from which He might easily pass from the jurisdiction of
Antipas. **Capernaum.** A town on the N.W. shore of the
Sea of Galilee. It was the scene of considerable traffic, and had
a large Gentile element in its population. In passing from
Nazareth to Capernaum Jesus left a retired mountain home for
a busy and populous neighbourhood, 'the manufacturing district
of Palestine.'

14. by Isaiah. Read the whole of the prophecy (Is. viii.
11–ix. 6).

15. Galilee of the Gentiles. See above, *v.* 12.

16. The immediate historical reference of the prophecy was to
the invasion of Tiglath-pileser (or Pul), whom Ahaz called in to
assist him against Rezin and Pekah. It fell with great severity on
the northern tribes (2 Kings xv. 29). Yet even they are promised a great deliverance, in the first instance, by the destruction
of Sennacherib, from temporal distress (cp. Is. chs. x. and xi.
with ch. ix. 1–6) ; secondly, by the advent of the Messiah, from
spiritual darkness.

From that time began Jesus to preach, and to say, 17
Repent ye ; for the kingdom of heaven is at hand.

18-22. The Call of Peter and Andrew and of the Sons of
    Zebedee—the first group of four in the Apostolic College.
    See Mark i. 16-20. In Luke, Simon is mentioned without
    any introduction, ch. iv. 38. The narrative of Luke v.
    3-11 possibly belongs to a different occasion, though *v.* 11
    corresponds with *v.* 22 of this chapter. St Luke adds that
    the sons of Zebedee were partners with "Simon. John i.
    35-42 refers to a previous summons. We learn there that
    Andrew was a disciple of John the Baptist, and that
    Bethsaida was the city of Andrew and Peter.

And walking by the sea of Galilee, he saw two brethren, 18
Simon who is called Peter, and Andrew his brother, casting a net into the sea ; for they were fishers. And he saith 19
unto them, Come ye after me, and I will make you fishers
of men. And they straightway left the nets, and followed 20
him. And going on from thence he saw other two 21
brethren, James the *son* of Zebedee, and John his brother,
in the boat with Zebedee their father, mending their nets ;
and he called them. And they straightway left the boat 22
and their father, and followed him.

23-25. Jesus preaches the Gospel and cures Diseases in Galilee.
    Special instances of cure are recorded in Mark i. 13 and
    foll. ; Luke v. 31 and foll.

And Jesus went about in all Galilee, teaching in their 23
synagogues, and preaching the gospel of the kingdom,

---

18. a net. *a casting-net*, mentioned here only in N.T. The
fisheries on the Sea of Galilee, once so productive, are now
deserted.

19. fishers of men. A condensed parable explicitly drawn
out, ch. xiii. 47-50. Cp. Jer. xvi. 16.

22. and their father. St Mark (i. 20) adds ' with the hired
servants.' We may infer that Zebedee and his sons and their
partners were raised above the lowest social rank.

23. in their synagogues. The synagogue, built on a hill or
on the highest place in the city, distinguished sometimes by a
tall pole corresponding to a modern steeple, was as familiar and
conspicuous in a Jewish town as the church is in an English

and healing all manner of disease and all manner of sick-
24 ness among the people. And the report of him went
forth into all Syria : and they brought unto him all that
were sick, holden with divers diseases and torments,
possessed with devils, and epileptic, and palsied ; and
25 he healed them. And there followed him great multitudes
from Galilee and Decapolis and Jerusalem and Judæa and
from beyond Jordan.

---

village. Sometimes, however, the synagogue was placed on the
bank of a river. Sometimes it was constructed without a roof
and open to the sky. 1. Divine service was held in the
synagogue on the Sabbath, and also on the second and fifth day
of each week. 2. The service consisted in reading the Law
and the prophets by those who were called upon by the 'Angel
of the Church,' and in prayers offered up by the minister for the
people ; the people responding 'Amen' as with us. 3. But
the synagogues were not churches alone. Like Turkish mosques
they were also Courts of Law in which the sentence was not
only pronounced but executed, 'they shall scourge you in their
synagogues.' 4. Further, the synagogues were Public Schools,
'the boys that were scholars were wont to be instructed before
their masters in the synagogue' (Talmud). 5. Lastly, the
synagogues were the Divinity Schools or Theological Colleges
among the Jews. 6. The affairs of the synagogue were
administered by ten men, of whom three, called ' Rulers of the
Synagogue,' acted as judges, admitted proselytes and performed
other important functions. A fourth was termed the 'Angel of
the Church' or bishop of the congregation ; three others were
deacons or almoners. An eighth acted as 'interpreter,' rendering
the Hebrew into the vernacular ; the ninth was the master of
the Divinity School, the tenth his interpreter ; see ch. x. 27.
It is interesting to trace in the arrangements of the synagogue
the germs of the organisation of the Christian Church.

24. into all Syria. The fame passes to the north and east,
rather than to the south. Galilee is connected by trade and
affinity with Damascus rather than with Jerusalem. **possessed
with devils.** See on ix. 32. **palsied,** i.e. paralysed. The
Christian Church has followed her divine Founder's example in
this tendance of bodily ailment. The founding of hospitals and
the care of the sick are distinguishing features of Christianity
and among the most blessed fruits of it. A deeper respect for
life and a deeper sense of purity have followed as necessary
consequences.

25. Decapolis. A group of ten cities. The cities included

Chs. V.—VII. The Sermon on the Mount is a discourse about the new life, showing its conditions; and about the Kingdom, showing its nature, legislation, and privileges. In regard to *heathenism* the sermon is a contrast, in regard to the *Jewish Law* it is a sublime fulfilment. Again, instead of curses there are blessings; instead of penalties, reward. Two questions are raised in regard to the Sermon on the Mount. (1) Is it a connected discourse, and not merely a collection of our Lord's sayings? (2) Is it to be identified with the Sermon on the Plain, Luke vi. 17-49? The first of these questions may without doubt be answered in the affirmative, the second with less certainty. 1. (a) This is the most natural inference from the Evangelist's words and from the manner in which the discourse is introduced. (b) An analysis points to a close connexion of thought and to a systematic arrangement of the different sections of the sermon. It is true that some of the sayings are found in a different connexion in St Luke's Gospel, but it is more than probable that our Lord repeated portions of His teaching on various occasions. 2. In favour of the identity of the two discourses it may be noted that: (a) The beginning and end are identical as well as much of the intervening matter. (b) The portions omitted—a comparison between the old and new legislation—are such as would be less adapted for St Luke's readers than for St Matthew's. On the other hand it is urged that (a) St Matthew describes the sermon as being delivered on the mountain while St Luke's words are 'stood in the plain.' But the 'mount' and the 'plain' are not necessarily distinct localities. The 'plain' or 'level place' was probably a platform on the high land. (b) The place in the order of events differs in St Luke. But it is probable that here as well as elsewhere St Matthew does not observe the order of time. The following analysis may be of use in showing the connexion. A. The subjects of the Kingdom, v. 3-16. (1) Their character and privileges, v. 3-12. (2) Their responsibility, v. 13-16. B. The Kingdom of Heaven in relation (1) to the Law, v. 17-48; and (2) to Pharisaic rules, vi. 1-34. (1) It is the highest fulfilment of the law in regard to (a) The Decalogue, v. 21-37. (b) The law of Retaliation, 38-42. (c) Love or Charity, 43-48. (2) It exceeds the righteousness of the Pharisees in regard to (a) Almsgiving, vi. 1-4; (b) Prayer, vi. 5-15; (c) Fasting, vi. 16-18; (d) Earthly possessions and daily cares, vi. 19-21; (e) Spiritual darkness and light, 22-23; (f) Singleness of service, 24; (g) Trust in God, 25-34. C. Characteristics of

---

in this group are variously named by different authors, they lay to the E. and S. of the Sea of Galilee; by some Damascus is mentioned as belonging to the group.

the Kingdom, vii. 1–27. (*a*) Truth in judgment, vii. 1–6.
(*b*) The Father's love for the Children of the Kingdom, 7–12.
(*c*) The narrow entrance therein, 13, 14. (*d*) The danger of
false guides to the narrow entrance, and the test of the true,
15–23: (*e*) A description of the true subjects of the Kingdom,
as distinguished from the false, 24–27.

5 And seeing the multitudes, he went up into the
mountain : and when he had sat down, his disciples came
2 unto him : and he opened his mouth and taught them,
saying,

A. The subjects of the Kingdom, 3–16. (1) Their character and
privileges, 3–12. (2) Their responsibility, 13–16.

3 Blessed are the poor in spirit : for theirs is the kingdom
of heaven.

---

1. the mountain, the high land bordering on the Lake,
behind Tell Hûm, which the inhabitants would naturally call
'the mountain.' **when he had sat down.** The usual position
of a Jewish Teacher. In the Talmud 'to sit' is nearly synony-
mous with 'to teach.' Christ is not preaching a sermon or
heralding the Gospel as in ch. iv. 23. 'The Sermon on the
Mount' is more properly the 'New Law.' Therefore He does
not stand like a modern or mediæval preacher as often represented,
but sits like an Oriental monarch or teacher. The difference
seems slight, but in the Ceremonial East it would mean a great
deal.

3–9. Of 'the Beatitudes'—so called from the opening word
' beati' in the Vulgate—the first seven may be regarded as groups
of characters on an ascending scale, tracing the Christian growth
step by step ; the two last have special reference to the disciples—
they supply the tests and the hopes of discipleship. First, two
passive qualities 'lowliness and meekness,' which mark the
character receptive of Christianity, then two activities or move-
ments of the soul; 'mourning,' which alienates it from earth ;
then divine ' hungering and thirsting,' which draw it to heaven.
This fourth Beatitude is the central point: righteousness is the
coping-stone of the soul seeking God, the foundation of the soul
which has found Him. Three graces of the Christian life follow,
' mercy,' the first-fruits of righteousness (see the close connexion
between the two ch. vi. 1 and comp. the fruits of righteousness
in the judgment scene ch. xxv.), ' purity of heart,' the soul cleansed
from all defilement sees God, and ' peace-making,' wherein the
soul that has seen God imitates the work of God—reconciliation.

3. poor in spirit. St Luke omits **in spirit**, showing that

Blessed are they that mourn : for they shall be com- 4
forted.

Blessed are the meek : for they shall inherit the earth. 5

Blessed are they that hunger and thirst after righteous- 6
ness : for they shall be filled.

Blessed are the merciful : for they shall obtain mercy. 7

Blessed are the pure in heart : for they shall see God. 8

Blessed are the peacemakers : for they shall be called 9
sons of God.

Blessed are they that have been persecuted for right- 10
eousness' sake : for theirs is the kingdom of heaven.

Blessed are ye when *men* shall reproach you, and persecute 11

---

the literal poor are primarily meant ; St Matthew shows that
they are not exclusively meant. The poor are opposed to the
spiritually proud and self-sufficient ; they have need of the riches
of Christ and feel their need.

4. they that mourn. Those who mourn for sin are primarily
intended, but the secondary meaning of 'all who are sorrowful'
is not excluded.

5. the meek. Meekness, or freedom from resentment when
suffering injustice, is essentially a Christian virtue. **shall inherit
the earth.** Ps. xxxvii. 11. In a literal sense the meek have
inherited the earth. History has no example of higher exaltation
than that of the Apostles, and the code which they promulgated
rules the world.

7. shall obtain mercy. This principle in the divine government that men shall be dealt with as they deal with their fellow-
men is taught in the parable of the Unmerciful Servant, ch. xviii.,
and underlies the fifth petition in the Lord's Prayer, ch. vi. 12.

8. pure in heart. Purity is a distinguishing virtue of Christianity. It finds no place in the teaching of pagan philosophy.

9. sons of God. These are most akin to the divine nature,
perfect as their Father which is in heaven is perfect, *v.* 48, cp.
1 John iii. 1.

10. they that have been persecuted, such as the prophets
of old, and the disciples who had already suffered for Christ.
Suffering persecution for Christ's sake is the seal and proof of
righteousness.

11. The nature of the persecution is indicated in this verse ;
not torture, imprisonment, and death, but reproach and calumny,
precisely the form of persecution to which the disciples must
have been now subjected.

you, and say all manner of evil against you falsely, for my
12 sake. Rejoice, and be exceeding glad : for great is your
reward in heaven : for so persecuted they the prophets
which were before you.

13 Ye are the salt of the earth : but if the salt have lost its
savour, wherewith shall it be salted? it is thenceforth
good for nothing, but to be cast out and trodden under
14 foot of men. Ye are the light of the world. A city set on
15 a hill cannot be hid. Neither do *men* light a lamp, and
put it under the bushel, but on the stand ; and it shineth
16 unto all that are in the house. Even so let your light
shine before men, that they may see your good works,
and glorify your Father which is in heaven.

B. (1) The Kingdom of Heaven is a fulfilment of the law,
17-48.

17 Think not that I came to destroy the law or the
18 prophets : I came not to destroy, but to fulfil. For

---

12. Rejoice. That which naturally brings distress and
despair to men, will bring delight in the Kingdom of God.

13-16. The disciples, though lowly and meek, are heirs of
the world. They must claim their inheritance, and not shrink
from a foremost position either from fear of persecution or from
a false idea of Christian poverty and humility.

13. the salt of the earth. Salt (1) preserves from corruption;
(2) gives taste to all that is insipid ; (3) is essential to all organised
life. So the Apostles alone can save the world from corruption;
the Gospel alone can give zest and meaning to Society; it is
essential to the life of the world. **to be trodden under foot of
men.** Thomson, *Land and Book*, 382, describes 'the sweeping
out of the spoiled salt and casting it into the streets' as 'actions
familiar to all men.'

14. the light of the world. See John viii. 12, where Jesus
says of Himself 'I am the light of the world.'

15. the bushel, i.e. the common measure found in every
Jewish house. **lamp.** The lamp in a Jewish house was not
set on a table, but on a tall pedestal or stand, sometimes made
with a sliding shaft.

17. to fulfil. To give the full and true meaning to the law :
not to extend or develop it so much as to teach the deep
underlying principles of it. Thus St Paul says, 'love is the
fulfilling of the law,' Rom. xiii. 10.

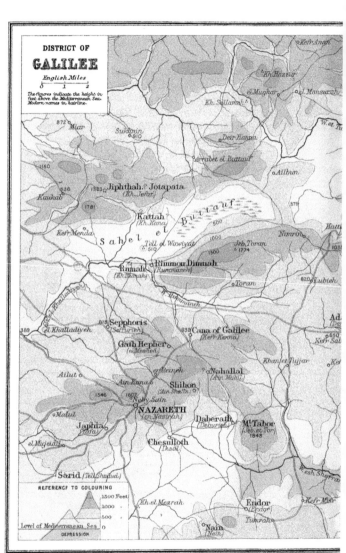

DISTRICT OF
GALILEE

English Miles
0   1   2

The figures indicate the height in
feet above the Mediterranean Sea.
Modern names in hairline.

Kefr Anan

Kh. Hazeur

'Mughar   el Mansurah

Kh. Sellameh

W. et Tu

872   Miar   Sukmin
                     910
                                    Deir Hanna

1150   Arrabet el Buttauf   Ailbun

530   Jiphthah. Jotapata
Kaukab   (Kh. Jefat)

1781

Kattah   el   Buttauf   379
Kefr Menda   (Kh. Kana)
              S a h e l   500
                    Tell el Wawiyat   1000   Hatti
                    510   Jeb. Toran   1035
                                1774
                          1500
              Rimmon Dimnah
Rumah   820 Yubleh
(Kh. Rumah) (Rumaneh)   Toran

                    W. el Melek

389 el Khattladiyeh
                                              Ad
915 Sepphoris   (Da
     (Seffurieh)   633 Cana of Galilee   650
                        (Kefr Kenna)   Kefr Sab
     Gath Hepher
     (el Meshhed)
                                         Khan et Tujjar   Kef
Ailut   el Meinveh   7 Nahallal
              Ain Runa.   (Ain Mahil)
              1602 Shihon
     1546   Neby Sain (Ain Sha'in)
Malul   NAZARETH
              (en Nasirah)   Daberath
Japhia   (Deburieh)   Mt Tabor
(Yafa)   (Jeb. et Tor)
el Mujeidil   Chesulloth   1843
                   (Iksal)

Sarid (Tell Shadud)   W. esh Sha

REFERENCE TO COLOURING
                          1500 Feet   Kh. el Mezrah
                          1000   Endor
                          500   (Endor)   Kefr Misr
Level of Mediterranean Sea   0   Tumrah
DEPRESSION   Nain
                                  (Nein)

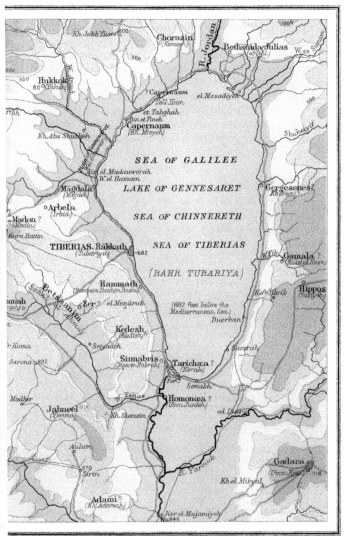

verily I say unto you, Till heaven and earth pass away, one jot or one tittle shall in no wise pass away from the law, till all things be accomplished. Whosoever therefore 19 shall break one of these least commandments, and shall teach men so, shall be called least in the kingdom of heaven : but whosoever shall do and teach them, he shall be called great in the kingdom of heaven. For I say 20 unto you, that except your righteousness shall exceed *the righteousness* of the scribes and Pharisees, ye shall in no wise enter into the kingdom of heaven.

(*a*) The teaching of Christ on the Decalogue, 21–37.

Ye have heard that it was said to them of old time, 21 Thou shalt not kill ; and whosoever shall kill shall be in danger of the judgement : but I say unto you, that every 22 one who is angry with his brother shall be in danger of the judgement ; and whosoever shall say to his brother, Raca, shall be in danger of the council ; and whosoever shall say, Thou fool, shall be in danger of the hell of fire.

---

jot, '*yod*' the smallest of the Hebr. characters, generally a silent letter, rather the adjunct of a letter than an independent letter. Still there are instances where an important difference of meaning depends on the question whether *yod* should be present or absent in a word. **tittle.** The English word means *a point*; the Greek word means literally *a horn.* Here the extremity of a letter, a little point in which one letter differs from another. For instances see the Cambridge Greek Testament.

20. righteousness, '*observance of the law.*' Unless ye observe the law with greater exactness than the Pharisees, ye shall not enter the kingdom of heaven. The Pharisaic righteousness consisted in extended and minute external observances, to exceed that righteousness was to reach the spiritual meaning of the law.

21. to them of old time, a correction for 'by them of old time,' A.V.

22. in danger of the judgement...the council, i.e. 'liable to the judgment of the lower court...of the higher court or Sanhedrin.' See note on ch. xxvi. 3. **Raca.** A word of contempt, said to be from a root meaning to 'spit.' **hell of fire,** or '*Gehenna of fire,*' i.e. burning Gehenna.' *Gehenna* is the Greek form of the Hebrew Ge-Hinnom or 'Valley of Hinnom,' sometimes called 'Valley of the sons of Hinnom,' also 'Tophet' (Jer. vii. 31).

23 If therefore thou art offering thy gift at the altar, and
there rememberest that thy brother hath aught against
24 thee, leave there thy gift before the altar, and go thy way,
first be reconciled to thy brother, and then come and offer
25 thy gift. Agree with thine adversary quickly, whiles thou
art with him in the way ; lest haply the adversary deliver
thee to the judge, and the judge deliver thee to the officer,
26 and thou be cast into prison. Verily I say unto thee,
Thou shalt by no means come out thence, till thou have
paid the last farthing.

27 Ye have heard that it was said, Thou shalt not commit
28 adultery : but I say unto you, that every one that looketh
on a woman to lust after her hath committed adultery
29 with her already in his heart. And if thy right eye

It was a deep narrow glen S.W. of Jerusalem, once the scene of
the cruel worship of Molech ; but Josiah, in the course of his
reformation, 'defiled Tophet, that no man might make his son
or his daughter to pass through the fire to Molech' (2 Kings
xxiii. 10). After that time pollutions of every kind, among them
the bodies of criminals who had been executed, were thrown into
the valley. From this defilement and from its former desecration
Gehenna was used to express the abode of the wicked after death.
The words 'of fire' are added, either because of the ancient
rites of Molech, or, if a Rabbinical tradition is to be credited,
because fires were always burning in the valley.

23. offering thy gift at the altar, such as a lamb or a pair
of doves. Note the tense of incomplete action. **hath aught
against thee**, hath cause of complaint against thee just or unjust,
if the quarrel is still not made up.

24. before the altar. Stay the sacrifice, though begun, for
God will not accept it unless the heart be free from anger, and
the conscience from offence.

25, 26.   The illustration is drawn from a legal process.   It
would be wise for the debtor to arrange with the creditor while
he is on the way to the court ; otherwise the judge's sentence
and a hopeless imprisonment await him. Sin is the debt (here
especially anger, a source of murder), the sense of sin or the
conscience is the adversary. Let the sinner come to terms with
his conscience by confession of sin and prayer for forgiveness
while he has opportunity, lest he be brought unrepentant and
unforgiven to the tribunal of the judge.

29. thy right eye. Suggested by the preceding verse. The

causeth thee to stumble, pluck it out, and cast it from
thee : for it is profitable for thee that one of thy members
should perish, and not thy whole body be cast into hell.
And if thy right hand causeth thee to stumble, cut it off, 30
and cast it from thee : for it is profitable for thee that
one of thy members should perish, and not thy whole
body go into hell.　It was said also, Whosoever shall put 31
away his wife, let him give her a writing of divorcement :
but I say unto you, that every one that putteth away his 32
wife, saving for the cause of fornication, maketh her an
adulteress : and whosoever shall marry her when she is
put away committeth adultery.

Again, ye have heard that it was said to them of old 33
time, Thou shalt not forswear thyself, but shalt perform
unto the Lord thine oaths : but I say unto you, Swear 34
not at all ; neither by the heaven, for it is the throne

---

eye and the hand are not only in themselves good and serviceable,
but *necessary*.　Still they may become the occasion of sin to us.
So pursuits and pleasures innocent in themselves may bring
temptation, and involve us in sin.　These must be resigned,
however great the effort implied in ' cast it from thee.'

causeth thee to stumble.　The Greek word also means to
entrap by means of a bait, so to allure to destruction, and
figuratively; as here, to tempt to sin.

31.　a writing of divorcement.　See note on ch. i. 19.　The
greatest abuses had arisen in regard to divorce, which was
permitted on very trivial grounds.　One Rabbinical saying was
' If any man hate his wife, let him put her away.'　Copies of
these bills of divorce are still preserved.

32.　when she is put away, or, *divorced*.

33.　Thou shalt not forswear thyself.　The reference is to the
third commandment, 'Thou shalt not take my name in vain,' i.e.
on a falsehood.　Cp. also Levit. xix. 12, ' Ye shall not swear by my
name falsely, neither shalt thou profane the name of thy God.'

34.　for it is the throne of God.　Such was the prevalent hypocrisy that the Jews of the day thought that they
escaped the sin of perjury if in their oaths they avoided using
the name of God.　One of the Rabbinical sayings was ' As
heaven and earth shall pass away, so passeth away the oath
taken by them.'　Our Lord shows that a false oath taken by

35 of God ; nor by the earth, for it is the footstool of his
feet ; nor by Jerusalem, for it is the city of the great
36 King. Neither shalt thou swear by thy head, for thou
37 canst not make one hair white or black. But let your
speech be, Yea, yea ; Nay, nay: and whatsoever is more
than these is of the evil *one*.

(*b*) The law of Retaliation 38-42.

38 Ye have heard that it was said, An eye for an eye, and
39 a tooth for a tooth: but I say unto you, Resist not him
that is evil: but whosoever smiteth thee on thy right
40 cheek, turn to him the other also. And if any man would
go to law with thee, and take away thy coat, let him have
41 thy cloke also. And whosoever shall compel thee to go
42 one mile, go with him twain. Give to him that asketh
thee, and from him that would borrow of thee turn not
thou away.

---

heaven, by earth, or by Jerusalem is none the less a profanation
of God's name.

38. An eye for an eye. Jewish history, however, records
no instance of the law being literally carried out. A fine was
substituted for the retributive penalty. But the principle of retaliation underlay the enactments of the law, and it is against
the principle that Christ's words are directed.

39. Resist not him that is evil, i.e. do not seek to retaliate
evil for evil. **smiteth thee.** See ch. xxvi. 67. **turn to him the
other also.** To be understood with the limitation imposed on
the words by our Lord's personal example, John xviii. 22, 23.

40. coat, '*tunic*,' the under-garment. It had sleeves, and
reached below the knees, somewhat like a modern shirt. **cloke,**
the upper garment. A large square woollen robe, resembling
the modern Arab *abba* or *abayeh*. The poorest people wore a
tunic only. Among the richer people many wore two tunics
besides the upper garment. Wealth is often shown in the East
not only by the quality but also by the amount of clothing worn.

41. compel. The Greek word is derived from the Persian
and signifies *to press into service as a courier* for the royal post,
then, generally, 'to force to be a guide,' 'to requisition,' 'com-
mandeer,' men or cattle. This was one of the exactions which
the Jews suffered under the Romans.

42. that would borrow of thee. Forced loans have been a

(c) Love or Charity, 43-48.

Ye have heard that it was. said, Thou shalt love thy 43
neighbour, and hate thine enemy: but I say unto you, 44
Love your enemies, and pray for them that persecute
you; that ye may be sons of your Father which is in 45
heaven: for he maketh his sun to rise on the evil and the
good, and sendeth rain on the just and the unjust. For 46
if ye love them that love you, what reward have ye? do
not even the publicans the same? And if ye salute your 47
brethren only, what do ye more *than others*? do not even
the Gentiles the same? Ye therefore shall be perfect, as 48
your heavenly Father is perfect.

B. (2) The Kingdom of Heaven in regard to Pharisaic rules.
   1-34.
(a) Almsgiving. 1-4.

Take heed that ye do not your righteousness before 6

---

mode of oppression in every age, from which, perhaps, no people
have suffered more than the Jews.

43. Thou shalt love thy neighbour, Levit. xix. 18, 'Thou
shalt love thy neighbour as thyself.' The second clause does
not occur in Levit., but was a Rabbinical inference. Heathen
writers bear testimony to this unsocial characteristic of the Jews.

45. that ye may be &c. See note on *v.* 9. To act thus
would be to act like God, who blesses those who curse Him and
are His enemies, by the gifts of sun and rain. This is divine.
Mere return of love for love is a human, even a heathen virtue.

46. publicans, tax-gatherers; not collectors of a regular tax
fixed by government, as with us, but men who by a payment to
the State purchased the right of exacting as much as they could
from the people. In making these exactions the publicans
practised every kind of cruelty and oppression. As a rule
therefore only the least patriotic and the most degraded of the
population undertook these functions, which naturally rendered
them odious to their fellow-citizens. It is this system pursued
in the Turkish Empire that produces much frightful misery and
illegal oppression. In Galilee the publicans would be in the
service of Herod Antipas.

1. righteousness, a better supported reading than 'alms'
A.V. The two words had nearly the same meaning with
the Jews, partly because the poor had a right to share in

men, to be seen of them: else ye have no reward with your Father which is in heaven.

2 When therefore thou doest alms, sound not a trumpet before thee, as the hypocrites do in the synagogues and in the streets, that they may have glory of men. Verily

3 I say unto you, They have received their reward. But when thou doest alms, let not thy left hand know what

4 thy right hand doeth: that thine alms may be in secret: and thy Father which seeth in secret shall recompense thee.

(*b*) Rules for prayer. 5-9.

5 And when ye pray, ye shall not be as the hypocrites: for they love to stand and pray in the synagogues and in the corners of the streets, that they may be seen of men. Verily I say unto you, They have received their reward.

---

the produce of the land; partly because almsgiving is the most natural and obvious external work of righteousness.

2. sound not a trumpet. The chests for alms in the Synagogue and also in the Temple treasury were called *shopharoth* (trumpets) from their shape. Possibly the words of the text contain a reference to these *shopharoth*. Those who dropped their coins into the 'trumpets' with a ringing sound might be said 'to sound their trumpet.' But perhaps the expression means simply 'avoid ostentation in almsgiving.' **hypocrites.** The Greek word means (1) Lit. 'one who answers'; then from dialogues on the stage (2) 'an actor,' hence (3) those who play a part in life, whose actions are not the true reflection of their thoughts, whose religion is external and unreal. Such men begin by deceiving others, but end in self-deception. It is against these that our Lord's severest reproofs are delivered. **They have received.** Their reward is *now* and *on earth*.

3. when thou doest alms. Observe the singular number here and *v.* 6; the duties of prayer and almsgiving are taught in their personal and individual aspect.

4. shall recompense thee, 'openly' of A.V. omitted on the best authority. The insertion gave a false antithesis, as the contrast is not between secret act and open reward, but between reward by God and reward by man.

5. to stand. There is no stress on this word, for the posture of standing was as closely connected with prayer as that of sitting was with teaching.

But thou, when thou prayest, enter into thine inner cham- 6
ber, and having shut thy door, pray to thy Father which
is in secret, and thy Father which seeth in secret shall
recompense thee. And in praying use not vain repetitions, 7
as the Gentiles do: for they think that they shall be heard
for their much speaking. Be not therefore like unto 8
them: for your Father knoweth what things ye have
need of, before ye ask him. After this manner therefore 9
pray ye:

9–15. The Lord's Prayer. St Luke xi. 2–4, where the
prayer is found in a different connexion, and is given by
our Lord in answer to a request from the disciples to teach
them to pray, 'even as John taught his disciples.'

Our Father which art in heaven, Hallowed be thy name.
Thy kingdom come. Thy will be done, as in heaven, so on 10
earth. Give us this day our daily bread. And forgive us our 11
———————————————————————————— 12

6. pray to thy Father which is in secret. Christ was the
first to enjoin clearly secret and silent prayer. Certainly to pray
aloud and in public appears to have been the Jewish practice.

7. use not vain repetitions. It is not the length of time
spent in prayer or the fervent or reasonable repetition of forms
of prayer that is forbidden, but the mechanical repetition of set
words, and the belief that the efficacy of prayer consists in such
repetition.

9. Our Father. It is of the essence of Christian prayer that
God should be addressed as a Father to whose love we appeal,
not as a God whose anger we appease. The analogy removes
nearly all the real difficulties on the subject of prayer. A wise
earthly father does not grant *all* requests, but all which are for
the good of his children and which are in his power to grant.
Again, the child asks without fear, yet no refusal shakes his
trust in his father's love or power. **Hallowed** '*Held sacred*,'
'*revered*.' Each of these petitions implies an obligation to carry
out on our own part what we pray God to accomplish.

11. bread. Primarily in a literal sense, subsistence as distinct
from luxury; but the spiritual meaning cannot be excluded,
Christ the Bread of Life is the Christian's daily food. The
address to God as Father influences each petition—to feed, to
forgive and to protect his children, are special acts of a father's
love. **daily.** The Greek word translated 'daily' is unknown
to the Classics and in N.T. occurs in the Lord's Prayer only.
For a discussion of the meaning and history of this word see

13 debts, as we also have forgiven our debtors. And bring
us not into temptation, but deliver us from the evil *one*.
14 For if ye forgive men their trespasses, your heavenly
15 Father will also forgive you. But if ye forgive not men
their trespasses, neither will your Father forgive your
trespasses.

(*c*) Truth about Fasting, 16-18.

16   Moreover when ye fast, be not, as the hypocrites, of a
sad countenance: for they disfigure their faces, that they
may be seen of men to fast. Verily I say unto you, They
17 have received their reward. But thou, when thou fastest,

---

note in Cambridge Greek Testament. 'Daily' fairly expresses
the general meaning of the word which signifies dependence
each succeeding moment on the Father's aid.

12. debts. Sin is a debt—a shortcoming in the service due
to God or a harm to fellow-men that requires reparation.
St Paul gives vivid expression to the thought Col. ii. 14, 'the
bond against us'—'the account standing against us.' It is
contemplated as a thing left undone, rather than an act of
transgression.

13. deliver, lit. *draw to thyself, rescue* as from an enemy.
from the evil one (1) i.e. Satan, or (2) from evil. The Greek
bears either rendering, but the neuter is preferable and gives a
deeper sense. We pray to be delivered from all that is included
under the name of evil, not only from external evil but from the
principle of evil within us.

The doxology 'for thine is the kingdom &c.' which appears in
A.V. is not supported by high MS. authority. It is probably an
insertion from the liturgy.

14. trespasses. Another conception of sin, either (1) a false
step, a blunder, or (2) a fall beside the way (cp. Heb. vi. 6), so
a transgression.

16. Fasting, in itself a natural result of grief, as any one who
has witnessed deep sorrow knows, easily degenerates into a form
without reality.

disfigure. Either (1) make unseen, 'veil,' or (2) cause to
disappear, so 'destroy,' hence (3) 'mar,' by leaving the face
unwashen, or by throwing ashes on the head. The first meaning
(1) is well established, that of (2) 'destroying' is the prevailing
one in LXX., the sense of (3) 'disfiguring,' or 'marring' has
less support. **that they may be seen of men to fast,** a good
change from the rendering of A.V. 'that they may appear unto
men to fast.'

anoint thy head, and wash thy face; that thou be not 18
seen of men to fast, but of thy Father which is in secret:
and thy Father, which seeth in secret, shall recompense
thee.

(*d*) True Riches, 19-21.

Lay not up for yourselves treasures upon the earth, 19
where moth and rust doth consume, and where thieves
break through and steal: but lay up for yourselves 20
treasures in heaven, where neither moth nor rust doth
consume, and where thieves do not break through nor
steal: for where thy treasure is, there will thy heart be 21
also.

(*e*) Spiritual Darkness and Light, 22, 23.

The lamp of the body is the eye: if therefore thine 22
eye be single, thy whole body shall be full of light.   But 23
if thine eye be evil, thy whole body shall be full of dark-

---

17. anoint thy head. As if feasting rather than fasting.

19. moth and rust. Oriental wealth consisted to a great·
extent in stores of linen, embroidered garments, &c., which were
handed down and left as heirlooms.   **moth.** The English word =
'the devourer.'

rust. Money was frequently buried in the ground in those
unsettled times, and so would be more liable to rust.   Banks in
the modern sense were unknown.   **break through.** An expression applicable to the mud walls of Oriental huts.

21. where thy treasure is. The words gain point if we
think of the hoards buried in the *earth*.

22. The lamp. The eye is not itself the light, but contains
the light; it is the 'lamp' of the body, the light-conveying
principle. If the eye or lamp is single, it admits the influx of
the pure light only; if an eye be evil, i.e. affected with disease,
the body can receive no light at all. The whole passage is on
the subject of the *singleness* of service to God. In the current
phraseology 'a good eye' meant a bountiful heart, 'an evil eye'
a covetous heart. This gives to our Lord's words the thought,
'covetousness darkens the soul more than anything else, it is a
medium through which the light cannot pass.' The connexion in
which the words occur in Luke xi. 34 is instructive. The inference
there is that the spiritual perception of the Pharisees is dimmed,
so that they cannot recognize Christ.

C.

3

ness. If therefore the light that is in thee be darkness, how great is the darkness!

(*f*) Singleness of Service, 24.

24 No man can serve two masters: for either he will hate the one, and love the other; or else he will hold to one, and despise the other.

(*g*) Trust in God, 25-34. The parallel passage (Luke xii. 22-31) follows immediately the parable of the Rich Fool.

25 Ye cannot serve God and mammon. Therefore I say unto you, Be not anxious for your life, what ye shall eat, or what ye shall drink; nor yet for your body, what ye shall put on. Is not the life more than the food, and the
26 body than the raiment? Behold the birds of the heaven, that they sow not, neither do they reap, nor gather into barns; and your heavenly Father feedeth them. Are not
27 ye of much more value than they? And which of you by
28 being anxious can add one cubit unto his stature? And

---

23. the light that is in thee. If the light be darkened by the diseased and impervious medium which prevents it gaining an entrance all will be darkness within. Covetousness permits no ray of divine light to enter.

24. serve two masters. Strictly, *be a slave to two masters*. The absolute subjection of the slave must be considered. The interests of the 'two masters' are presupposed to be diverse. **mammon.** An Aramaic and a Punic word signifying '*wealth*.' It is said, on hardly sufficient authority, to have been personified as a god. This would strengthen the antithesis.

25. Therefore, i.e. because this double service is impossible there must be no distraction of thought. **Be not anxious.** The argument in the verse is : such anxiety is unnecessary; God gave the life and the body; will He not give the smaller gifts of food and clothing?

26. they sow not &c. There is no argument here against forethought or labour. In one sense 'trusting to providence' is idleness and a sin. God has appointed labour as the means whereby man provides for his wants. Even birds show forethought, and search in faith for the food which God has provided for them.

27. add one cubit unto his stature. The word translated stature sometimes signifies 'duration of life,' so that the meaning

why are ye anxious concerning raiment? Consider the
lilies of the field, how they grow; they toil not, neither do
they spin: yet I say unto you, that even Solomon in all 29
his glory was not arrayed like one of these. But if God 30
doth so clothe the grass of the field, which to-day is, and
to-morrow is cast into the oven, *shall he* not much more
clothe you, O ye of little faith? Be not therefore anxious, 31
saying, What shall we eat? or, What shall we drink? or,
Wherewithal shall we be clothed? For after all these 32
things do the Gentiles seek; for your heavenly Father
knoweth that ye have need of all these things. But seek 33
ye first his kingdom, and his righteousness; and all these
things shall be added unto you. Be not therefore anxious 34
for the morrow: for the morrow will be anxious for itself.
Sufficient unto the day is the evil thereof.

7. C. Characteristics of the Kingdom, 1–27. After contrasting
the New Law with the Mosaic Law and with Pharisaic rules
and conduct, Jesus proceeds to lay down rules for the
guidance of His disciples in the Christian life. (a) Truth
in judgment, 1–6. The passage occurs in St Luke's report
of the Sermon on the Mount (ch. vi. 37, 38), with a different
context, and a further illustration of 'full measure.'

Judge not, that ye be not judged. For with what $\frac{7}{2}$

---

may be 'add a cubit to his life.' Comp. Ps. xxxix. 5, 'Thou
hast made my days as an handbreath.' On the whole, however,
it is better to take 'cubit' and 'stature' in the literal sense.

28. raiment. The birds are an example of God's care in
providing food, the flowers of His care in providing apparel.
The Creator promises that the care shown to the lowliest of His
works shall be extended to the noblest.   **the lilies of the field.**
Either used generally of any bright and beautiful flower, or of
some special variety, the Hulêh lily, as Dr Thomson thinks, or
the *anemone coronaria*, according to Canon Tristram.

30. cast into the oven. In Eastern countries the oven is
often a circular hole made in the ground with cemented sides.
Into that is thrown the fuel-grass, or thorns, or dried dung, and
the thin bread-cakes are baked on the sides. Sometimes the
oven is a jar-shaped vessel of baked clay raised above the ground,
and is either fixed or movable.

1. judge not. The censorious spirit is condemned; it is

judgement ye judge, ye shall be judged: and with what
3 measure ye mete, it shall be measured unto you. And
why beholdest thou the mote that is in thy brother's eye,
but considerest not the beam that is in thine own eye?
4 Or how wilt thou say to thy brother, Let me cast out the
mote out of thine eye; and lo, the beam is in thine own
5 eye? Thou hypocrite, cast out first the beam out of thine
own eye; and then shalt thou see clearly to cast out the
mote out of thy brother's eye.

6 Give not that which is holy unto the dogs, neither cast
your pearls before the swine, lest haply they trample them
under their feet, and turn and rend you.

(b) The Father's love for the children of the Kingdom, 7-12.

7 Ask, and it shall be given you; seek, and ye shall find;

---

opposed to the 'forbearance,' 'fairness in judgment,' that allows
for faults, a characteristic ascribed to Jesus Christ Himself, 2 Cor.
x. 1; cp. also Rom. xiv. 3 foll.

2. judgement. Either (1) in the sense of a judicial sentence,
or (2) a rule or principle of judging, apparently the meaning here.

3. mote. A 'twig,' 'splinter,' dry particle of hay, &c.

4. the beam is in thine own eye. Which (1) ought to prevent
condemnation of another for a less grave offence; and which (2)
would obscure the spiritual discernment, and so render thee an
incapable judge. The Pharisaic sin of hypocrisy (see next verse)
was deeper and more fatal to the spiritual life than the sins which
the Pharisee condemned. This metaphor or parable of the mote
and the beam is one which may have been drawn from the
carpenter's shop.

6. The connexion between this verse and the preceding section
is not quite obvious. It seems to be this. Although evil and
censorious judgment is to be avoided, discrimination is needful.
The Christian must be judicious, not judicial.

that which is holy. Some have seen in the expression a
reference to the holy flesh of the offering (Hag. ii. 12). But
this allusion is very doubtful; see Meyer on this passage. **the
dogs...swine.** Unclean animals; see the proverb quoted 2 Pet.
ii. 22. See note on ch. xv. 26. **pearls.** The only gems
mentioned in the Gospels, twice named by Jesus: here, where
they signify the deepest spiritual thoughts of God and heaven,
and ch. xiii. 46, where 'the pearl of great price' is the kingdom
of heaven itself.

knock, and it shall be opened unto you: for every one 8
that asketh receiveth; and he that seeketh findeth; and
to him that knocketh it shall be opened. Or what man 9
is there of you, who, if his son shall ask him for a loaf,
will give him a stone; or if he shall ask for a fish, will 10
give him a serpent? If ye then, being evil, know how to 11
give good gifts unto your children, how much more shall
your Father which is in heaven give good things to them
that ask him? All things therefore whatsoever ye would 12
that men should do unto you, even so do ye also unto
them: for this is the law and the prophets.

(*c*) The narrow entrance, 13, 14.

Enter ye in by the narrow gate: for wide is the gate, 13
and broad is the way, that leadeth to destruction, and
many be they that enter in thereby. For narrow is the 14
gate, and straitened the way, that leadeth unto life, and
few be they that find it.

(*d*) The danger of false guides to the narrow entrance, and the
test of the true, 15-23.

Beware of false prophets, which come to you in sheep's 15

9. **a loaf...a stone...a fish...a serpent.** The things contrasted
have a certain superficial resemblance, but in each case one
thing is good, the other unclean, or even dangerous.
12. **therefore.** The practical result of what has been said
both in regard to judgment and to prayer is mutual charity.
The thought of the divine judgment teaches forbearance; the
thought of the divine goodness teaches kindness.
13, 14. These verses are linked to the preceding by the
thought of prayer, for it is by prayer chiefly that the narrow
entrance must be gained.
13. **Enter ye in by the narrow gate,** Luke xiii. 24, 25. The
illustration seems to be drawn from a mansion having a large
portal at which many enter, and a narrow entrance known to
few, with broad and narrow ways leading respectively to each.
14. **few be they that find it.** An answer to one of the
disputed questions of the day, Luke xiii. 43. It was a question
that had been canvassed most earnestly in the reflective period
after the cessation of prophecy. An answer to it would be
demanded of every great teacher.
15. **false prophets.** Who will not help you to find the

16 clothing, but inwardly are ravening wolves. By their
fruits ye shall know them. Do *men* gather grapes of
17 thorns, or figs of thistles? Even so every good tree
bringeth forth good fruit; but the corrupt tree bringeth
18 forth evil fruit. A good tree cannot bring forth evil fruit,
19 neither can a corrupt tree bring forth good fruit. Every
tree that bringeth not forth good fruit is hewn down, and
20 cast into the fire. Therefore by their fruits ye shall know
21 them. Not every one that saith unto me, Lord, Lord,
shall enter into the kingdom of heaven; but he that doeth
22 the will of my Father which is in heaven. Many will say
to me in that day, Lord, Lord, did we not prophesy by
thy name, and by thy name cast out devils, and by thy
23 name do many mighty works? And then will I profess
unto them, I never knew you: depart from me, ye that
work iniquity.

(e) A description of the true subjects of the Kingdom as
distinguished from the false, 24–27.

24 Every one therefore which heareth these words of mine,
and doeth them, shall be likened unto a wise man,
25 which built his house upon the rock: and the rain
descended, and the floods came, and the winds blew,
and beat upon that house; and it fell not: for it was
26 founded upon the rock. And every one that heareth
these words of mine, and doeth them not, shall be likened
unto a foolish man, which built his house upon the sand:
27 and the rain descended, and the floods came, and the

---

narrow way.   **in sheep's clothing.** Not in a literal sense, but
figuratively, ' wearing the appearance of guilelessness and truth.'
   19. Every tree &c. See note ch. iii. 10.
   22. in that day. A well-known Hebraism for '*the last day.*'
   24. The wise and foolish builders. See Luke vi. 47–49.
   26. every one that heareth. Both classes of men hear the
word. So far they are alike. Moreover the two houses have
externally the same appearance. The great day of trial shows
the difference.
   27. the rain descended. The imagery is from a mountain

winds blew, and smote upon that house; and it fell: and
great was the fall thereof.

And it came to pass, when Jesus ended these words, 28
the multitudes were astonished at his teaching: for he 29
taught them as *one* having authority, and not as their
scribes.

8 1-4. A Leper is cleansed. Mark i. 40-44, and Luke v. 12.
This incident affords one of the most marked instances of
parallelism. The special acts and words of Jesus are described in identical terms. St Matthew places this miracle
after the Sermon on the Mount, and first in a series of
various miracles, proving power to do as well as to teach.
If the Sermon on the Mount were removed from the text
St Matthew's sequence would appear identical with that of
the other Synoptics, a most interesting example of the
manner in which this Evangelist inserts the discourses of
Jesus in the 'Catechetical' order.

And when he was come down from the mountain, great 8
multitudes followed him. And behold, there came to him 2
a leper and worshipped him, saying, Lord, if thou wilt,
thou canst make me clean. And he stretched forth his 3
hand, and touched him, saying, I will; be thou made

---

country, where in summer the wide sandy torrent-bed is dry; in
autumn and winter the streams rush down the mountain sides,
filling the river channels and sweeping away every obstacle.
   29. the scribes. Whose highest boast it was that they never
spoke save in the words of a Rabbi. The Scribes, as an
organised body, originated with Ezra, who was in a special sense
the '*Sopher*' or Scribe. A scribe's education began as early as
in his fifth year. At thirteen he became a 'son of the precept,'
Bar-mitsvah. If deemed fit, he became a disciple. At thirty he
was admitted as a teacher, having tablets and a key given him.
See note, ch. xvi. 19.
   2. a leper. Leprosy is to be regarded as especially symbolic
of sin: (1) the beginning of the disease is almost unnoticed,
(2) it is essentially *unclean*—the leper is *cleansed*, the sick are
healed, (3) it is contagious, (4) in its worst form it is incurable
except by the touch of Christ, (5) it separated a man and classed
him with the dead. **worshipped him.** The tense in the original
marks that persistency in prayer, which Jesus had just promised
should win acceptance; while the leper's words imply a faith
which is another condition of acceptance.

4 clean. And straightway his leprosy was cleansed. And
Jesus saith unto him, See thou tell no man; but go thy
way, shew thyself to the priest, and offer the gift that
Moses commanded, for a testimony unto them.

5-13. Cure of a Centurion's Servant. St Luke vii. 1-10, where
the incident is placed immediately after the Sermon on the
Mount.

5   And when he was entered into Capernaum, there came
6 unto him a centurion, beseeching him, and saying, Lord,
my servant lieth in the house sick of the palsy, grievously
7 tormented. And he saith unto him, I will come and heal
8 him. And the centurion answered and said, Lord, I am
not worthy that thou shouldest come under my roof: but
9 only say the word, and my servant shall be healed. For

---

4. that Moses commanded. 'Two birds alive and clean,
and cedar wood, and scarlet and hyssop.' And on the eighth
day 'two he lambs without blemish, and one ewe lamb of the
first year without blemish, and three tenth deals of fine flour
for a meat offering, mingled with oil, and one log of oil'; or if
poor, 'he shall take one lamb for a trespass offering to be waved,
and one tenth deal of fine flour mingled with oil for a meat
offering, and a log of oil; and two turtledoves, or two young
pigeons, such as he is able to get.' Levit. xiv. 4, 10, 21, 22.
for a testimony unto them. Either (1) to the priests or (2) to
the people who were following Jesus ; in either case to show that
Jesus came to fulfil the law.

5. a centurion, i.e. a captain or commander of a century—a
company nominally composed of a hundred men, the sixtieth
part of a legion in the Roman army. This centurion was
probably an officer in the army of Herod Antipas, which would
be modelled after the Roman fashion, and not, as is often
understood, a Roman centurion.

6. my servant or '*slave*'; the Greek word is a more
affectionate term than the word translated servant in *v.* 9.

8. the centurion answered. The argument lies in a comparison between the centurion's command and the authority of
Jesus. 'If I who am under authority command others, how
much more hast thou power to command who art under no
authority? If I can send my soldiers or my slave to execute my
orders, how much more canst thou send thy ministering spirits
to do thy bidding?'

I also am a man under authority, having under myself
soldiers: and I say to this one, Go, and he goeth; and to
another, Come, and he cometh; and to my servant, Do
this, and he doeth it.   And when Jesus heard it, he 10
marvelled, and said to them that followed, Verily I say
unto you, I have not found so great faith, no, not in
Israel.   And I say unto you, that many shall come from 11
the east and the west, and shall sit down with Abraham,
and Isaac, and Jacob, in the kingdom of heaven: but the 12
sons of the kingdom shall be cast forth into the outer
darkness: there shall be the weeping and gnashing of
teeth.   And Jesus said unto the centurion, Go thy way; 13
as thou hast believed, *so* be it done unto thee.   And the
servant was healed in that hour.

14-17.   The Cure of Peter's Mother-in-law of a Fever, Mark i.
29-31; Luke iv. 38, 39.   St Luke's description bears special
marks of scientific accuracy.   Both St Mark and St Luke
mention that the incident took place when 'he came out of
the synagogue'; and St Mark adds that he went into the
house of Simon and Andrew with James and John.

And when Jesus was come into Peter's house, he saw 14
his wife's mother lying sick of a fever.   And he touched 15
her hand, and the fever left her; and she arose, and

---

9.   this (soldier)...**servant** (slave).   Observe a distinction in
the centurion's orders; his *soldiers* come and go, i.e. march when
he bids them.   His *slave* he orders to do this, i.e. perform any
servile work.   In the household of the centurion Cornelius we
find as here *slaves* and *soldiers* (Acts x. 7).

11.   sit down, i.e. *recline at a feast.*   The image of a banquet
is often used to represent the joy of the kingdom of heaven.
Luke xiv. 15, xxii. 29, 30; Rev. xix. 9.   Cp. Isaiah xxv. 6.

12.   the outer darkness, i.e. the darkness outside the house
in which the banquet is going on.

14.   Peter's house.   From John i. 44 we learn that Bethsaida
was the city of Andrew and Simon Peter.   Either then (1) they
had changed their home to Capernaum, or (2) Bethsaida was
close to Capernaum.   St Peter alone of the Apostles is expressly
named as being married.   **lying.**   Lit. *struck down*, the word
denotes the great and sudden prostration characteristic of fever.

15.   left her.   St Luke has ' immediately she arose.'   To the

16 ministered unto him. And when even was come, they
brought unto him many possessed with devils: and he
cast out the spirits with a word, and healed all that were
17 sick: that it might be fulfilled which was spoken by
Isaiah the prophet, saying, Himself took our infirmities,
and bare our diseases.

18-22. Fitness for Discipleship. Luke ix. 57-62. St Luke
adds a third instance, and places the scene of the incident
in Samaria.

18 Now when Jesus saw great multitudes about him, he
19 gave commandment to depart unto the other side. And
there came a scribe, and said unto him, Master, I will
20 follow thee whithersoever thou goest. And Jesus saith
unto him, The foxes have holes, and the birds of the
heaven *have* nests; but the Son of man hath not where
21 to lay his head. And another of the disciples said unto
22 him, Lord, suffer me first to go and bury my father. But

---

physician the completeness and suddenness of the cure prove
the miraculous nature of it.

16. with a word. Not by a touch, as in the case of leprosy
and fever. Christ never laid His hand on demoniacs.

17. Isaiah liii. 4.

19. a scribe. The accession of a Scribe to the cause of
Christ must have appeared to the people as a great success.
Language of the most extravagant adulation is used to express
the dignity and influence of the Scribes. Yet Jesus discourages
him. We are not told whether, thus brought face to face with
privation and hardship, he was daunted like the young ruler
(ch. xix. 16), or persevered like the sons of Zebedee (ch. xx.
22).

20. Son of man. See Dan. vii. 13. By assuming this title
Jesus manifests Himself as the second Adam, as One who is
essentially man, who took man's nature upon Him, who is man's
representative before God, showing the possibilities of purified
human nature, and so making atonement practicable. The title
'Son of man,' so frequently used by our Lord of Himself, is not
applied to Him except by Stephen (Acts vii. 56), 'I see the
heavens opened, and the Son of man standing on the right hand
of God.'

Jesus saith unto him, Follow me; and leave the dead to
bury their own dead.

23–27. The Storm on the Lake. Mark iv. 35–41; Luke viii.
22–25. St Mark, as usual, has some interesting details:
'it was evening—there were other boats with Him—a great
storm of wind—the waves beat into the boat—He was asleep
on the cushion in the hinder part of the boat.'

And when he was entered into a boat, his disciples 23
followed him. And behold, there arose a great tempest 24
in the sea, insomuch that the boat was covered with the
waves : but he was asleep. And they came to him, and 25
awoke him, saying, Save, Lord; we perish. And he saith 26
unto them, Why are ye fearful, O ye of little faith? Then
he arose, and rebuked the winds and the sea; and there
was a great calm. And the men marvelled, saying, What 27
manner of man is this, that even the winds and the sea
obey him?

28–34. The Gadarene Demoniacs. St Mark v. 1–20; St
Luke viii. 26–39. St Mark and St Luke make mention

---

22. leave the dead to bury their own dead. The word
'dead' is used first in a figurative, secondly in a literal sense,
as in John xi. 25, 26. In a figurative sense by the 'dead' are
intended those who are outside the kingdom, who are dead to
the true life. Perhaps no incident marks more decisively the
height of self-abandonment required by Jesus of His followers.
In this instance the disciple is called upon to renounce for
Christ's sake the last and most sacred of filial duties. The
unswerving devotion to Christ is illustrated in the parallel
passage (Luke ix. 62) by 'the man who puts his hand to the
plough.'

23. a boat. In most MSS. *the* boat or fishing-boat, i.e. the
boat which Jesus always used.

24. he was asleep. The expression in the original is very
impressive. 'He—the Master—continued to sleep.' It is the
only place where the sleep of Jesus is named.

26. Why are ye fearful. Cowardice and want of faith are
classed together as grievous sins in Rev. xxi. 8, 'the fearful and
unbelieving.'

27. the men. The disciples, and other fishermen who were
also on the Lake: see account in Mark.

of one demoniac only. St Mark relates the incident at greater length and with more particularity. St Matthew omits the name 'legion,' the prayer not to be sent into the 'abyss' (Luke), the request of one of the demoniacs to be with Jesus, and the charge which Jesus gives him to tell his friends what great things the Lord had done for him. The sequence observed in the Synoptics of these two miracles manifesting power over the physical and spiritual world is noticeable. It would be a natural connexion in a catechetical form.

28 And when he was come to the other side into the country of the Gadarenes, there met him two possessed with devils, coming forth out of the tombs, exceeding 29 fierce, so that no man could pass by that way. And behold, they cried out, saying, What have we to do with thee, thou Son of God? art thou come hither to torment 30 us before the time? Now there was afar off from them a 31 herd of many swine feeding. And the devils besought him, saying, If thou cast us out, send us away into the 32 herd of swine. And he said unto them, Go. And they came out, and went into the swine: and behold, the whole herd rushed down the steep into the sea, and perished in 33 the waters. And they that fed them fled, and went away into the city, and told everything, and what was befallen to 34 them that were possessed with devils. And behold, all the city came out to meet Jesus: and when they saw him, they besought *him* that he would depart from their borders.

9 1–8. Cure of a Man afflicted with Paralysis. Mark ii. 1–12 ; Luke v. 18–26. Both St Mark and St Luke notice the

---

28. Gadarenes. Gadara, the capital of Peræa, was some distance to the South of the Lake. Gergesa, the modern Khersa, was close to the Eastern shore ; where a steep descent to the verge of the Lake exactly corresponds with the circumstances of the miracle.   **tombs,** hewn out of the mountain-sides, formed convenient dwelling-places for the demoniacs.

32. the steep. The slope of Gergesa, familiar to St Matthew and to the readers of his Gospel.

33. they that fed them. It does not appear whether these were Jews or Gentiles, more probably the latter ; if the former, they were transgressing the law.

crowding of the people to hear Jesus, and narrate the means
by which the sufferer was brought into His presence.

And he entered into a boat, and crossed over, and **9**
came into his own city. And behold, they brought to 2
him a man sick of the palsy, lying on a bed: and Jesus
seeing their faith said unto the sick of the palsy, Son, be
of good cheer; thy sins are forgiven. And behold, certain 3
of the scribes said within themselves, This man blasphemeth. And Jesus knowing their thoughts said, Where- 4
fore think ye evil in your hearts? For whether is easier, 5
to say, Thy sins are forgiven; or to say, Arise, and walk?
But that ye may know that the Son of man hath power 6
on earth to forgive sins (then saith he to the sick of the
palsy), Arise, and take up thy bed, and go unto thy house.
And he arose, and departed to his house. But when the 7
multitudes saw it, they were afraid, and glorified God, 8
which had given such power unto men.

9. The call of St Matthew. Mark ii. 14; Luke v. 27, 28.
St Mark has 'Levi, the son of Alphæus,' St Luke 'a
publican named Levi.' Probably the name Matthew, 'Gift
of Jehovah,' was adopted by the Apostle when he became
a follower of Jesus.

And as Jesus passed by from thence, he saw a man, 9
called Matthew, sitting at the place of toll: and he saith
unto him, Follow me. And he arose, and followed him.

---

1. his own city. Capernaum, the city where He dwelt,
thus designated here only.

2. sick of the palsy. Not in this case 'grievously tormented'
(see ch. viii. 6), therefore suffering from a less severe type of
paralysis.   **their faith.** The faith of those who brought
him as well as his own. Cp. Mark ix. 23, 24.

3. This man blasphemeth, i.e. pretends to a divine power
which he does not possess. The scribes said this because they
had no visible proof of Christ's power to forgive sins. But when
the paralytic rose and walked at Christ's bidding they were left
to infer the invisible miracle by seeing the visible miracle.

6. take up thy bed. The Oriental frequently spreads a mat
upon the ground and sleeps in the open air, in the morning he
rolls up his mat and carries it away.

9.   the place of toll, or *custom-house.*

10–13. A Meal in the Evangelist's House. Mark ii. 15–17; Luke v. 29–32.

10 And it came to pass, as he sat at meat in the house, behold, many publicans and sinners came and sat down 11 with Jesus and his disciples. And when the Pharisees saw it, they said unto his disciples, Why eateth your 12 Master with the publicans and sinners? But when he heard it, he said, They that are whole have no need of a 13 physician, but they that are sick. But go ye and learn what *this* meaneth, I desire mercy, and not sacrifice: for I came not to call the righteous, but sinners.

14–17. A question about Fasting. Mark ii. 18–22; Luke v. 33–39. It is not quite clear whether this further incident took place at Levi's feast. St Luke leads us to draw that inference.

14 Then come to him the disciples of John, saying, Why do we and the Pharisees fast oft, but thy disciples fast 15 not? And Jesus said unto them, Can the sons of the bridechamber mourn, as long as the bridegroom is with them? but the days will come, when the bridegroom shall 16 be taken away from them, and then will they fast. And

---

10. in the house. St Luke says 'and Levi made him a great feast,' which makes it clear that the meal was in Levi's house. **many publicans.** The fact that the tax-gatherers were numerous enough to form a large class of society points significantly to the oppression of the country.

11. The Pharisees were not guests, but came into the house or perhaps into the court while the feast was going on—a custom still prevalent in the East.

13. I desire mercy, I require mercy rather than sacrifice, Hosea vi. 6. It is a protest by the prophet against the unloving, insincere formalist of his day. **to call...sinners.** The addition of '*to repentance*' in A.V. is against the best MS. authority.

15. See note, *v.* 6. 'The children of the bridechamber' were the bridegroom's friends or groomsmen who went to conduct the bride from her father's house (see **note,** ch. xxv. 1). **the bridegroom.** The Jews symbolised the 'congregation' or 'church' by the image of a bride. Jesus sets Himself forth as the Bridegroom of the Christian Church. **will they fast.** Herschell (quoted in *Scripture Manners and Customs*) observes

no man putteth a piece of undressed cloth upon an old
garment; for that which should fill it up taketh from the
garment, and a worse rent is made. Neither do *men* put 17
new wine into old wine-skins: else the skins burst, and
the wine is spilled, and the skins perish: but they put
new wine into fresh wine-skins, and both are preserved.

18-26. The Daughter of Jairus, 18, 19 and 23-26; Mark v.
  22-24 and 35-43. Luke viii. 41, 42 and 49-56. The
  Woman cured of an Issue of Blood, 20-22. Mark v.
  25-34; Luke viii. 43-48. Related with more detail by
  St Mark and St Luke. She had spent all her living on
  physicians. Jesus perceives that virtue had gone out of
  Him. The woman tells all the truth before the people.

While he spake these things unto them, behold, there 18
came a ruler, and worshipped him, saying, My daughter
is even now dead: but come and lay thy hand upon her,
and she shall live. And Jesus arose, and followed him, 19

---

that many Jews who keep voluntary fasts, if invited to a marriage,
are specially exempted from the observance of them. Jesus first
gives a special answer to the question about fasting. There is
a time of sorrow in store for My disciples when fasting will have
a real meaning, *now* in My presence they can but rejoice.
  16. no man putteth &c. Jesus says in effect to John's
disciples: 'Your question implies ignorance of My teaching.
My doctrine is not merely a reformed Judaism like the teaching
of John and Pharisaism, it is a new life to which such questions
as these concerning ceremonial fasting are quite alien.'
  undressed cloth. The old garment is Judaism. Christianity
is not to be pieced on to Judaism to fill up its deficiencies.
This would make the rent—the divisions of Judaism—still more
serious.   **rent.** The Greek word is used of the '*schisms*'
in the Corinthian Church, 1 Cor. i. 10, and has so passed into
ecclesiastical language.
  17. new wine into old wine-skins. The Oriental bottles
are skins of sheep or goats. Old bottles would crack and leak.
The new wine is the new law, the freedom of Christianity. The
new bottles are those fitted to live under that law. The old
wine is Judaism, the old bottles those who, trained in Judaism,
cannot receive the new law, who say 'the old is better' (or
'good'), Luke v. 39.
  18. a ruler. From Mark and Luke we learn that he was
a chief ruler of the synagogue, Jairus by name.

20 and *so did* his disciples. And behold, a woman, who had
an issue of blood twelve years, came behind him, and
21 touched the border of his garment: for she said within
herself, If I do but touch his garment, I shall be made
22 whole. But Jesus turning and seeing her said, Daughter,
be of good cheer; thy faith hath made thee whole. And
23 the woman was made whole from that hour. And when
Jesus came into the ruler's house, and saw the flute-
24 players, and the crowd making a tumult, he said, Give
place: for the damsel is not dead, but sleepeth. And
25 they laughed him to scorn. But when the crowd was put
forth, he entered in, and took her by the hand; and the
26 damsel arose. And the fame hereof went forth into all
that land.

> 27-31. A Cure of two Blind Men. Peculiar to St Matthew.
> Archbp Trench alludes to the fact that cases of blindness
> are far more numerous in the East than in Western
> countries. 'The dust and flying sand enter the eyes,
> causing inflammations......the sleeping in the open air, and
> the consequent exposure of the eyes to the noxious nightly
> dews, is another source of this malady.'

27 And as Jesus passed by from thence, two blind men
followed him, crying out, and saying, Have mercy on us,

---

20. border of his garment. See ch. xiv. 36 and xxii. 5.

23. St Mark and St Luke mention the message to Jairus on
the way, that his daughter was already dead, and name the
three disciples whom Jesus permits to enter the house with Him.
The minstrels are mentioned by St Matthew only. Lane
(*Modern Egyptians*) says "the women of the family raise the
cries of lamentation called '*welweleh*' or '*wilwal*'; uttering the
most piercing shrieks and calling upon the name of the deceased."

the crowd making a tumult. To join in lamentation for the
dead and to assist in the preparation for the funeral rites were
reckoned among the most meritorious works of charity. Here
perhaps the professional mourners are meant. Amos (v. 16) al-
ludes to those who are 'skilful of lamentation.' See also Jer. ix. 17.

24. is not dead, but sleepeth. These words are reported
without variation by the three Synoptists; it is open to question
whether they ought not to be taken of literal sleep. A different
word is used for the sleep of death (John xi. 11; Acts vii. 60).

thou son of David.　And when he was come into the 28
house, the blind men came to him: and Jesus saith unto
them, Believe ye that I am able to do this?　They say
unto him, Yea, Lord.　Then touched he their eyes, saying, 29
According to your faith be it done unto you.　And their 30
eyes were opened.　And Jesus strictly charged them,
saying, See that no man know it.　But they went forth, 31
and spread abroad his fame in all that land.

32–34.　Cure of a Dumb Man possessed by an evil spirit.
　　St Luke xi. 14, 15.

And as they went forth, behold, there was brought to 32
him a dumb man possessed with a devil.　And when the 33
devil was cast out, the dumb man spake: and the multitudes marvelled, saying, It was never so seen in Israel.
But the Pharisees said, By the prince of the devils casteth 34
he out devils.

35–38.　A third circuit in Galilee.　The Preaching of Jesus.
　　The Harvest of the World.　This passage forms the preface
　　to the mission of the Twelve.　The connexion points to a
　　regular sequence of thought in St Matthew's plan.　The

27.　son of David.　See note ch. i. 1.　The thought of the
kingdom of heaven had been closely linked with the reign of a
son of David, but doubtless with many Jews the glory of the
Asmonean dynasty (the Maccabees) and the established power
of the Herods had tended to obscure this expectation.　To have
clung to it was an act of faith.

32.　possessed with a devil.　The word translated 'devil' in
this and similar passages must be carefully distinguished from
the word so translated in the account of the temptation (ch. iv. 1)
and elsewhere.　The possession of the human soul by spiritual
powers or beings is distinguished from ordinary diseases in this
and other passages.　The reality of such possession was not
questioned at the ·time; and at this day there are certain
symptoms in disease and madness which are more naturally
described by the words of the Evangelists in their account of
'demoniacal possession' than by any others.　See note in
Cambridge Greek Testament for a fuller account of the word.

34.　By the prince of the devils casteth he out devils.
The answer to this charge is given ch. xii. 25–30.

work of Christ is described as the model for the work of
the Twelve; cp. *v.* 35 with ch. x. 7, 8. The pity of Jesus for
the lost and shepherdless flock was the *motive* for the
mission; cp. *v.* 36 with ch. x. 6. The thought of the harvest
of God and the labourers, *vv.* 37 and 38, is raised again in
the charge, ch. x. 10.

35 And Jesus went about all the cities and the villages,
teaching in their synagogues, and preaching the gospel
of the kingdom, and healing all manner of disease and all
36 manner of sickness. But when he saw the multitudes, he
was moved with compassion for them, because they were
distressed and scattered, as sheep not having a shepherd.
37 Then saith he unto his disciples, The harvest truly is
38 plenteous, but the labourers are few. Pray ye therefore
the Lord of the harvest, that he send forth labourers into
his harvest.

10. The Mission of the Twelve, 1-4, and the Charge to them,
5-42. Mark iii. 14-19, and vi. 7-13. Luke vi. 12-16;
ix. 1-6.

10 And he called unto him his twelve disciples, and gave
them authority over unclean spirits, to cast them out, and
to heal all manner of disease and all manner of sickness.
2 Now the names of the twelve apostles are these: The

---

37. The harvest truly is plenteous. The same expression
occurs Luke x. 2 on the occasion of sending forth the Seventy;
cp. also John iv. 35, 'look on the fields, that they are white
already unto harvest.'
38. send forth. The Greek verb, lit. *to thrust forth*, denotes
the enthusiastic impulse of mission work.
1. his twelve disciples. The first passages in St Mark and
St Luke record the *choice* or *calling* of the Twelve, this chapter
and Mark vi. and Luke ix. narrate *the* mission or *a* mission of
the disciples. Possibly they were sent forth more than once.
The number twelve was doubtless in reference to the twelve
tribes of Israel, which, as the type of the Christian Church,
survive unbroken and undispersed.
2. apostles, the only passage in this Gospel where the word
occurs. The literal meaning, *sent forth*, or *envoys*, though
scarcely recognized by classical authors, was not new. The title

first, Simon, who is called Peter, and Andrew his brother;
James the *son* of Zebedee, and John his brother; Philip, 3
and Bartholomew; Thomas, and Matthew the publican;

---

of 'apostles' was given in a special sense to the Twelve, but
was not confined to them. Matthias was added to the number
of the Twelve, Paul was 'called to be an apostle,' James the
Lord's brother, and Barnabas, are designated by the same title.
It had even a wider signification: cp. among other passages
Rom. xvi. 7. The name is applied to Jesus Christ, Heb. iii. 1,
He came to do the will of Him that *sent Him*. There are four
lists of the Apostles recorded, one by each of the Synoptic
Evangelists, one in the Acts of the Apostles. No two of these
lists perfectly coincide. This will be seen from the tabular view
below.

Matt. x. 3.	*Mark* iii. 16.	*Luke* vi. 14.	*Acts* i. 13.
1. Simon Peter.	Simon Peter.	Simon Peter.	Peter.
2. Andrew.	James the son of Zebedee.	Andrew.	John.
3. James the son of Zebedee.	John the brother of James.	James.	James.
4. John his brother.	Andrew.	John.	Andrew.
5. Philip.	Philip.	Philip.	Philip.
6. Bartholomew.	Bartholomew.	Bartholomew.	Thomas.
7. Thomas.	Matthew.	Matthew.	Bartholomew.
8. Matthew the Publican.	Thomas.	Thomas.	Matthew.
9. James the son of Alphæus.	James son of Alphæus.	James the son of Alphæus.	James son of Alphæus.
10. Thaddæus.	Thaddæus.	Simon the Zealot.	Simon the Zealot.
11. Simon the Cananæan.	Simon the Cananæan.	Judas (son) of James.	Judas (son) of James.
12. Judas Iscariot.	Judas Iscariot.	Judas Iscariot.	

It will be observed from a comparison of these lists that the
twelve names fall into three divisions, each containing four
names which remain in their respective divisions in all the lists.
Within these divisions, however, the order varies. But Simon
Peter is placed first, and Judas Iscariot last, in all. Again,
Philip invariably heads the second, and James the son of Alphæus
the third division. The classification of the apostolate is the
germ of Christian organisation. It implies diversity of work
and dignity suited to differences of intelligence and character.
The first group of four are twice named as being alone with
Jesus, Mark i. 29, and xiii. 3; Peter and the sons of Zebedee on
three occasions, see ch. xvii. 1.

3. Bartholomew = *son of Tolmai*, probably to be identified
with Nathanael. (1) St John, who twice mentions the name of
Nathanael, never mentions that of Bartholomew; (2) the three
Synoptists mention Bartholomew but not Nathanael. (3) Philip

4 James the *son* of Alphæus, and Thaddæus; Simon the Cananæan, and Judas Iscariot, who also betrayed him.

> 5-42. Christ's Charge to the Apostles. This discourse falls
> naturally into two divisions; of which the first (*vv.* 5-15)
> has reference to the immediate present, the second relates
> rather to the Church of the future. The subdivisions of
> the first part are: (1) Their mission field, 5, 6. (2) Their
> words and works, 7, 8. (3) Their equipment, 9, 10.
> (4) Their approach to cities and houses, 11-15.

5 These twelve Jesus sent forth, and charged them, saying,
Go not into *any* way of the Gentiles, and enter not into
6 any city of the Samaritans: but go rather to the lost
7 sheep of the house of Israel. And as ye go, preach,
8 saying, The kingdom of heaven is at hand. Heal the

---

is closely connected with Nathanael and also with Bartholomew.
(4) Lastly, Nathanael is mentioned with six other disciples as if
like them he belonged to the Twelve. (John xxi. 2.)

4. Simon the Cananæan. Cananæan has the same meaning
as zealot, one being an Aramaic the other a Greek word. The
fierce party of the Zealots professed a rigid attachment to the
Mosaic law; they acknowledged no king save God. Under
Judas the Gaulonite they rose in rebellion at the time of the
census. **Iscariot** = *Man of Kerioth*, in the tribe of Judah;
accordingly (if this be the case) the only non-Galilæan among
the Apostles. For other accounts of the name see *Dict. of Bible.*

5. the Samaritans were foreigners descended from the alien
population introduced by the Assyrian king (probably Sargon),
2 Kings xvii. 24, to supply the place of the exiled Israelites. In
Luke xvii. 18, our Lord calls a Samaritan 'this stranger,' i.e.
this man of alien or foreign race. The bitterest hostility existed
between Jew and Samaritan, which has not died out to this
day. The origin of this international ill-feeling is related
Ezra iv. 2, 3. Their religion was a corrupt form of Judaism.
For, being plagued with lions, the Samaritans summoned a priest
to instruct them in the religion of the Jews. Soon, however,
they lapsed from a pure worship, and in consequence of their
hatred to the Jews, purposely introduced certain innovations.
Their rival temple on Mount Gerizim was destroyed by John
Hyrcanus about 129 B.C. Samaria was the stepping-stone to
the Gentile world. After the Ascension the charge to the
Apostles was to be witnesses 'in Jerusalem, and in all Judæa
and Samaria, and unto the uttermost part of the earth.'

sick, raise the dead, cleanse the lepers, cast out devils: freely ye received, freely give.   Get you no gold, nor 9 silver, nor brass in your purses; no wallet for *your* 10 journey, neither two coats, nor shoes, nor staff: for the labourer is worthy of his food.   And into whatsoever 11 city or village ye shall enter, search out who in it is worthy; and there abide till ye go forth.   And as ye 12 enter into the house, salute it.   And if the house be 13 worthy, let your peace come upon it: but if it be not worthy, let your peace return to you.   And whosoever 14

---

8. cleanse the lepers. Leprosy is not classed with the other diseases.   As especially symbolical of a sin-stricken man, the leper requires cleansing or purification.

9. Get you no gold &c.   The disciples must not furnish themselves with the ordinary equipment of an Eastern traveller. **gold...silver...brass....** Of the three metals named the brass or copper represents the native currency.   The coinage of Herod the Great was copper only.   But Greek and Roman money was also current.   The Roman *denarius*, a silver coin, is frequently mentioned (ch. xviii. 28, xx. 2).   The farthing, *v.* 29, is the Roman *as*, the 16th part of a denarius; the Greek *drachma* of nearly the same value as a denarius, and the *stater* (ch. xvii. 27), were also in circulation.

10. no wallet, such as David wore when he went to meet Goliath.   **two coats,** i.e. 'two tunics.'   It was a mark of luxury to wear more than one tunic, or to wear *shoes* instead of sandals.   See **Mark vi. 9.**   The latter were often made with soles of wood, or rushes, or bark of palm-trees.

12. as ye enter into the house, 'when ye are entering into the house,' i.e. the house of him who is indicated as 'worthy.' The injunction to remain in the same house was, perhaps, partly to avoid feasting from house to house, partly for the sake of secrecy—a necessary precaution in after-times.   Such 'worthy' hosts of the Church afterwards were Lydia at Philippi ('If ye have judged me to be faithful to the Lord, come into my house and abide there,' Acts xvi. 15), Jason at Thessalonica, Gaius perhaps at Derbe, see Rom. xvi. 23.   This kind of general hospitality is still recognized as a duty in the East, where indeed it may be regarded as a necessity.   **salute it.**   Saying 'Peace be unto you' (*Shalom l'cha*), the usual salutation at this day.   This of course explains 'peace' in the next verse.   The ordinary and conventional salutation acquires a sacred depth of meaning on the lips of Christ, Luke xxiv. 36 and John xiv. 27.

shall not receive you, nor hear your words, as ye go forth
out of that house or that city, shake off the dust of your
15 feet.   Verily I say unto you, It shall be more tolerable
for the land of Sodom and Gomorrah in the day of
judgement, than for that city.

> 16-42.   The Church of the Future.   (1) The Apostolic
> character, 16.   (2) Persecution, 17-25.   (3) Consolation—
> the care of the Father, 26-31.   (4) The reward, 32.
> (5) The Christian choice, 33-39.   (6) The hosts of the
> Church, 40-42.

16   Behold, I send you forth as sheep in the midst of
wolves: be ye therefore wise as serpents, and harmless
17 as doves.   But beware of men: for they will deliver you
up to councils, and in their synagogues they will scourge
18 you; yea and before governors and kings shall ye be
brought for my sake, for a testimony to them and to the
19 Gentiles.   But when they deliver you up, be not anxious
how or what ye shall speak: for it shall be given you in
20 that hour what ye shall speak.   For it is not ye that
speak, but the Spirit of your Father that speaketh in you.

---

14. shake off the dust. As St Paul did at Antioch in
Pisidia, Acts xiii. 51. The cities of Israel that rejected the
Gospel should be regarded as heathen. The very dust of them
was a defilement as the dust of a heathen land.

15. Comp. ch. xi. 24.

16. wise...and harmless. The qualities required for the
safety of the unarmed traveller. Prudence and simplicity are
the defence of the weak. Wise = '*prudent*,' full of precaution,
possessing such 'practical wisdom' as Paul had when he claimed
the rights of Roman citizenship at Philippi.

17. beware of men, comp. ch. xvii. 22, 'The Son of man
shall be delivered up into the hands of men.'

synagogues, i.e. provincial synagogue-tribunals. See note,
ch. iv. 23.

18. governors. Such as Felix and Festus at Cæsarea, the
Prætors or Duumviri at Philippi (Acts xvi. 20), the Politarchs
at Thessalonica (Acts xvii. 6).   **kings.** As Herod Agrippa
or the Roman Emperor.

And brother shall deliver up brother to death, and the 21
father his child: and children shall rise up against parents,
and cause them to be put to death. And ye shall be 22
hated of all men for my name's sake: but he that endureth
to the end, the same shall be saved. But when they 23
persecute you in this city, flee into the next: for verily I
say unto you, Ye shall not have gone through the cities of
Israel, till the Son of man be come.

A disciple is not above his master, nor a servant above 24
his lord. It is enough for the disciple that he be as his 25
master, and the servant as his lord. If they have called
the master of the house Beelzebub, how much more *shall
they call* them of his household! Fear them not therefore: 26
for there is nothing covered, that shall not be revealed;
and hid, that shall not be known. What I tell you in the 27

---

21. brother...brother, father...his child. The history of
persecutions for religion affords many instances of this.

22. he that endureth to the end &c. The parallel expression
Luke xxi. 19 is made clear by this verse, 'by your patience ye
shall win your souls' (R.V.), i.e. win your true life by enduring
to the end.

23. till the Son of man be come. The passage in Luke xxi.,
which is to a great extent parallel to this, treats of the destruction
of Jerusalem; and no one who carefully weighs our Lord's words
can fail to see that in a real sense He came in the destruction
of Jerusalem. That event was in truth the judgment of Christ
falling on the unrepentant nation. In this sense the Gospel had
not been preached to all the cities of Israel before Christ came.
But all these words point to a more distant future. The work
of Christian missions is going on, and will still continue until
Christ comes again to a final judgment.

25. Beelzebub. Baal Zebub = '*Lord of flies*,' i.e. 'averter
of flies' (a serious plague in hot countries)—the name of the
Philistine god worshipped at Ekron (2 Kings i. 2, 3), and used
by the Jews to designate the chief of the evil spirits. For
'Beelzebul,' the form in the Greek text, see notes *ad loc.* in
Cambridge Greek Testament.

26. for there is nothing covered &c. Two reasons against
fear are implied: (1) If you fear, a day will come which will
reveal your disloyalty; (2) Fear not, for one day the unreality
of the things that terrify you will be made manifest.

darkness, speak ye in the light: and what ye hear in the
28 ear, proclaim upon the housetops. And be not afraid of
them which kill the body, but are not able to kill the soul:
but rather fear him which is able to destroy both soul and
29 body in hell. Are not two sparrows sold for a farthing?
and not one of them shall fall on the ground without your
30 Father: but the very hairs of your head are all numbered.
31 Fear not therefore; ye are of more value than many
32 sparrows.   Every one therefore who shall confess me
before men, him will I also confess before my Father
33 which is in heaven. But whosoever shall deny me before
men, him will I also deny before my Father which is in
heaven.

34   Think not that I came to send peace on the earth: I came
35 not to send peace, but a sword. For I came to set a man
at variance against his father, and the daughter against
her mother, and the daughter in law against her mother
36 in law: and a man's foes *shall be* they of his own house-
37 hold. He that loveth father or mother more than me is

---

27. **what ye hear in the ear.** Lightfoot (*Hor. Heb.*) refers
this to a custom in the 'Divinity School' of the synagogue (see
ch. iv. 23), where the master whispered into the ear of the
interpreter, who repeated in a loud voice what he had heard.
the housetops. In the village districts of Syria proclamations
are frequently made from the housetops at the present day.
The announcement of the approaching Sabbath was made by
the minister of the synagogue from the roof of an exceeding high
house (Lightfoot, *Hor. Heb.*) just as the Turkish 'Muezzin'
proclaims the hour of prayer from the top of the mosque.

28. **in hell.** See note, ch. v. 22.

29. **sparrows.** The Greek word signifies any kind of small
bird.   **not one of them shall fall** &c. Two deductions may
be drawn—(1) That human life is more precious in God's sight
than the life of the lower animals (*v.* 31); (2) That kindness to
animals is part of God's law.

34. **not to send peace, but a sword.** History shows that
religion has been the great separating influence in the world, in
families, and in nations.

37. The connexion is this: there will be divisions in families;

not worthy of me; and he that loveth son or daughter
more than me is not worthy of me.   And he that doth 38
not take his cross and follow after me, is not worthy of
me.   He that findeth his life shall lose it; and he that 39
loseth his life for my sake shall find it.

40–42.   The Reception of the Apostles and Ministers of Jesus
Christ.

He that receiveth you receiveth me, and he that re- 40
ceiveth me receiveth him that sent me.   He that receiveth 41
a prophet in the name of a prophet shall receive a prophet's
reward; and he that receiveth a righteous man in the
name of a righteous man shall receive a righteous man's
reward.   And whosoever shall give to drink unto one of 42
these little ones a cup of cold water only, in the name of
a disciple, verily I say unto you, he shall in no wise lose
his reward.

---

my disciples must not hesitate to side with *me* rather than with
father or mother, or son or daughter.   The new life changes
the old relationships: everything is viewed now in reference to
Christ, to whom His followers are related as mother and sisters
and brethren.

38. he that doth not take his cross.   These are deeply
interesting and solemn words.   The cross is named for the first
time by the Saviour.   The expression recurs ch. xvi. 24, following
upon the announcement of the Passion to the disciples.   By the
Roman custom criminals were compelled to bear the cross to the
place of execution.

39. He that findeth his life &c.   This means that whoever
will sacrifice the lower pleasures and self-indulgences of life will
find a higher and more blessed life in this world and the next.

40. receiveth.   Whoever welcomes the Apostles and listens
to them, listens to the voice of Jesus Christ and of God the
Father Himself, and They 'will make their abode with him,'
John xiv. 23.

42. one of these little ones.   These are the young disciples,
who are babes in Christ.   The lowest in the scale—Apostles—
Prophets—the saints—the young disciples.   The simplest act of
kindness done to one of Christ's little ones *as such* shall have its
reward.

11 1. Jesus preaches the Gospel, probably unaccompanied by the Twelve.

11 And it came to pass, when Jesus had made an end of commanding his twelve disciples, he departed thence to teach and preach in their cities.

2–19. Concerning John the Baptist. His message to Jesus, 2–6. His position as a Prophet, 7–14. His relation to Jesus and to his contemporaries, 15–19. St Luke vii. 18–35.

2 Now when John heard in the prison the works of the
3 Christ, he sent by his disciples, and said unto him, Art
4 thou he that cometh, or look we for another? And Jesus answered and said unto them, Go your way and tell John
5 the things which ye do hear and see: the blind receive their sight, and the lame walk, the lepers are cleansed, and the deaf hear, and the dead are raised up, and the
6 poor have good tidings preached to them. And blessed is he, whosoever shall find none occasion of stumbling in
7 me. And as these went their way, Jesus began to say unto· the multitudes concerning John, What went ye out into the wilderness to behold? a reed shaken with the

---

2. in the prison. At Machærus. See note, ch. xiv. 3.

3. he that cometh, one of the designations of the Messiah; in every age the prophet said, ' He cometh.' See note ch. i. 18. **another.** A *different* Messiah, whose 'works' shall not be those of love and healing. John had perhaps expected a quicker overthrow of the enemies of Christ, and a speedier coming of the kingdom of God. Therefore he sends the message to confirm his own and his disciples' faith.

5. Comp. Isaiah xxxv. 5 and lxi. 1. The first passage describes the work of God, who '*will come* and save you.' **the poor have good tidings preached to them.** In earthly kingdoms envoys are sent to the rich and great. Compare the thought implied in the disciples' words, ' Who then can be saved?' If it is difficult for the rich to enter the kingdom, how much more for the poor?

6. And blessed is he. Blessed are all who see that these works of mine are truly the works of the Messiah. Some had thought only of an avenging and triumphant Christ.

7. a reed shaken with the wind. A weak or wavering

wind? But what went ye out for to see? a man clothed 8
in soft *raiment*? Behold, they that wear soft *raiment*
are in kings' houses. But wherefore went ye out? to see 9
a prophet? Yea, I say unto you, and much more than a
prophet. This is he, of whom it is written,   10

Behold, I send my messenger before thy face,
Who shall prepare thy way before thee.

Verily I say unto you, Among them that are born of 11
women there hath not arisen a greater than John the
Baptist: yet he that is but little in the kingdom of heaven
is greater than he. And from the days of John the Baptist 12
until now the kingdom of heaven suffereth violence, and
men of violence take it by force. For all the prophets 13
and the law prophesied until John. And if ye are willing 14
to receive *it*, this is Elijah, which is to come. He that 15
hath ears to hear, let him hear. But whereunto shall I 16
liken this generation? It is like unto children sitting in

---

man might be compared to the tall reeds growing by the side
of the Jordan, which every breeze shakes and bends. But this
was not the character of John the Baptist.

9. more than a prophet. John was more than a prophet
because he not only foretold the coming of Christ like the other
prophets, but beheld Him and proclaimed His advent. Besides
this John was himself the subject of prophecy.

11. he that is but little. Those who through Christ are
brought nearer to God and have clearer spiritual knowledge,
have higher privileges than the greatest of those who lived before
the time of Christ.

12. from the days of John. It was from the time of John's
preaching that men began to press into the kingdom, and the
earnest won their way in. For the preaching of John was the
epoch to which all prophecy tended.   **suffereth violence.**
Is forced, broken into, as a ship enters a harbour by breaking
the boom stretched across the harbour's mouth. John's preaching
was the signal for men to press into the kingdom—to adopt
eagerly the new rule and life heralded by John and set forth by
Christ.   **men of violence take it by force.** The invaders,
those who force their way in—the eager and enthusiastic followers
of Christ—seize the kingdom, win it as a prize of war.

14. this is Elijah. See Malachi iv. 5.

16. It is like unto children. The simplest explanation of

17 the marketplaces, which call unto their fellows, and say,
We piped unto you, and ye did not dance; we wailed,
18 and ye did not mourn. For John came neither eating
19 nor drinking, and they say, He hath a devil. The Son of
man came eating and drinking, and they say, Behold, a
gluttonous man, and a winebibber, a friend of publicans
and sinners! And wisdom is justified by her works.

20-24. The Cities that repented not. St Luke x. 13-15, where
the words form part of the charge to the seventy disciples.
It is instructive to compare the connexion suggested by the
two evangelists. In St Matthew the link is the rejection
of Christ by the Jews—then by these favoured cities; in
St Luke, the rejection of the Apostles as suggestive of the
rejection of Jesus.

20 Then began he to upbraid the cities wherein most of
his mighty works were done, because they repented not.
21 Woe unto thee, Chorazin! woe unto thee, Bethsaida! for
if the mighty works had been done in Tyre and Sidon
which were done in you, they would have repented long
22 ago in sackcloth and ashes. Howbeit I say unto you, it
shall be more tolerable for Tyre and Sidon in the day of
23 judgement, than for you. And thou, Capernaum, shalt

---

this comparison is to see in the children who mourned a likeness
to John the Baptist, who was stern and austere in his life and
preaching. The children who piped are like Jesus, who lived
among men, and entered into their joys. The Jews of that day
listened neither to the preaching of John nor of Christ.

19. wisdom is justified by her works. The results or
'works' of divine wisdom show clearly how truly wise it is.
The wisdom of God however little understood now will be
manifested in the end.

21. Chorazin is identified with Kerazeh, two and a half
miles N. of Tell Hûm. The ruins here are extensive and
interesting; among them a synagogue built of hard black basalt
and houses with walls still six feet high. **Bethsaida.** This is
probably Bethsaida Julias on the east bank of the Jordan (see
map), so named by Herod Philip in honour of Julia, daughter of
Augustus. The supposition of a second Bethsaida on the western
shore of the Lake near Capernaum is now generally abandoned.

thou be exalted unto heaven? thou shalt go down unto
Hades : for if the mighty works had been done in Sodom
which were done in thee, it would have remained until
this day.   Howbeit I say unto you, that it shall be more 24
tolerable for the land of Sodom in the day of judgement,
than for thee.

25–27. The Revelation to 'Babes.' St Luke x. 21–22, where
the words are spoken on the return of the Seventy.

At that season Jesus answered and said, I thank thee, 25
O Father, Lord of heaven and earth, that thou didst hide
these things from the wise and understanding, and didst
reveal them unto babes : yea, Father, for so it was well- 26
pleasing in thy sight.   All things have been delivered 27
unto me of my Father: and no one knoweth the Son,
save the Father; neither doth any know the Father, save
the Son, and he to whomsoever the Son willeth to reveal
him.

28–30. Rest for the heavy laden. These words of Jesus are
preserved by St Matthew only. The connecting thought
is, those alone shall know who desire to learn, those alone

---

23. exalted unto heaven. This means either that Capernaum
had exalted herself, prided herself on her superiority to other
cities; or else, that Capernaum was exalted, highly honoured
by the presence of Christ; comp. Is. xiv. 13–15, and Obadiah
3, 4.

25. that thou didst hide, not by an arbitrary and harsh
will, but in accordance with a law of divine wisdom. Truth is
not revealed to the philosophical theorist, but the humility that
submits to observe and follow the method of nature and working
of God's laws is rewarded by the discovery of truth.   **from
the wise and understanding.** The secrets of the kingdom are
not revealed to those who are wise in their own conceit, but to
those who have the meekness of infants and the child-like
eagerness for knowledge. In a special Jewish sense 'the wise
and understanding' are the Scribes and Pharisees.

26. was well-pleasing, lit. *was thy good pleasure*, in the
sense of resolve or determination. The divine plan of discovery
and revelation is a subject of thankfulness.

shall have rest who feel their burden. The babes are those
who feel ignorant, the laden those who feel oppressed.

28 Come unto me, all ye that labour and are heavy laden,
29 and I will give you rest. Take my yoke upon you, and
learn of me; for I am meek and lowly in heart: and ye
30 shall find rest unto your souls. For my yoke is easy, and
my burden is light.

> **12** 1-13. The observance of the Sabbath. 1. The disciples
> pluck ears of corn on the Sabbath. 2. A man with a
> withered hand cured on the Sabbath. St Mark ii. 23-28,
> iii. 1-5; St Luke vi. 1-11.

12   At that season Jesus went on the sabbath day through
the cornfields; and his disciples were an hungred, and
2 began to pluck ears of corn, and to eat. But the Pharisees, when they saw it, said unto him, Behold, thy disciples
do that which it is not lawful to do upon the sabbath.
3 But he said unto them, Have ye not read what David did,

---

28. Come unto me. Jesus does not give rest to all the
heavy laden, but to those of them who show their want of relief
by coming to Him.   **labour and are heavy laden.** The
figure is from beasts of burden which either plough or draw
chariots, wagons, &c.

29. learn of me, i.e. '*become my disciples*'; an idea also
conveyed by the word 'yoke,' which was used commonly among
the Jews for the yoke of instruction.

meek and lowly. Thus Jesus describes His own character.
Cp. 2 Cor. x. 1, 'the meekness and gentleness of Christ.'
rest unto your souls. Cp. Jer. vi. 16, 'Thus saith the Lord,
Stand ye in the ways, and see, and ask for the old paths, where
is the good way, and walk therein, and ye shall find rest for
your souls. But they said, We will not walk therein.' Christ
does not promise rest from bodily toil.

1. began to pluck ears of corn. The Pharisees, who seem
to have been watching their opportunity, make the objection
as soon as the disciples *began* what by Pharisaic rules was an
unlawful act.

2. that which it is not lawful to do. This was not a rule of
the Mosaic law, but one which had been added by the Pharisees.

3. Ahimelech, the priest at Nob, gave David and his
companions five loaves of the shewbread (1 Sam. xxi. 1-7).

when he was an hungred, and they that were with him; how he entered into the house of God, and did eat the 4 shewbread, which it was not lawful for him to eat, neither for them that were with him, but only for the priests? Or 5 have ye not read in the law, how that on the sabbath day the priests in the temple profane the sabbath, and are guiltless? But I say unto you, that one greater than the 6 temple is here. But if ye had known what this meaneth, 7 I desire mercy, and not sacrifice, ye would not have condemned the guiltless. For the Son of man is lord 8 of the sabbath.

And he departed thence, and went into their synagogue: 9 and behold, a man having a withered hand. And they 10 asked him, saying, Is it lawful to heal on the sabbath day? that they might accuse him. And he said unto 11 them, What man shall there be of you, that shall have one sheep, and if this fall into a pit on the sabbath day, will he not lay hold on it, and lift it out? How much 12 then is a man of more value than a sheep! Wherefore it is lawful to do good on the sabbath day. Then saith 13

'It is no improbable conjecture that David came to Nob either on the Sabbath itself, or when the Sabbath was but newly gone.'

4. shewbread. Sometimes called '*bread of the presence*' or '*continual bread*' because it was set forth continually every Sabbath before the Lord. For an account of the shewbread see Levit. xxiv. 5-9.

5. profane the sabbath. By labour in removing the shewbread, preparing fire for the sacrifice, and performing the whole temple service.

7. I desire mercy, and not sacrifice. Quoted a second time, see ch. ix. 13. There is something more binding than the Law, and that is the principle which underlies the Law. The Law rightly understood is the expression of God's love to man. That love allowed the act of David, and the labour of the priests; 'Shall it not permit my disciples to satisfy their hunger?'

12. How much then is a man of more value than a sheep! Comp. 'ye are of more value than many sparrows,' ch. x. 31.

he to the man, Stretch forth thy hand. And he stretched
it forth ; and it was restored whole, as the other.

14-21.   The Pharisees plot against Jesus, who retires.   Mark
     iii. 6-12; Luke vi. 11, 12.

14 But the Pharisees went out, and took counsel against
15 him, how they might destroy him.   And Jesus perceiving
   it withdrew from thence: and many followed him ; and
16 he healed them all, and charged them that they should
17 not make him known: that it might be fulfilled which was
   spoken by Isaiah the prophet, saying,

18   Behold, my servant whom I have chosen;
       My beloved in whom my soul is well pleased :
       I will put my Spirit upon him,
       And he shall declare judgement to the Gentiles.

19   He shall not strive, nor cry aloud ;
       Neither shall any one hear his voice in the streets.

20   A bruised reed shall he not break,
       And smoking flax shall he not quench,
       Till he send forth judgement unto victory.

21   And in his name shall the Gentiles hope.

---

14. took counsel against him. St Mark adds that the
Herodians joined the Pharisees. .

15. withdrew from thence. See ch. x. 23. Jesus follows
the principle which He laid down for His disciples' guidance.

17. spoken by Isaiah the prophet. Is. xlii. 1-4.

18. my servant. In Isaiah's prophecy, either (1) 'the
chosen one,' whom Jehovah raised 'from the north' (Is. xli. 25)
to do His will, and bring about His people's deliverance from
the Babylonish Captivity, or (2) the nation of Israel, the worker
out of Jehovah's purposes; in either case in an ultimate sense
the Messiah.   **judgement.** Here 'the divine rule of life,'
'religion.'

19, 20. These verses describe the gentleness and forbearance
of Christ. He makes no resistance or loud proclamation like an
earthly prince. The bruised reed and the feebly-burning wick
may be referred to the failing lives which Jesus restores and the
sparks of faith which He revives.

20. Till he send forth judgement unto victory, i.e. 'until he

22, 23. Cure of a man who was blind and dumb. Luke xi.
14–16. St Luke omits to mention that the man was blind
as well as dumb.

Then was brought unto him one possessed with a devil, 22
blind and dumb: and he healed him, insomuch that the
dumb man spake and saw. And all the multitudes were 23
amazed, and said, Is this the son of David?

24–30. The Charge, 'He casteth out devils by Beelzebub.'
The Answer of Jesus. Mark iii. 22–27; Luke xi. 15.

But when the Pharisees heard it, they said, This man 24
doth not cast out devils, but by Beelzebub the prince of
the devils. And knowing their thoughts he said unto 25
them, Every kingdom divided against itself is brought to
desolation; and every city or house divided against itself
shall not stand: and if Satan casteth out Satan, he is 26
divided against himself; how then shall his kingdom
stand? And if I by Beelzebub cast out devils, by whom 27
do your sons cast them out? therefore shall they be your
judges. But if I by the Spirit of God cast out devils, then 28
is the kingdom of God come upon you. Or how can one 29
enter into the house of the strong *man*, and spoil his
goods, except he first bind the strong *man*? and then he
will spoil his house. He that is not with me is against 30
me; and he that gathereth not with me scattereth.

---

makes his judgment (see *v.* 18) triumph—until he brings it to
victory.' For 'send forth' see ch. ix. 38.

24. Beelzebub. See ch. x. 25.

27. by whom do your sons cast them out? The children
are the disciples of the Pharisees, who either really possessed
the power of casting out evil spirits, or pretended to have that
power. In either case the argument of Jesus was unanswerable.

29. Not only is Satan not an ally, but he is an enemy and a
vanquished enemy.

30. He that is not with me is against me. The thought of
the contest between Christ and Satan is continued. Satan is
not divided against himself, neither can Christ be. Neutrality
is impossible in the Christian life. It must be for Christ or
against Christ.

31-37. Blaspheming against the Holy Ghost.

31 Therefore I say unto you, Every sin and blasphemy shall
be forgiven unto men; but the blasphemy against the
32 Spirit shall not be forgiven. And whosoever shall speak
a word against the Son of man, it shall be forgiven him;
but whosoever shall speak against the Holy Spirit, it shall
not be forgiven him, neither in this world, nor in that
33 which is to come. Either make the tree good, and its
fruit good; or make the tree corrupt, and its fruit corrupt:
34 for the tree is known by its fruit. Ye offspring of vipers,
how can ye, being evil, speak good things? for out of the
35 abundance of the heart the mouth speaketh. The good
man out of his good treasure bringeth forth good things.
and the evil man out of his evil treasure bringeth forth

31. **Therefore.** The conclusion of the whole is—you are on
Satan's side, and *knowingly* on Satan's side, in this decisive
struggle between the two kingdoms, and this is blasphemy
against the Holy Ghost—an unpardonable sin.

32. **whosoever shall speak against the Holy Spirit.** To
speak against the Holy Spirit is to speak against the clear voice
of conscience, to call good evil and light darkness, to pursue
goodness as such with malignity and hatred. Such sin, or
sinful state, cannot be forgiven, since from its very nature it
excludes the idea of repentance. Jesus, who saw the heart,
knew that the Pharisees were insincere in the charge which they
brought against Him. They were attributing to Satan what
they knew to be the work of God. Their former attacks against
the Son of man had excuse; for instance, they might have
differed conscientiously on the question of Sabbath observance,
now they have no excuse. *vv.* 32-37 are peculiar to St Matthew.

33. **Either make the tree good** &c. The meaning and
connexion are; 'Be honest for once; represent the tree as good,
and its fruit as good, or the tree as evil, and its fruit as evil;
either say that I am evil and that my works are evil, or, if you
admit that my works are good, admit that I am good also and
not in league with Beelzebub.'

34. **how can ye, being evil, speak good things?** Closely
connected with the preceding thought, but further illustrated by
two figures—the overflow as of a cistern, and the abundance of
a treasury.

35. Cp. ch. ii. 11.

evil things. And I say unto you, that every idle word 36
that men shall speak, they shall give account thereof in
the day of judgement. For by thy words thou shalt be 37
justified, and by thy words thou shalt be condemned.

38-42. The Pharisees ask for a Sign. St Luke xi. 16, 29-32.
St Luke omits, or at least does not state explicitly, the
special application of the sign given in v. 40, to understand
which required a knowledge of the Jewish prophets which
would be lacking to St Luke's readers.

Then certain of the scribes and Pharisees answered 38
him, saying, Master, we would see a sign from thee. But 39
he answered and said unto them, An evil and adulterous
generation seeketh after a sign; and there shall no sign
be given to it but the sign of Jonah the prophet: for as 40
Jonah was three days and three nights in the belly of the
whale; so shall the Son of man be three days and three
nights in the heart of the earth. The men of Nineveh 41
shall stand up in the judgement with this generation, and

36, 37. A usual explanation of this passage is that a man's
words shall be the ground of his acquittal or condemnation,
because words are the index of the heart and character. But as
the Greek expression for **words** in v. 37 is the same as that for
account in v. 36 another explanation is: 'By the account thou
givest thyself, by thine own defence, thou shalt be acquitted or
condemned.' Cp. 'out of thine own mouth will I judge thee,
thou wicked servant,' Luke xix. 22. See notes in Cambridge
Greek Testament.

38. we would see a sign from thee. This is the second
expedient taken by the Pharisees after their resolution to destroy
Jesus.

39. adulterous. Estranged from God; a figure often used
by the Prophets to express the defection of Israel from Jehovah.
Cp. ch. xvi. 4 and Is. i. 21 and lvii. 3.

40. Jonah is a sign, (1) as affording a type of the Resurrection,
(2) as a preacher of righteousness to a people who needed
repentance as this generation needs it. **the belly of the
whale.** The O.T. rendering is more accurate, *the fish's belly*
(Jonah ii. 1), *a great fish* (Jonah i. 17). It is scarcely needful to
note that there are no whales in the Mediterranean.

41. shall stand up in the judgement with, i.e. *shall stand up
in the day of judgment beside.* When on the day of judgment

shall condemn it: for they repented at the preaching of
42 Jonah; and behold, a greater than Jonah is here. The
queen of the south shall rise up in the judgement with
this generation, and shall condemn it: for she came from
the ends of the earth to hear the wisdom of Solomon;
and behold, a greater than Solomon is here.

> 43-45. A Figure to illustrate the surpassing Wickedness of the
> day. Luke xi. 24-26, where the connexion is different.
> St Luke, as usual, omits the direct application to Israel.

43 But the unclean spirit, when he is gone out of the man,
passeth through waterless places, seeking rest, and findeth
44 it not. Then he saith, I will return into my house whence I
came out; and when he is come, he findeth it empty, swept,
45 and garnished. Then goeth he, and taketh with himself
seven other spirits more evil than himself, and they enter
in and dwell there: and the last state of that man becometh worse than the first. Even so shall it be also
unto this evil generation.

---

the Ninevites stand side by side with the men of that generation,
they will by their penitence condemn the impenitent Jews.

42. The queen of the south. For an account of the queen
of Sheba or Southern Arabia, see 1 Kings x. 1.

43-45. This short parable explains the supreme wickedness
of the present generation. And herein lies the connexion.
The Jews of former times were like a man possessed by a single
demon, the Jews of the day are like a man possessed by many
demons. And this is in accordance with a moral law. If the
expulsion of sin be not followed by real amendment of life, and
perseverance in righteousness, a more awful condition of sinfulness
will result. See note *v.* 45.

43. waterless places. *The waterless desert*, uninhabited by
man, was regarded by the Jews as the especial abode of evil
spirits.

44. empty. Properly '*at leisure.*' There must be no
leisure in the Christian life; to have cast out a sin does not make
a man safe from sin.

45. Even so shall it be also unto this evil generation.
Israel had cast forth the demon of idolatry—the sin of its earlier
history, but worse demons had entered in—the more insidious
and dangerous sins of hypocrisy and hardness of heart.

46-50. Jesus is sought by His Mother and Brethren. The
true Mother and Brethren of Jesus. Mark iii. 31-35;
Luke viii. 19-21. The account is given with very slight
variation by the three Synoptists. But see Mark iii. 21 and
30, 31, where a *motive* is suggested—'When His friends
heard of it, they went out to lay hold on Him: for they
said, He is beside Himself' (*v.* 21). It would seem that
the Pharisees, on the pretext that Jesus had a demon, had
persuaded His friends to secure Him. This was another
device to destroy Jesus, see *vv.* 14 and 38.

While he was yet speaking to the multitudes, behold, 46
his mother and his brethren stood without, seeking to
speak to him. And one said unto him, Behold, thy 47
mother and thy brethren stand without, seeking to speak
to thee. But he answered and said unto him that told 48
him, Who is my mother? and who are my brethren?
And he stretched forth his hand towards his disciples, 49
and said, Behold, my mother and my brethren! For 50
whosoever shall do the will of my Father which is in
heaven, he is my brother, and sister, and mother.

13 1-9. Jesus teaches in Parables. The Parable of the Sower.
Mark iv. 1-9; Luke viii. 4-9.

On that day went Jesus out of the house, and sat by **13**
the sea side. And there were gathered unto him great 2

---

47. thy brethren. The 'brethren' of Jesus are generally
thought to have been the sons of Joseph by a former marriage.
50. which is in heaven. The addition is important. 'Not
those who do the will of my earthly father, but those who do
the will of my heavenly Father are brethren.' The essence of
sonship is obedience, and obedience to God constitutes brother-
hood to Jesus, Who came to do 'the will of Him that sent Me,'
John vi. 38.
1. sat. The usual position of a Jewish teacher.   **by the
sea side.** At the N. end of the Lake of Gennesaret there are
small creeks or inlets 'where the ship could ride in safety only a
few feet from the shore, and where the multitudes seated on both
sides and before the boat could listen without distraction or
fatigue. As if on purpose to furnish seats, the shore on both
sides of these narrow inlets is piled up with smooth boulders of
basalt.' Thomson, *Land and Book*, p. 356.

multitudes, so that he entered into a boat, and sat ; and
3 all the multitude stood on the beach. And he spake to
them many things in parables, saying, Behold, the sower
4 went forth to sow ; and as he sowed, some *seeds* fell by
the way side, and the birds came and devoured them :
5 and others fell upon the rocky places, where they had not
much earth : and straightway they sprang up, because
6 they had no deepness of earth : and when the sun was
risen, they were scorched ; and because they had no root,
7 they withered away. And others fell upon the thorns ; and
8 the thorns grew up, and choked them : and others fell
upon the good ground, and yielded fruit, some a hundred-
9 fold, some sixty, some thirty. He that hath ears, let him
hear.

10–17. The Reason why Jesus teaches in Parables. Mark iv.
10–12 ; Luke viii. 10.

10 And the disciples came, and said unto him, Why
11 speakest thou unto them in parables ? And he answered
and said unto them, Unto you it is given to know the

---

3. in parables. Up to this time Jesus had preached repentance, proclaiming the kingdom, and setting forth the laws of it
in direct terms. He now indicates by parables the reception,
growth, characteristics, and future of the kingdom. The reason
for this manner of teaching is given below, *vv.* 10–15. **parable**
(Hebr. *mashal*) = 'a *likeness*' or '*comparison.*' Parables differ
from fables in being pictures of possible occurrences—frequently
of actual daily occurrences,—and in teaching *religious* truths
rather than *moral* truths. See below *v.* 10 and *v.* 33.
4. by the way side, i.e. along the narrow footpath dividing
one field from another.
5. rocky places. Places where the underlying rock was
barely covered with earth. The hot sun striking on the thin
soil and warming the rock beneath would cause the corn to
spring up rapidly and then as swiftly to wither.
10. in parables. The parable is suited (1) to the uninstructed,
as being attractive in form and as revealing spiritual truth exactly
in proportion to the capacity of the hearer; and (2) to the
divinely wise as wrapping up a secret which he can penetrate
by his spiritual insight.

mysteries of the kingdom of heaven, but to them it is not given. For whosoever hath, to him shall be given, and 12 he shall have abundance: but whosoever hath not, from him shall be taken away even that which he hath. There- 13 fore speak I to them in parables; because seeing they see not, and hearing they hear not, neither do they under- stand. And unto them is fulfilled the prophecy of Isaiah, 14 which saith,

> By hearing ye shall hear, and shall in no wise under-
> stand;
> And seeing ye shall see, and shall in no wise perceive:
> For this people's heart is waxed gross,   15
> And their ears are dull of hearing,
> And their eyes they have closed;
> Lest haply they should perceive with their eyes,
> And hear with their ears,
> And understand with their heart,
> And should turn again,
> And I should heal them.

But blessed are your eyes, for they see; and your ears, 16

---

11. mysteries. Secrets known only to the initiated—the inner teaching of the gospel. St Paul regards as 'mysteries,' the spread of the gospel to the Gentiles, Eph. iii. 3, 4, 9; the doctrine of the resurrection, 1 Cor. xv. 51; the conversion of the Jews, Rom. xi. 25; the relation of Christ to His Church, Eph. v. 32.

12. Cp. ch. xxv. 29.

13. Therefore speak I to them in parables. Jesus teaches in parables, *because*, as it is, the people do not understand, &c., i.e. (1) either He teaches them in the simplest and most attractive form, so as by degrees to lead them on to deeper knowledge, or (2) He teaches in parables because it is not fitting that divine truths should be at once patent to the unreflective and indifferent multitude.

14. Is. vi. 9, 10. The words form part of the mission of Isaiah.

15. this people's heart is waxed gross. The heart, regarded by the ancients as the seat of intelligence, has become gross or fat, and so closed against the perception of spiritual truth.

17 for they hear. For verily I say unto you, that many
prophets and righteous men desired to see the things
which ye see, and saw them not; and to hear the things
which ye hear, and heard them not.

18–23. The Parable of the Sower is explained. Mark iv.
14–20; Luke viii. 11–15.

18
19 Hear then ye the parable of the sower. When any one
heareth the word of the kingdom, and understandeth it
not, *then* cometh the evil *one*, and snatcheth away that
which hath been sown in his heart. This is he that was
20 sown by the way side. And he that was sown upon the
rocky places, this is he that heareth the word, and
21 straightway with joy receiveth it; yet hath he not root
in himself, but endureth for a while; and when tribulation
or persecution ariseth because of the word, straightway
22 he stumbleth. And he that was sown among the thorns,
this is he that heareth the word; and the care of the
world, and the deceitfulness of riches, choke the word,
23 and he becometh unfruitful. And he that was sown upon
the good ground, this is he that heareth the word, and
understandeth it; who verily beareth fruit, and bringeth
forth, some a hundredfold, some sixty, some thirty.

---

19. On some the word of God makes no *impression*, as we
say; some hearts are quite unsusceptible of good.

20. straightway. The unstable and volatile nature is as
quick to be attracted by the gospel at first, as it is to abandon it
afterwards when the trial comes.

21. tribulation or persecution. Jesus forecasts the persecution of Christians, and the time when 'the love of the many
shall wax cold,' ch. xxiv. 12.   **stumbleth,** or 'is tempted and
falls,' as a bird is tempted by a bait and falls into a snare. See
note, ch. v. 29.

23. The word will be more fruitful in some hearts than in
others. Even the Apostles exemplified this. The triple division
in their number seems to point to differences of gifts and spiritual
fruitfulness.

24–30. The Parable of the Tares. Confined to St Matthew.

Another parable set he before them, saying, The 24
kingdom of heaven is likened unto a man that sowed
good seed in his field : but while men slept, his enemy 25
came and sowed tares also among the wheat, and went
away. But when the blade sprang up, and brought forth 26
fruit, then appeared the tares also. And the servants of 27
the householder came and said unto him, Sir, didst thou not
sow good seed in thy field ? whence then hath it tares ?
And he said unto them, An enemy hath done this. And 28
the servants say unto him, Wilt thou then that we go and
gather them up ? But he saith, Nay ; lest haply while ye 29
gather up the tares, ye root up the wheat with them. Let 30
both grow together until the harvest : and in the time of
the harvest I will say to the reapers, Gather up first the
tares, and bind them in bundles to burn them : but gather
the wheat into my barn.

31–33. (1) The Parable of the Mustard Seed. (2) The Parable
of the Leaven which leavened the Meal. (1) Mark iv.
30–32. (1) and (2) Luke xiii. 18–21. The 'mystery' or
secret of the future contained in these two parables has
reference to the growth of the Church ; the first regards the
growth in its external aspect, the second in its inner working.

Another parable set he before them, saying, The 31
kingdom of heaven is like unto a grain of mustard seed,
which a man took, and sowed in his field : which indeed 32
is less than all seeds ; but when it is grown, it is greater

---

25. while men slept, i.e. during the night. The expression
is not introduced into the Lord's explanation of the parable.
tares. Probably the English 'darnel'; in the earlier stages of
its growth this weed very closely resembles wheat. This
resemblance gives an obvious point to the parable. The good
and the evil are often indistinguishable in the visible Church.
The Day of Judgment will separate. Men have tried in every
age to make the separation beforehand, but have failed.
26. appeared, '*were manifest*,' when the good corn made
fruit : before that they were indistinguishable.
32. less than all seeds. Not absolutely the least, but least

than the herbs, and becometh a tree, so that the birds of
the heaven come and lodge in the branches thereof.

33 Another parable spake he unto them ; The kingdom of
heaven is like unto leaven, which a woman took, and hid
in three measures of meal, till it was all leavened.

34, 35. Teaching by parables foreshewn in prophecy.

34 All these things spake Jesus in parables unto the
multitudes ; and without a parable spake he nothing
35 unto them : that it might be fulfilled which was spoken
by the prophet, saying,

I will open my mouth in parables ;
I will utter things hidden from the foundation of the
world.

36-43. Explanation of the Parable of the Tares, in St Matthew
only.

36 Then he left the multitudes, and went into the house :
and his disciples came unto him, saying, Explain unto us

---

in proportion to the plant that springs from the seed. Moreover
the mustard seed was used proverbially of anything excessively
minute.

lodge in the branches, i.e. settle for the purpose of rest or
shelter or to eat the seeds, of which goldfinches and linnets are
very fond. (Tristram, *Nat. Hist. of Bible*, p. 473.) **lodge,** lit.
dwell in tents. If we think of the leafy huts constructed for the
feast of tabernacles the propriety of the word will be seen.

33. leaven. Except in this one parable, leaven is used of
the working of evil; cp. Gal. v. 9; 1 Cor. v. 6; and 1 Cor. v. 7.
So, too, in the Rabbinical writings. This thought probably
arose from the prohibition of leaven during the paschal season.
But the secrecy and the all-pervading character of leaven aptly
symbolize the growth of Christianity, (1) as a society penetrating
everywhere by a subtle and mysterious operation; (2) as an
influence unfelt at *first* growing up within the human soul.
three measures. '*Three seahs.*' In Gen. xviii. 6, Abraham
bids Sarah 'make ready three *seahs* of fine meal, knead it and
make cakes upon the hearth.' **foundation of the world.** The
remainder of the psalm (lxxviii.) is a review of the history of
Israel from the Exodus to the reign of David. This indicates the
somewhat wide sense given to 'parables' and 'dark sayings.'

the parable of the tares of the field. And he answered 37
and said, He that soweth the good seed is the Son of
man ; and the field is the world ; and the good seed, 38
these are the sons of the kingdom ; and the tares are
the sons of the evil *one* ; and the enemy that sowed them 39
is the devil: and the harvest is the end of the world; and
the reapers are angels. As therefore the tares are gathered 40
up and burned with fire ; so shall it be in the end of the
world. The Son of man shall send forth his angels, and 41
they shall gather out of his kingdom all things that cause
stumbling, and them that do iniquity, and shall cast them 42
into the furnace of fire : there shall be the weeping and
gnashing of teeth. Then shall the righteous shine forth 43
as the sun in the kingdom of their Father. He that hath
ears, let him hear.

44. The Parable of the Hid Treasure, in this Gospel only.

The kingdom of heaven is like unto a treasure hidden 44
in the field ; which a man found, and hid ; and in his joy
he goeth and selleth all that he hath, and buyeth that
field.

---

41. all things that cause stumbling. Everything that
ensnares or tempts men to destruction; see ch. v. 29.

43. shine forth as the sun. Cp. Dan. xii. 3, 'Then they
that be wise shall shine as the brightness of the firmament.'

44. treasure hidden in the field. In ancient times, and in
an unsettled country like Palestine, where there were no banks,
in the modern sense, it was a common practice to conceal
treasures in the ground. Even at this day the Arabs are keenly
alive to the chance of finding such buried stores. The dishonesty
of the purchaser must be excluded from the thought of the
parable. The *unexpected* discovery, the consequent excitement
and joy, and the eagerness to buy at any sacrifice, are the points
to be observed in the interpretation.   **which a man found.**
Here the kingdom of heaven presents itself unexpectedly,
'Christ is found of one who sought Him not.' The woman of
Samaria, the jailer at Philippi, the centurion by the Cross are
instances.   **selleth all that he hath.** This is the renunciation
which is always needed for the winning of the kingdom, cp.
ch. x. 38. Thus St Paul gave up position, St Matthew wealth,

45, 46. The Parable of the Pearl of Great Price, in St Matthew only.

45 Again, the kingdom of heaven is like unto a man that
46 is a merchant seeking goodly pearls : and having found
one pearl of great price, he went and sold all that he had,
and bought it.

47-50. The Parable of the Net, in St Matthew only.

47 Again, the kingdom of heaven is like unto a net, that
48 was cast into the sea, and gathered of every kind : which,
when it was filled, they drew up on the beach ; and they
sat down, and gathered the good into vessels, but the bad
49 they cast away. So shall it be in the end of the world :
the angels shall come forth, and sever the wicked from
50 among the righteous, and shall cast them into the furnace
of fire : there shall be the weeping and gnashing of teeth.

Barnabas lands. **buyeth that field.** Puts himself in a position
to attain the kingdom.

45, 46. Here the story is of one who succeeds in getting what
he strives to obtain. The Jewish or the Greek 'seekers after
God,' possessing many pearls, but still dissatisfied, sought others
yet more choice, and finding one, true to the simplicity in Christ,
renounce all for that; the one his legalism, the other his philosophy.
Nathanael, Apollos, Timotheus, Justin Martyr are amongst those
who thus sought and found.

47. a net. A *drag-net* or *seine* (the English word comes
from the Greek through *sagena* of the Vulgate). One end of the
seine is held on the shore, the other is hauled off by a boat and
then returned to the land. In this way a large number of fishes
of all kinds is enclosed. The teaching of this parable partly
coincides with that of the parable of the Tares (*vv.* 24-30). In
both are exhibited the mixture of good and evil in the visible
Church, and the final separation of them. But here the thought
is specially directed to the ingathering of the Church. The
ministers of Christ will of necessity draw converts of diverse
character, good and evil, and actuated by different motives.
From the parable of the Tares we learn not to reject any from
within the Church, in the hope of expelling the element of evil.
It is a parable of the settled Church. This is a missionary
parable. It teaches that, as a matter of history or of fact, no
external test will serve to exclude the unworthy convert.

51, 52. The Scribes of the Kingdom of Heaven.

Have ye understood all these things? They say unto 51
him, Yea. And he said unto them, Therefore every scribe 52
who hath been made a disciple to the kingdom of heaven
is like unto a man that is a householder, which bringeth
forth out of his treasure things new and old.

53-58. The Prophet in his own Country; a second rejection at
Nazareth, Mark vi. 1-6; comp. Luke iv. 16-30. In Mark
the incident is placed between the cure of Jairus' daughter
and the mission of the Twelve; in Luke our Lord's discourse
in the synagogue is given at length. But many commentators
hold with great probability that St Luke's narrative refers
to a different and earlier visit to Nazareth.

And it came to pass, when Jesus had finished these 53
parables, he departed thence. And coming into his own 54
country he taught them in their synagogue, insomuch
that they were astonished, and said, Whence hath this
man this wisdom, and these mighty works? Is not this 55
the carpenter's son? is not his mother called Mary? and
his brethren, James, and Joseph, and Simon, and Judas?
And his sisters, are they not all with us? Whence then 56

---

52. made a disciple to the kingdom of heaven. The new
law requires a new order of Scribes who shall be instructed in
the kingdom of heaven—instructed in its mysteries, its laws, its
future—as the Jewish Scribes are instructed in the observances
of the Mosaic Law.   **new and old.** Just as the householder
brings from his stores or treasury precious things which have
been heirlooms for generations, as well as newly-acquired treasures;
the disciples following their Master's example will exhibit the
true teaching of the old law, and add thereto the new lessons of
Christianity.

54. his own country. Nazareth and the neighbourhood.

55. his brethren. See note, ch. xii. 47. The brethren of
the Lord were probably not in the number of the Twelve. This
seems to be rendered nearly certain by St John's assertion
(vii. 5), 'For even his brethren did not believe on him,' and is
strengthened by the way in which the brethren's names are
introduced, as though they were more familiar than Jesus to the
men of Nazareth; it seems to be implied that they were still
living there. Of His sisters nothing further is known.

57 hath this man all these things? And they were offended
in him.   But Jesus said unto them, A prophet is not
without honour, save in his own country, and in his own
58 house. And he did not many mighty works there because
of their unbelief.

> **14** 1–12. Herod the Tetrarch puts to death John the Baptist.
> Mark vi. 14–29, where the further conjectures as to the
> personality of Jesus are given, 'Others said, It is Elijah.
> And others said, It is a prophet, even as one of the prophets,'
> and the whole account is narrated in the vivid dramatic
> manner of St Mark.   St Luke relates the cause of the im-
> prisonment, iii. 19, 20; the conjectures as to Jesus, ix. 7–9.

14   At that season Herod the tetrarch heard the report
2 concerning Jesus, and said unto his servants, This is
John the Baptist; he is risen from the dead; and there-
3 fore do these powers work in him. For Herod had laid
hold on John, and bound him, and put him in prison for

---

1. At that season.   During the missionary journey of the
Twelve. See Mark vi. 14–29.   **Herod.** Herod Antipas, tetrarch
of Galilee and Peræa.   He was a son of Herod the Great and
Malthakè, a Samaritan, who was also the mother of Archelaus
and Olympias.   He was thus of Gentile origin, and his early
associations were Gentile, for he was brought up at Rome with
his brother Archelaus.   He married first a daughter of Aretas,
king of Arabia, and afterwards, while his first wife was still
living, he married Herodias, wife of his half-brother Philip,—
who was living in a private station, and must not be confused
with Philip the tetrarch of Ituræa.   For Herod's design against
our Lord, see Luke xiii. 31; and for the part which he took in
the Passion, see Luke xxiii. 6–12.   **tetrarch.** Literally,
the ruler of a fourth part or district into which a province was
divided.   Afterwards the name was extended to denote generally
a petty king.

2. risen from the dead.   A proof that Herod did not hold
the Sadducean doctrine, that there is no resurrection.   **and
therefore.**   In consequence of having risen from the dead he is
thought to be possessed of larger powers.

3. in prison.   At Machærus, in Peræa, on the eastern side
of the Dead Sea, near the southern frontier of the tetrarchy.
Here Antipas had a palace and a prison under one roof, as was
common in the East.

the sake of Herodias, his brother Philip's wife. For John 4 said unto him, It is not lawful for thee to have her. And 5 when he would have put him to death, he feared the multitude, because they counted him as a prophet. But 6 when Herod's birthday came, the daughter of Herodias danced in the midst, and pleased Herod. Whereupon he 7 promised with an oath to give her whatsoever she should ask. And she, being put forward by her mother, saith, 8 Give me here in a charger the head of John the Baptist. And the king was grieved ; but for the sake of his oaths, 9 and of them which sat at meat with him, he commanded it to be given ; and he sent, and beheaded John in the 10 prison. And his head was brought in a charger, and 11 given to the damsel : and she brought it to her mother. And his disciples came, and took up the corpse, and 12 buried him ; and they went and told Jesus.

---

4. It is not lawful for thee to have her. 'Boldly to rebuke vice' is fixed upon as the leading characteristic of the Baptist in the Collect for St John the Baptist's Day.

5. when he would have put him to death. From St Mark we learn that Herodias was eager to kill John, while Herod, partly from fear of his prisoner, partly from interest in him, refused to take away his life.

6. the daughter of Herodias. Salome ; she was afterwards married to her uncle Herod-Philip, the tetrarch, and on his death to Aristobulus, grandson of Herod the Great. **danced.** Some sort of pantomimic dance is meant.

8. charger. *A flat wooden trencher* on which meat was served. The word 'charger' is connected with *cargo* and with French *charger*, and signified originally that on which a load is placed, hence a dish.

9. the king. A title which Antipas had in vain tried to acquire : it was probably addressed to him by his courtiers. **was grieved.** He still feared the popular vengeance, and perhaps did not himself desire the death of John, see Mark vi. 20. **for the sake of his oaths.** Plural because he had sworn repeatedly.

12. took up the corpse &c. There is in this some proof of forbearance, if not of kindness, on Herod's part. He did not persecute John's disciples, or prevent them paying the last offices to their master.

13-21. Jesus retires to a Desert Place, where He feeds Five
Thousand. Mark vi. 31-44; Luke ix. 10-17; John vi. 5-14.
This is the only miracle narrated by all the Evangelists. In
St John it prepares the way for the memorable discourse on
the 'Bread of Life.' St John also mentions, as a result of
this miracle, the desire of the people 'to take him by force
and make him a king.'

13   Now when Jesus heard *it*, he withdrew from thence in
a boat, to a desert place apart : and when the multitudes
heard *thereof*, they followed him on foot from the cities.
14 And he came forth, and saw a great multitude, and he
15 had compassion on them, and healed their sick.   And
when even was come, the disciples came to him, saying,
The place is desert, and the time is already past ; send
the multitudes away, that they may go into the villages,
16 and buy themselves food.   But Jesus said unto them,
They have no need to go away ; give ye them to eat.
17 And they say unto him, We have here but five loaves, and
18 two fishes.   And he said, Bring them hither to me.   And
19 he commanded the multitudes to sit down on the grass ;
and he took the five loaves, and the two fishes, and looking
up to heaven, he blessed, and brake and gave the loaves
20 to the disciples, and the disciples to the multitudes.   And
they did all eat, and were filled: and they took up that
which remained over of the broken pieces, twelve baskets

---

15. when even was come.   In the Jewish division of the
day there were two evenings.   According to the most probable
view the space of time called 'between the evenings' (Ex. xii. 6)
was from the ninth to the twelfth hour (Jos. *B. J.* VI. 9. 3).
Hence the first evening ended at 3 o'clock, the second began at
sunset.   In this verse the first evening is meant, in *v.* 23 the
second.
20. the broken pieces, i.e. *the portions* broken off for distri-
bution.   **twelve baskets.**   The same word is used for baskets
in the four accounts of this miracle, and also by our Lord, when
He refers to the miracle (ch. xvi. 9); whereas a different word
is used in describing the feeding of four thousand and in the
reference made to that event by our Lord (ch. xvi. 10).

full. And they that did eat were about five thousand 21
men, beside women and children.

22-33. The disciples cross from the scene of the miracle to
Bethsaida. Mark vi. 45-52 ; John vi. 15-21. St Matthew
alone narrates St Peter's endeavour to walk on the sea.

And straightway he constrained the disciples to enter 22
into the boat, and to go before him unto the other side,
till he should send the multitudes away. And after he 23
had sent the multitudes away, he went up into the mountain apart to pray: and when even was come, he was
there alone. But the boat was now in the midst of the 24
sea, distressed by the waves; for the wind was contrary.
And in the fourth watch of the night he came unto them, 25
walking upon the sea. And when the disciples saw him 26
walking on the sea, they were troubled, saying, It is an
apparition ; and they cried out for fear. But straightway 27
Jesus spake unto them, saying, Be of good cheer; it is I ;
be not afraid. And Peter answered him and said, Lord, 28
if it be thou, bid me come unto thee upon the waters.
And he said, Come. And Peter went down from the 29
boat, and walked upon the waters, to come to Jesus. But 30
when he saw the wind, he was afraid; and beginning to

---

22. **the boat.** See note viii. 23.

23. **he was there alone.** This is a simple but sublime
thought :—the solitary watch on the lonely mountain, the com-
munion in prayer with the Father throughout the beautiful
Eastern night.

24. **distressed by the waves.** The expression is forcible, *tor-
tured by the waves*, writhing in throes of agony, as it were. These
sudden storms are very characteristic of the Lake of Gennesaret.

25. **in the fourth watch,** i.e. early in the morning. At
this time the Jews had adopted the Greek and Roman custom
of four night watches. Formerly they divided the night into
three watches.

29. **And he said, Come.** The boat was so near that the
voice of Jesus could be heard even through the storm, though
the wind was strong and the oarsmen labouring and perhaps
calling out to one another. The hand of the Saviour was quite
close to the sinking disciple.

31 sink, he cried out, saying, Lord, save me. And immediately Jesus stretched forth his hand, and took hold of
him, and saith unto him, O thou of little faith, wherefore
32 didst thou doubt? And when they were gone up into the
33 boat, the wind ceased. And they that were in the boat
worshipped him, saying, Of a truth thou art the Son
of God.

> 34-36. Jesus cures sick folk in the land of Gennesaret. Mark
> vi. 53-56, where the stir of the neighbourhood and eagerness
> of the people are vividly portrayed.

34   And when they had crossed over, they came to the
35 land, unto Gennesaret. And when the men of that place
knew him, they sent into all that region round about, and
36 brought unto him all that were sick; and they besought
him that they might only touch the border of his garment:
and as many as touched were made whole.

> **15** 1-20. The true religion and the false. A discourse to the
> Pharisees, the people, and the disciples. Mark vii. 1-23.

15   Then there come to Jesus from Jerusalem Pharisees
2 and scribes, saying, Why do thy disciples transgress the

---

32. the wind ceased. Lit. *rested from weariness.*

34. when they had crossed over. Having crossed the bay
from Tiberias to the neighbourhood of Capernaum.   **Gennesaret.** By this is meant the plain of Gennesaret, two miles and
a half in length and about one mile in breadth.   Modern
travellers speak of 'its charming bays, and its fertile soil rich
with the scourings of the basaltic hills.'

36. the border of his garment. The hem of the garment
had a certain sanctity attached to it. It was the distinguishing
mark of the Jew : cp. Numbers xv. 38, 39, 'that they add to the
fringes of the borders (or corners) a thread of blue.'   **as many
as touched were made whole.** Cp. the case of the woman with
an issue of blood, ch. ix. 20-22.

1-20. These twenty verses sum up the great controversy of
the N.T., that between the religion of the letter and external
observances and the religion of the heart, between what
St Paul calls 'the righteousness which is of the law and the
righteousness which is of God by (or grounded upon) faith,'
Phil iii. 9.

tradition of the elders? for they wash not their hands when they eat bread. And he answered and said unto 3 them, Why do ye also transgress the commandment of God because of your tradition? For God said, Honour 4 thy father and thy mother: and, He that speaketh evil of father or mother, let him die the death. But ye say, 5 Whosoever shall say to his father or his mother, That wherewith thou mightest have been profited by me is given *to God*; he shall not honour his father. And ye 6 have made void the word of God because of your tradition. Ye hypocrites, well did Isaiah prophesy of 7 you, saying,

This people honoureth me with their lips ;   8
But their heart is far from me.
But in vain do they worship me,   9
Teaching *as their* doctrines the precepts of men.

And he called to him the multitude, and said unto them, 10 Hear, and understand: Not that which entereth into the 11 mouth defileth the man ; but that which proceedeth out of the mouth, this defileth the man. Then came the 12 disciples, and said unto him, Knowest thou that the

---

2. the tradition of the elders. The elders, or presbyters, were the Jewish teachers, or scribes, such as Hillel or Shammai. The traditions were the rules or observances of the unwritten law, which they enjoined on their disciples.

5. That wherewith thou mightest have been profited by me (i.e. the sum which might have gone to your support) **is given to God**, or *Corban* (St Mark), i.e. *devoted to God*. The scribes held that these words, even when pronounced in spite and anger against parents who needed succour, excused the son from his natural duty.

8, 9. Isaiah xxix. 13.

10. he called to him the multitude. The moment our Lord turns to the people His teaching is by parables. This appeal to the multitude·as worthier than the Pharisees to receive the divine truths is significant of the popular character of the kingdom of heaven.

11. defileth. Literally, *maketh common*; cp. 'common or unclean,' Acts x. 14.

Pharisees were offended, when they heard this saying?
13 But he answered and said, Every plant which my heavenly
14 Father planted not, shall be rooted up. Let them alone:
they are blind guides. And if the blind guide the blind,
15 both shall fall into a pit. And Peter answered and said
16 unto him, Declare unto us the parable. And he said, Are
17 ye also even yet without understanding? Perceive ye not,
that whatsoever goeth into the mouth passeth into the
18 belly, and is cast out into the draught? But the things
which proceed out of the mouth come forth out of the
19 heart; and they defile the man. For out of the heart
come forth evil thoughts, murders, adulteries, fornications,
20 thefts, false witness, railings: these are the things which
defile the man: but to eat with unwashen hands defileth
not the man.

> 21–28. The daughter of a Canaanite woman is cured. Mark
> vii. 24–30. This narrative of faith without external observ-
> ance or knowledge of the Law affords a suggestive contrast
> to the preceding discourse. It is not related as we might
> have expected by the Gentile St Luke. St Mark has
> various points of particular description not given here.

21   And Jesus went out thence, and withdrew into the parts
22 of Tyre and Sidon. And behold, a Canaanitish woman

---

12. the Pharisees were offended. A proof of the influence
of the Pharisees. The disciples believed that Christ would be
concerned to have offended those who stood so high in popular
favour.

13. Every plant &c. The plant which is planted and culti-
vated by human hands, and not by God, means the teaching of
the Pharisees, the additions which they made to the divine law.

14. shall fall into a pit. Palestine abounded in dangers of
this kind, from unguarded wells, quarries and pitfalls. Blindness
also was from various causes very prevalent. See note ch. ix.
27–31.

21. withdrew. Perhaps to avoid the hostility which this
attack upon the Pharisees would arouse.

parts of Tyre and Sidon. It is important to notice that Jesus
crossed the borders of Palestine and passed through a Gentile land.

22. a Canaanitish woman. Called in Mark *a Greek, a
Syrophœnician by nation.* The two expressions are nearly

came out from those borders, and cried, saying, Have
mercy on me, O Lord, thou son of David ; my daughter
is grievously vexed with a devil. But he answered her 23
not a word. And his disciples came and besought him,
saying, Send her away; for she crieth after us. But he 24
answered and said, I was not sent but unto the lost sheep
of the house of Israel. But she came and worshipped 25
him, saying, Lord, help me. And he answered and said, 26
It is not meet to take the children's bread and cast it to
the dogs. But she said, Yea, Lord : for even the dogs 27
eat of the crumbs which fall from their masters' table.

---

identical, for the term land of Canaan, literally the *low lands*
or *netherlands*, at first applied to the whole of Palestine, was
confined in later times to the maritime plain of Phœnicia. The
importance of the narrative lies in the fact that this woman was
a foreigner and a heathen—a descendant of the worshippers of
Baal. **Have mercy on me.** Identifying herself with her
daughter. Cp. the prayer of the father of the lunatic child :
'Have compassion on *us* and help *us*,' Mark ix. 22. **son of
David.** A title that proves the expectation that the Messiah
should spring from the house of David. It is the particular
Messianic prophecy which would be most likely to reach foreign
countries. The Tyrian woman's appeal to the descendant of
Hiram's friend and ally has a special significance.

23. Send her away. By granting what she asks, by yielding,
like the unjust judge, to her importunity.

24. the lost sheep of the house of Israel. Jesus came to
save all, but His personal ministry was confined, with few
exceptions, to the Jews. The thought of Israel as a flock of
sheep lost upon the mountain is beautifully drawn out, Ezekiel
xxxiv., 'My sheep were scattered upon all the face of the earth,
and there was none that did search or seek after them' (*v.* 6).
Read the whole chapter.

26. the children's bread. The 'children' are the Jews;
the 'dogs' are the Gentiles. This was the name applied by the
Jews to all outside the chosen race, the dog being in the East a
symbol of impurity. St Paul, regarding the Christian Church as
the true Israel, terms the Judaizing teachers 'dogs,' Phil. iii. 2.
The same name of scorn still exists in the East between
Mussulman and Christian populations.

27. Yea, Lord: for even the dogs &c., i.e. even the Gentiles
have a share in their heavenly Father's gifts. The 'masters' in
the parable must be interpreted to mean God.

28 Then Jesus answered and said unto her, O woman, great
is thy faith : be it done unto thee even as thou wilt. And
her daughter was healed from that hour.

> 29–31. Jesus returns to the high land of Galilee, and cures
> many blind, dumb, and lame. Mark vii. 31–37, where, not
> content with the general statement, the Evangelist describes
> one special case of healing.

29 And Jesus departed thence, and came nigh unto the
sea of Galilee ; and he went up into the mountain, and sat
30 there. And there came unto him great multitudes, having
with them the lame, blind, dumb, maimed, and many
others, and they cast them down at his feet ; and he
31 healed them : insomuch that the multitude wondered,
when they saw the dumb speaking, the maimed whole,
and the lame walking, and the blind seeing : and they
glorified the God of Israel.

> 32–38. Four thousand men, besides women and children, are
> miraculously fed. Mark viii. 1–9.

32 And Jesus called unto him his disciples, and said, I
have compassion on the multitude, because they continue
with me now three days and have nothing to eat : and I
would not send them away fasting, lest haply they faint
33 in the way. And the disciples say unto him, Whence
should we have so many loaves in a desert place, as to
34 fill so great a multitude? And Jesus saith unto them,
How many loaves have ye? And they said, Seven, and a
35 few small fishes. And he commanded the multitude to
36 sit down on the ground ; and he took the seven loaves
and the fishes ; and he gave thanks and brake, and gave
37 to the disciples, and the disciples to the multitudes. And
they did all eat, and were filled : and they took up that
which remained over of the broken pieces, seven baskets

---

29. the mountain, i.e. the high land, as distinguished from
the low land, which He had left.

37. that which remained over of the broken pieces. See
ch. xiv. 20. **seven baskets.** A word implying a different kind
of basket from that mentioned ch. xiv. 20, where see note.

full. And they that did eat were four thousand men, 38
beside women and children.

39-**16** 4. Jesus at Magdala, or Magadan, is tempted to give a
   sign. Mark viii. 10-12; Luke xii. 54-57.

And he sent away the multitudes, and entered into the 39
boat, and came into the borders of Magadan.

And the Pharisees and Sadducees came, and tempting **16**
him asked him to shew them a sign from heaven. But 2
he answered and said unto them, When it is evening, ye
say, *It will be* fair weather: for the heaven is red. And 3
in the morning, *It will be* foul weather to-day : for the
heaven is red and lowring. Ye know how to discern the
face of the heaven; but ye cannot *discern* the signs of the
times. An evil and adulterous generation seeketh after a 4
sign; and there shall no sign be given unto it, but the
sign of Jonah. And he left them, and departed.

5-12. The leaven of the Pharisees and of the Sadducees.
   Mark viii. 14-21, where the rebuke of Christ is given more
   at length in stirring language; and Luke xii. 1, where the
   context and occasion are different.

And the disciples came to the other side and forgot to 5
take bread. And Jesus said unto them, Take heed and 6
beware of the leaven of the Pharisees and Sadducees.
And they reasoned among themselves, saying, We took 7
no bread. And Jesus perceiving it said, O ye of little 8

---

1. the Pharisees and the Sadducees. The coalition between
these opposing sects can only be accounted for by the uniting
influence of a strong common hostility against Jesus.
   3. the signs of the times. The meaning of passing events—
some of which point in many ways to the fulfilment of prophecy,
and to the presence of Christ among men; others to the overthrow of the national existence through the misguided passions
of the people, and the absence of true spiritual life.
   4. the sign of Jonah. See ch. xii. 39-41.
   6. the leaven. Teaching, which like leaven is corrupt and
penetrating, cp. 1 Cor. v. 7, where the reference is to the putting
away of leaven before the passover.
   7. We took no bread. The Pharisees had rules of their

faith, why reason ye among yourselves, because ye have
9 no bread? Do ye not yet perceive, neither remember the
five loaves of the five thousand, and how many baskets ye
10 took up? Neither the seven loaves of the four thousand,
11 and how many baskets ye took up? How is it that ye do
not perceive that I spake not to you concerning bread?
But beware of the leaven of the Pharisees and Sadducees.
12 Then understood they how that he bade them not beware
of the leaven of bread, but of the teaching of the Pharisees
and Sadducees.

> 13-20. The great confession of St Peter, and the promise given
> to him. Mark viii. 27-30: the question is put 'while they
> were on the way,' the words 'the Son of the living God' are
> omitted, as also the blessing on Peter. Luke ix. 18-21:
> Jesus was engaged in prayer alone; the words of the
> confession are 'the Christ of God'; the blessing on Peter is
> omitted.

13 Now when Jesus came into the parts of Cæsarea
Philippi, he asked his disciples, saying, Who do men
14 say that the Son of man is? And they said, Some *say*
John the Baptist ; some, Elijah : and others, Jeremiah,
15 or one of the prophets. He saith unto them, But who
16 say ye that I am? And Simon Peter answered and said,
17 Thou art the Christ, the Son of the living God. And

---

own as to what kind of leaven it was lawful to use, and
what kind it was right to avoid. Hence it was not strange that
the disciples should imagine that their Master was laying down
similar rules for their guidance.

13. Cæsarea Philippi. The most northerly point in the
Holy Land reached by our Lord. The city was rebuilt by
Herod Philip, who called it by his own name to distinguish it
from Cæsarea Stratonis on the sea-coast, the seat of the Roman
government, and the scene of St Paul's imprisonment. The
Greek name of this Cæsarea was Paneas, which survives in the
modern Banias. Cæsarea was beautifully placed on a rocky
terrace under Mount Hermon, a few miles east of Dan, the old
frontier city of Israel. The cliffs near this spot, where the
Messiah was first acknowledged, bear marks of the worship of
Baal and of Pan.   **the Son of man.** See note ch. viii. 20.

16. Thou art the Christ, the Son of the living God. This

Jesus answered and said unto him, Blessed art thou,
Simon Bar-Jonah : for flesh and blood hath not revealed
it unto thee, but my Father which is in heaven.   And I 18
also say unto thee, that thou art Peter, and upon this
rock I will build my church ; and the gates of Hades
shall not prevail against it.   I will give unto thee the keys 19
of the kingdom of heaven : and whatsoever thou shalt

---

confession not only sees in Jesus the promised Messiah, but in
the Messiah recognizes the divine nature.

17.   Bar-jonah, 'son of Jonah,' or '*son of John*.' The Greek
form may stand for either name, but the reading adopted by the
best editors John i. 42, 'son of John,' seems conclusive in favour
of the latter rendering.   **flesh and blood hath not revealed.**
Not man, but God; 'flesh and blood' was a common Hebrew
expression in this contrast.

18.   thou art Peter, and upon this rock &c. The Greek
word for *rock* is nearly the same as the Greek name Peter.
This play on the words can be seen in a French rendering:
'Tu es Pierre, et sur cette pierre je bâtirai mon église.'   The
central truth on which the Church of Christ is built is the divine
nature of Christ.   St Peter therefore, as having been the first to
see and acknowledge this truth, is the rock on which the Church
is built.   Elsewhere we read that the Church is founded on the
Apostles and Prophets (Eph. ii. 20), and on Christ Himself
(2 Cor. iii. 11); so that the *personal* reference to St Peter should
not be pressed.

my church. The Greek word for Church (*ecclesia*) occurs
twice in St Matthew, and not elsewhere in the Gospels.   From
the analogy of the corresponding Hebrew word, *ecclesia* in a
Christian sense may be defined as the congregation of the faithful
throughout the world, united under Christ as their Head.   The
use of the word by Christ implied at least two things: (1) That
He was founding an organized society, not merely preaching a
doctrine: (2) That the Jewish Church was the point of departure
for the Christian Church, and in part its prototype.   It is one
among many links in this Gospel between Jewish and Christian
thought.

the gates of Hades. The expression symbolises the power of
the unseen world, especially the power of death: cp. Rev. i. 18,
1 Cor. xv. 55. *Hades* is used for the Hebrew *Sheôl*, the abode
of departed spirits, in which were the two divisions, *Paradise*
and *Gehenna*.

19.   the keys of the kingdom of heaven. A key was given
to a scribe when admitted to his office as a symbol of his

bind on earth shall be bound in heaven : and whatsoever
20 thou shalt loose on earth shall be loosed in heaven. Then
charged he the disciples that they should tell no man that
he was the Christ.

21–23. The Passion is foretold. Mark viii. 31–33; Luke ix.
    22. St Luke omits the rebuke to St Peter.

21   From that time began Jesus to shew unto his disciples,
how that he must go unto Jerusalem, and suffer many
things of the elders and chief priests and scribes, and be
22 killed, and the third day be raised up. And Peter took
him, and began to rebuke him, saying, Be it far from thee,
23 Lord: this shall never be unto thee. But he turned, and
said unto Peter, Get thee behind me, Satan : thou art a

---

authority to open the treasury of the divine oracles (ch. xiii. 52).
Peter was to be a scribe in the kingdom of heaven. He has
received authority to teach the truths of the kingdom. **whatsoever thou shalt bind** &c. 'To bind' (cp. ch. xxiii. 4) is to
impose an obligation as binding; 'to loose' is to declare a
precept not binding. The decisions of Peter, as an authorized
scribe of the kingdom of God, will be ratified in heaven. Such
decisions of the scribes of the kingdom of heaven were the
sentence pronounced by James, Acts xv. 19, and the judgments
of Paul in the Corinthian Church.

20. that they should tell no man that he was the Christ.
Lest the Galilæan enthusiasm should endeavour to make Him a
king.

21. From that time. An important note of time. Now
that the disciples have learned to acknowledge Jesus to be the
Messiah, He is able to instruct them in the true nature of the
Kingdom. **must.** The Greek word conveys the idea of duty,
of a course of life not led haphazard, but determined by principle,
of the divine plan which rules the life and work of Christ from
first to last. **elders and chief priests and scribes**=*the
Sanhedrin.* See ch. ii. 4, and xxvi. 3. **be killed.** As yet
there is no mention of the Roman judge or of the death upon the
cross; this truth is broken gradually, see *v.* 24.

23. Get thee behind me, Satan. Peter takes the place of
the tempter, and argues for the false kingdom instead of for the
true (see notes ch. iv. 8–10). **a stumblingblock,** or a snare
to allure me, as tempting me to forsake the divine plan of self-
denial and sacrifice. **thou mindest not the things of God,**

stumblingblock unto me : for thou mindest not the things
of God, but the things of men.

24-28. Self-renouncement required in Christ's followers. Their
   reward. Mark viii. 34-ix. 1; Luke ix. 23-27.

Then said Jesus unto his disciples, If any man would come 24
after me, let him deny himself, and take up his cross, and
follow me.   For whosoever would save his life shall lose 25
it: and whosoever shall lose his life for my sake shall find
it.   For what shall a man be profited, if he shall gain the 26
whole world, and forfeit his life? or what shall a man give
in exchange for his life?   For the Son of man shall come 27
in the glory of his Father with his angels ; and then shall
he render unto every man according to his deeds.   Verily 28
I say unto you, There be some of them that stand here,
which shall in no wise taste of death, till they see the Son
of man coming in his kingdom.

17 1-13. The Transfiguration. Mark ix. 2-13 ; Luke ix. 28-36.

And after six days Jesus taketh with him Peter, and **17**
James, and John his brother, and bringeth them up into a

---

but the things of men, i.e. thine are not God's thoughts but
man's thoughts; thou art not on God's side but on man's.
   25. whosoever would save his life shall lose it. See note
ch. x. 39. Let Christ's follower lose his lower life on his cross,
crucify his earthly affections, and he shall win the higher and
spiritual life here and hereafter.
   would save. *Should resolve to save.*
   26. and forfeit his life. The Greek word translated 'life'
signifies life in all its senses, here ' the soul,' which is life in
its highest sense.
   27. For. The reason given why the higher life—the soul—is
of priceless value: (1) The Judge is at hand who will condemn
self-indulgence and all the works of the lower life, and will
reward those who have denied themselves. (2) Further (*v.* 28)
this judgment shall not be delayed—it is very near.
   28. It is thought by most that the event spoken of as 'the
Coming of the Son of Man' was the fall of Jerusalem A.D. 70—a
great crisis in the history of the Church, and a judgment on the
nation which rejected Christ.
   1. Peter, and James, and John. The three who were chosen

2 high mountain apart: and he was transfigured before
them: and his face did shine as the sun, and his garments
3 became white as the light. And behold, there appeared
4 unto them Moses and Elijah talking with him. And Peter
answered, and said unto Jesus, Lord, it is good for us to
be here: if thou wilt, I will make here three tabernacles;
one for thee, and one for Moses, and one for Elijah.
5 While he was yet speaking, behold, a bright cloud over-
shadowed them: and behold, a voice out of the cloud,
saying, This is my beloved Son, in whom I am well
6 pleased; hear ye him. And when the disciples heard it,
7 they fell on their face, and were sore afraid. And Jesus
came and touched them and said, Arise, and be not
8 afraid. And lifting up their eyes, they saw no one, save
Jesus only.

---

to be with their Master on two other occasions, (1) the raising
of Jairus' daughter, (2) the Agony in the Garden of Gethsemane.

a high mountain. An old tradition placed the scene of the
Transfiguration on Mount Tabor. It is known, however, that
the summit of Tabor was at this period occupied by a fortress,
and there is no hint given of Jesus being in that neighbourhood.
Many regard one of the spurs of Hermon, or even its summit
(Conder, *Tent Work*, &c. 266), as the most likely spot. Cæsarea
Philippi, the last-named locality, lies under Hermon.

2. was transfigured. The word implies more than a mere
change of the outward semblance.   **as the light.** A hint that
the Transfiguration took place at night, which is also rendered
probable by the statement of St Luke that the three Apostles
were 'heavy with sleep,' that they 'kept awake,' that they
descended 'the next day,' ch. ix. 32 and 37.

3. Moses and Elijah. The representatives of the Law and
the Prophets. The whole history of the Jewish Church is
brought in one glance, as it were, before the Apostles' eyes
in its due relation to Christ. St Luke names the subject of
converse: they 'spake of His decease which He was about to
accomplish at Jerusalem' (ix. 31).

4. By **tabernacles** are meant little huts made out of boughs
of trees or shrubs, such as were made at the Feast of Tabernacles.

5. This is my beloved Son. Words that recall the baptism
of Jesus; ch. iii. 17, where see note.

8. Jesus only. Christ, who came to fulfil the Law and the

And as they were coming down from the mountain, 9
Jesus commanded them, saying, Tell the vision to no
man, until the Son of man be risen from the dead. And 10
his disciples asked him, saying, Why then say the scribes
that Elijah must first come? And he answered and said, 11
Elijah indeed cometh, and shall restore all things : but I 12
say unto you, that Elijah is come already, and they knew
him not, but did unto him whatsoever they listed. Even
so shall the Son of man also suffer of them. Then 13
understood the disciples that he spake unto them of John
the Baptist.

14-20. A lunatic child is cured. Mark ix. 14-29, where in
  v. 29 the words of v. 21, A.V., of this Chapter are found.
  Luke ix. 37-42.

And when they were come to the multitude, there came 14
to him a man, kneeling to him, and saying, Lord, have 15
mercy on my son : for he is epileptic, and suffereth grievously : for oft-times he falleth into the fire, and oft-times
into the water. And I brought him to thy disciples, and 16
they could not cure him. And Jesus answered and said, 17
O faithless and perverse generation, how long shall I be

Prophets, is left alone. To His voice alone the Church will
listen.
  11. restore all things. To restore is strictly to bring back
to a lost perfection, then, to develope, raise, to introduce a purer,
nobler epoch; here, specially, to proclaim the kingdom of God.
Cp. Acts iii. 21, 'the times of restoration of all things.'
  12. Elijah is come already. Jesus shows that the prophecy
in Malachi iv. 5 was fulfilled in St John the Baptist.
  15. he is epileptic. This is the only special instance of cure
in the case of an epileptic. They are mentioned as a class,
ch. iv. 24. St Mark describes the child as foaming, gnashing
with his teeth, and pining away. St Luke mentions that he
'crieth out.' All these were epileptic symptoms; 'the child was
a possessed epileptic lunatic.'
  17. O faithless and perverse generation. Addressed to the
scribes and the multitude thronging round, as representing the
whole nation. The disciples, if not specially addressed, are by
no means excluded from the rebuke.

with you? how long shall I bear with you? bring him
18 hither to me. And Jesus rebuked him; and the devil
went out from him: and the boy was cured from that
19 hour. Then came the disciples to Jesus apart, and said,
20 Why could not we cast it out? And he saith unto them,
Because of your little faith: for verily I say unto you, If
ye have faith as a grain of mustard seed, ye shall say unto
this mountain, Remove hence to yonder place; and it
shall remove; and nothing shall be impossible unto you.

22, 23. The second announcement of the Passion. Mark ix.
31; Luke ix. 44. Both St Mark and St Luke add that the
disciples 'understood not this saying.' It was difficult for
them to abandon cherished hopes of an earthly kingdom,
and 'might not Jesus be speaking in parables of a figurative
death and resurrection?' See note, ch. xvi. 21.

22 And while they abode in Galilee, Jesus said unto them,
The Son of man shall be delivered up into the hands of
23 men; and they shall kill him, and the third day he shall
be raised up. And they were exceeding sorry.

24-27. Jesus pays the half-shekel of the sanctuary. Peculiar
to St Matthew.

24 And when they were come to Capernaum, they that
received the half-shekel came to Peter, and said, Doth

20. **ye shall say unto this mountain** &c. Such expressions
are characteristic of the vivid imagery of Eastern speech generally.
To '*remove mountains*' is to make difficulties vanish. The Jews
used to say of an eminent teacher, he is 'a rooter-up of mountains.'

22, 23. Observe here the various phases in the prediction of
the Passion. The first (ch. xvi. 21) foretells the rejection of
Jesus as the Messiah by the Jews, and His death in the indefinite
passive, 'be killed.' The second speaks of the betrayal into the
hands of *men* (Matt., Mark, Luke); and 'they shall put him to
death.' The third (ch. xx. 17-19) particularises the share taken
by Jew and Gentile. The Sanhedrin shall condemn and deliver
to the Gentiles, 'to scourge and to crucify him.'

24. **the half-shekel.** This was not a tribute levied by Cæsar
or by Herod, but the half-shekel (Exod. xxx. 13) paid annually
by every Jew into the Temple treasury. The 'sacred tax' was
collected from Jews in all parts of the world.

not your master pay the half-shekel?   He saith, Yea.
And when he came into the house, Jesus spake first to 25
him, saying, What thinkest thou, Simon? the kings of
the earth, from whom do they receive toll or tribute?
from their sons, or from strangers?   And when he said, 26
From strangers, Jesus said unto him, Therefore the sons
are free.   But, lest we cause them to stumble, go thou to 27
the sea, and cast a hook, and take up the fish that first
cometh up ; and when thou hast opened his mouth, thou
shalt find a shekel : that take, and give unto them for me
and thee.

18 1-4.   A lesson in humility.   The kingdom of heaven and
    little children.   Mark ix. 33-37; Luke ix. 46-48.

In that hour came the disciples unto Jesus, saying, 18
Who then is greatest in the kingdom of heaven?   And 2
he called to him a little child, and set him in the midst of
them, and said, Verily I say unto you, Except ye turn, 3
and become as little children, ye shall in no wise enter
into the kingdom of heaven.   Whosoever therefore shall 4
humble himself as this little child, the same is the greatest
in the kingdom of heaven.

---

25. spake first to him.   So answering his thoughts.   **from
their sons,** or from those who do not belong to the family,
namely, subjects and tributaries.

26. the sons are free.   The deduction is, 'Shall He whom
thou hast rightly named the Son of God pay tribute to the
Temple of His Father?'

27. a shekel.   Lit. *a stater*, a Greek silver coin equivalent
to the Hebrew shekel.

1. In that hour.   The preceding incident and our Lord's
words had again excited hopes of a glorious kingdom on earth.
We may suppose that Jesus and St Peter were alone when the
last incident happened, they had entered the house (probably
Peter's) and were now joined by the other apostles who had
been disputing on the way.

3. shall in no wise enter.   Much less be great therein.

4. shall humble himself.   He who shall be most Christ-like
in humility (see Phil. ii. 7-9) shall be most like Christ in glory.

5, 6. Christ's little ones. Mark ix. 37-42. The thought of Jesus passes from the dispute among His disciples to the care of His little ones, the young in faith, who, if they have the weakness, have also the humility of little children.

5 And whoso shall receive one such little child in my name
6 receiveth me : but whoso shall cause one of these little ones which believe on me to stumble, it is profitable for him that a great millstone should be hanged about his neck, and *that* he should be sunk in the depth of the sea.

7-9. Of offences. Mark ix. 43-48. From offences—snares and hindrances to the faith of Christ's little ones—the discourse proceeds to offences in general—everything that hinders the spiritual life.

7 Woe unto the world because of occasions of stumbling ! for it must needs be that the occasions come ; but woe to
8 that man through whom the occasion cometh ! And if thy hand or thy foot causeth thee to stumble, cut it off, and cast it from thee : it is good for thee to enter into life maimed or halt, rather than having two hands or
9 two feet to be cast into the eternal fire. And if thine eye causeth thee to stumble, pluck it out, and cast it from thee : it is good for thee to enter into life with one eye, rather than having two eyes to be cast into the hell of fire.

10-14. Christ's care for His little ones illustrated by a parable. Luke xv. 3-7. After a brief digression (*vv.* 7-9), Christ's love for His young disciples again breaks out in words. Let no one despise them. They have unseen friends in the court of heaven, who are ever in the presence of the King himself. There, at any rate, they are not despised. It was for them especially that the Son of Man came to earth.

10 See that ye despise not one of these little ones ; for I say unto you, that in heaven their angels do always behold

---

8. **Hand, foot** and **eye** here represent sources or causes of temptation. Temptation may come in the shape of pursuits or pleasures innocent in themselves and even necessary to one but dangerous to another. The pursuit of pleasure or position which tempts to sin must be abandoned for Christ's sake.

the face of my Father which is in heaven. How think ye? 12
if any man have a hundred sheep, and one of them be
gone astray, doth he not leave the ninety and nine, and
go unto the mountains, and seek that which goeth astray?
And if so be that he find it, verily I say unto you, he 13
rejoiceth over it more than over the ninety and nine which
have not gone astray. Even so it is not the will of your 14
Father which is in heaven, that one of these little ones
should perish.

15–35. Forgiveness of sins. Luke xvii. 3, 4. God's forgiveness of sinners suggests the duty of forgiveness among men.

And if thy brother sin against thee, go, shew him his 15
fault between thee and him alone: if he hear thee, thou
hast gained thy brother. But if he hear *thee* not, take 16
with thee one or two more, that at the mouth of two
witnesses or three every word may be established. And 17
if he refuse to hear them, tell it unto the church: and if
he refuse to hear the church also, let him be unto thee as
the Gentile and the publican. Verily I say unto you, 18
What things soever ye shall bind on earth shall be bound
in heaven: and what things soever ye shall loose on earth
shall be loosed in heaven. Again I say unto you, that if 19

---

10. behold the face of my Father. The image is drawn
from the court of an Eastern king, where the favoured courtiers
enjoy the right of constant approach to the royal presence: cp.
Esther i. 14, 'Which saw the king's face, and sat first in the
kingdom.'

15. shew him his fault. *Rebuke him.* See Levit. xix. 17,
'Thou shalt not hate thy brother in thine heart: thou shalt
surely rebuke thy neighbour, and not bear sin because of him.'

17. the church. See note ch. xvi. 18. Here the reference
is to the Jewish Church or synagogue.

**18. What things soever ye shall bind on earth shall be bound
in heaven.** What was spoken to Peter alone is now spoken to
all the disciples, representing the Church. Whatsoever you as
a Church declare binding or declare not binding, that decision
shall be ratified in heaven.

19. The slight digression is continued. Christ thinks of His

two of you shall agree on earth as touching anything that
they shall ask, it shall be done for them of my Father
20 which is in heaven. For where two or three are gathered
together in my name, there am I in the midst of them.

21 Then came Peter, and said to him, Lord, how oft shall
my brother sin against me, and I forgive him? until seven
22 times? Jesus saith unto him, I say not unto thee, Until
23 seven times; but, Until seventy times seven. Therefore
is the kingdom of heaven likened unto a certain king,
24 which would make a reckoning with his servants. And
when he had begun to reckon, one was brought unto him,
25 which owed him ten thousand talents. But forasmuch as
he had not *wherewith* to pay, his lord commanded him to
be sold, and his wife, and children, and all that he had,
26 and payment to be made. The servant therefore fell
down and worshipped him, saying, Lord, have patience
27 with me, and I will pay thee all. And the lord of that

Church. Not only shall your decisions be ratified, but your
requests shall be granted, provided ye agree.

20. two or three. In the smallest gathering of His followers
Christ will be present.

21. until seven times. Such numerical questions about the
duty of forgiveness are quite opposed to the Christian spirit.

22. Until seventy times seven, i.e. an infinite number of
times. There is no limit to forgiveness.

23. would make a reckoning with his servants. The
picture is drawn from an Oriental court. The provincial
governors, farmers of taxes, and other high officials, are summoned before a despotic sovereign to give an account of their
administration. **servants,** i.e. *subjects,* for all subjects of an
Eastern monarch from the highest to the lowest are 'slaves.'

24. ten thousand talents. Even if silver talents are meant,
the sum is enormous—at least two million pounds of our money.
It was probably more than the whole annual revenue of Palestine
at this time. The modern kingdoms of Norway or Greece or
Denmark hardly produce a larger national income. The vast
amount implies the hopeless character of the debt of sin.

25. he had not wherewith to pay. He had wasted in
extravagance the provincial revenues, or the proceeds of taxa-
tion.

servant, being moved with compassion, released him, and
forgave him the debt. But that servant went out, and 28
found one of his fellow-servants, which owed him a hundred pence: and he laid hold on him, and took *him* by
the throat, saying, Pay what thou owest. So his fellow- 29
servant fell down and besought him, saying, Have patience
with me, and I will pay thee. And he would not: but 30
went and cast him into prison, till he should pay that
which was due. So when his fellow-servants saw what 31
was done, they were exceeding sorry, and came and told
unto their lord all that was done. Then his lord called 32
him unto him, and saith to him, Thou wicked servant, I
forgave thee all that debt, because thou besoughtest me :
shouldest not thou also have had mercy on thy fellow- 33
servant, even as I had mercy on thee? And his lord was 34
wroth, and delivered him to the tormentors, till he should
pay all that was due. So shall also my heavenly Father 35

---

27. forgave him the debt. With the almost reckless
generosity of an Eastern court that delights to exalt or
debase with swift strokes. The pardon is free and uncon-
ditional.

28. found. Perhaps even sought him out. **one of his
fellow-servants**. By this is meant the debt of man to man,
offences which men are bound to forgive one another. **a
hundred pence**, i.e. *denarii*. The *denarius* was a day's wage
(ch. xx. 2). The sum therefore is about three months' wages
for an ordinary labourer, by no means a hopeless debt as the
other was; see note ch. xxvi. 7.

31. they were exceeding sorry. This seems to point to the
common conscience of mankind approving or anticipating the
divine sentence.

33. Cp. the Lord's Prayer, where forgiveness of others is put
forward as the claim for divine pardon.

34. The acquittal is revoked—a point not to be pressed in
the interpretation. The truth taught is the impossibility of the
unforgiving being forgiven, but the chief lesson is the example
of the divine spirit of forgiveness in the act of the king. This
example the pardoned slave should have followed. **the
tormentors**, i.e. the keepers of the prison, the gaolers, part of
whose duty it was to torture the prisoners.

do unto you, if ye forgive not every one his brother from
your hearts.

19 1, 2. Jesus goes to Judæa from Galilee. Mark x. 1.

19 And it came to pass when Jesus had finished these
words, he departed from Galilee, and came into the
2 borders of Judæa beyond Jordan; and great multitudes
followed him; and he healed them there.

> 3–12. The question of marriage and divorce. Mark x. 2–9.
> *vv.* 10–12 are peculiar to Matthew. St Mark mentions the
> part of the conversation contained in *v.* 9 as having taken
> place 'in the house,' *vv.* 10–12.

3 And there came unto him Pharisees, tempting him, and
saying, Is it lawful *for a man* to put away his wife for
4 every cause? And he answered and said, Have ye not
read, that he which made *them* from the beginning made
5 them male and female, and said, For this cause shall a
man leave his father and mother, and shall cleave to his
6 wife; and the twain shall become one flesh? So that
they are no more twain, but one flesh. What therefore
7 God hath joined together, let not man put asunder. They
say unto him, Why then did Moses command to give a
8 bill of divorcement, and to put *her* away? He saith unto
them, Moses for your hardness of heart suffered you to

---

35. from your hearts. A different principle from the
Pharisee's arithmetical rules of forgiveness.

3. to put away his wife for every cause. The words 'for
every cause' are omitted in Mark. In Matthew they contain
the pith of the question: 'Is the husband's right to divorce his
wife quite unlimited?'

4. from the beginning. An appeal from the law of Moses
to a higher and absolute law, which has outlived the law of
Moses.

7. a bill of divorcement. See ch. v. 31, 32.

8. for your hardness of heart. Having respect to, with a
view to, the hardness of your hearts towards God. So the law
was relatively good, not absolutely. A great principle. Even
now not all are capable of the higher religious life or of the
deepest truths.

put away your wives : but from the beginning it hath not
been so. And I say unto you, Whosoever shall put away 9
his wife, except for fornication, and shall marry another,
committeth adultery : and he that marrieth her when she
is put away committeth adultery. The disciples say unto 10
him, If the case of the man is so with his wife, it is not
expedient to marry. But he said unto them, All men 11
cannot receive this saying, but they to whom it is given.
For there are eunuchs, which were so born from their 12
mother's womb : and there are eunuchs, which were made
eunuchs by men : and there are eunuchs, which made
themselves eunuchs for the kingdom of heaven's sake.
He that is able to receive it, let him receive it.

13-15. Little children are brought to Christ. Mark x. 13-16;
　　Luke xviii. 15-17. In Luke the incident is placed immedi-
　　ately after the parable of the Pharisee and Publican; there
　　it is an illustration of humility. Here, and in Mark, the
　　connexion between the purity of married life and the love
　　of little children cannot be overlooked.

Then were there brought unto him little children, that 13
he should lay his hands on them, and pray: and the
disciples rebuked them. But Jesus said, Suffer the little 14
children, and forbid them not, to come unto me: for of

---

9. See ch. v. 32.
10. it is not expedient to marry. Nothing could prove
more clearly the revolution in thought brought to pass by Christ
than this. Even the disciples feel that such a principle would
make the yoke of marriage unbearable.
12. for the kingdom of heaven's sake. In old days some
men abstained from marriage in order to devote themselves to
the study of the Law, in later times men have done so for the
furtherance of Christianity.
13. It appears that it was customary for Jewish infants to be
taken to the synagogue to be blessed by the Rabbi. Smith's
Dict. of Bible, Art. 'Synagogue,' note E.
14. for such &c. Love, simplicity of faith, innocence,
and above all, humility, are the ideal characteristics of little
children, and of the subjects of the kingdom.

15 such is the kingdom of heaven. And he laid his hands on
them, and departed thence.

> 16–22. **The young rich ruler. Mark x. 17–22; Luke xviii.
> 18–23.** From Luke alone we learn that he was a '*ruler*';
> from Matthew alone that he was *young*. Each of the three
> Synoptists states that he was rich.

16   And behold, one came to him and said, Master, what
17 good thing shall I do, that I may have eternal life? And
he said unto him, Why askest thou me concerning that
which is good? One there is who is good : but if thou
18 wouldest enter into life, keep the commandments. He
saith unto him, Which? And Jesus said, Thou shalt not
kill, Thou shalt not commit adultery, Thou shalt not steal,
19 Thou shalt not bear false witness, Honour thy father and
thy mother: and, Thou shalt love thy neighbour as thyself.
20 The young man saith unto him, All these things have I
21 observed : what lack I yet? Jesus said unto him, If thou
wouldest be perfect, go, sell that thou hast, and give to
the poor, and thou shalt have treasure in heaven : and

---

15. laid his hands on them. No unmeaning act; therefore
infants are capable of receiving a blessing, though not *conscious*
of an obligation. It is the authorization of infant baptism.

16. what good thing shall I do &c. In this question,
'what shall I *do?*' the ruler touches the central error of the
Pharisaic system—that goodness consisted in exact conformity
to certain external rules of conduct. Jesus shows that it is not
by *doing* anything whatever that a man can inherit eternal life,
but by *being* something; not by observing Pharisaic rules, but
by being child-like.

17. Why askest thou me concerning that which is good?
The answer of Jesus would draw the ruler's thoughts to the One
Supreme Source of good; and show that the good in itself lies
beyond the reach of human effort. It was a rebuke to shallow-
ness and pride. The reading represented in A.V. 'Why callest
thou me good?' is rightly rejected.

21. go, sell &c. Jesus does indeed bid him do something, but to *do* that would be a proof of *being* perfect, it is *the*
test for his special case, not a universal rule. With most it is
more difficult to use wealth for Christ than to give it up for
Christ.

come, follow me. But when the young man heard the 22
saying, he went away sorrowful : for he was one that had
great possessions.

23-26. Of riches, and the kingdom of God. Mark x. 23-27;
　　Luke xviii. 24-27. These reflections follow naturally on
　　the last incident.

And Jesus said unto his disciples, Verily I say unto 23
you, It is hard for a rich man to enter into the kingdom
of heaven. And again I say unto you, It is easier for a 24
camel to go through a needle's eye, than for a rich man
to enter into the kingdom of God. And when the dis- 25
ciples heard it, they were astonished exceedingly, saying,
Who then can be saved? And Jesus looking upon *them* 26
said to them, With men this is impossible ; but with God
all things are possible.

27-30. The claim of the disciples. Mark x. 28-31; Luke xviii.
　　28-30.

Then answered Peter and said unto him, Lo, we have left 27

---

22. sorrowful. A conflict of opposite desires vexed his soul.
He wished to serve God and mammon. He was sorrowful
because he saw that the special sacrifice required to win eternal
life was too great for him. He was lost through the deceitfulness
of riches (ch. xiii. 22).

24. a camel to go through a needle's eye. An Eastern
proverb to express impossibility. Attempts have been made to
explain away the natural meaning of the words. Some have
said that by 'needle's eye' was meant a gate in Jerusalem:
others instead of the word for 'camel' read another Greek word
similar in sound, meaning 'a rope.' But neither of these explana-
tions rests on a good foundation.

25. were astonished exceedingly. The extreme amazement
of the disciples, which can find no echo in souls trained to
Christianity, is not quite easy to understand. But there was
present to the disciples, perhaps, a latent Jewish thought that
external prosperity was a sign of the favour of heaven. Salvation
seemed to belong by right to rulers of synagogues and other rich
people.

26. Jesus looking upon them. These heart-searching looks
of Christ doubtless gave an effect to His words which it is
impossible to recall, but which would never be effaced from the
memory of those who felt their meaning.

28 all, and followed thee ; what then shall we have? And
Jesus said unto them, Verily I say unto you, that ye which
have followed me, in the regeneration when the Son of
man shall sit on the throne of his glory, ye also shall sit
upon twelve thrones judging the twelve tribes of Israel
29 And every one that hath left houses, or brethren, or sisters,
or father, or mother, or children, or lands, for my name's
sake, shall receive a hundredfold, and shall inherit eternal
30 life.   But many shall be last *that are* first ; and first *that
are* last.

20 1-16.   The parable of the labourers in the vineyard.   Peculiar
to St Matthew.

20 For the kingdom of heaven is like unto a man that is a
householder, which went out early in the morning to hire

---

27. what then shall we have? Peter, still not perfect in
the Spirit of Christ, suggests a lower motive for following Christ.
The answer of Christ shows that all true sacrifice shall have
its reward, but not all that looks like sacrifice is really such,
therefore, 'Many that are first shall be last.'   Among the Twelve
there was a Judas.

28. the regeneration.   A return to life, a new birth.   It is
the renewed and higher life of the world regenerated by Christ,
succeeding the birth-pangs which the present generation must
suffer.   Again, it is the spiritual return of Israel from the bondage
of the Law, which the Apostle calls life from the dead, Rom. xi.
15.   **ye also shall sit upon twelve thrones.**   The Church of
Christ is the spiritual Israel.   And in this spiritual Israel the
Apostles have actually sat on thrones.   They are the kings and
judges of the Church of God.

1.   There are many possible applications of the parable, but
the only true explanation of its meaning to the disciples at the
time must be reached by considering the question to which it is
an answer.   The parable is addressed solely to the disciples.
The thread of thought may be traced in this way: It is impossible
for a rich man, one who trusts in riches, to enter the kingdom of
heaven.   The disciples, through Peter, say, 'We at any rate left
all and followed Thee; what shall we have therefore?'   Our
Lord's answer is (1) partly encouraging, (2) partly discouraging.
(1) All who have in a *true* sense given up all for Christ shall
have a great reward (ch. xix. 28, 29).   (2) But (*v.* 30) priority
of time is not everything.   The parable is given in explanation

labourers into his vineyard. And when he had agreed 2
with the labourers for a penny a day, he sent them into
his vineyard. And he went out about the third hour, and 3
saw others standing in the marketplace idle; and to them 4
he said, Go ye also into the vineyard, and whatsoever is
right I will give you. And they went their way. Again 5
he went out about the sixth and the ninth hour, and did
likewise. And about the eleventh *hour* he went out, and 6
found others standing; and he saith unto them, Why
stand ye here all the day idle? They say unto him, 7
Because no man hath hired us. He saith unto them, Go
ye also into the vineyard. And when even was come, the 8
lord of the vineyard saith unto his steward, Call the
labourers, and pay them their hire, beginning from the
last unto the first. And when they came that *were hired* 9

---

of this point. Not only will the disciples not be the only called,
but they may not reach a higher place or a higher reward than
some who follow them at an apparent disadvantage. Still, all
who work shall have their reward. But they must beware of a
spirit very prevalent among hard workers, and not think too
much of their own labours, or be displeased because others are
equally rewarded.

2. a penny. *A denarius*: see ch. xviii. 28. A 'florin' or a
'half-crown' would represent the meaning to English readers far
more accurately than the *penny* of the A.V., which gives a wholly
wrong impression.

4. whatsoever is right. This time there is no stipulated
sum. The labourers are invited to leave all to the justice of the
householder. It is a lesson in faith and an implied rebuke to
the spirit displayed in the question, 'What shall we have therefore?'

5. Again he went out. The householder himself goes forth
to summon labourers to his vineyard. Thus not only in the
beginning of the gospel, but in every age Christ Himself calls
labourers to His work. The Master never stands idle.

6. about the eleventh hour. The various hours may be
referred in the first instance to the call of a Paul, a Barnabas,
and a Timothy, who adopted the Cause later than the Twelve.
In a secondary and less immediate sense they seem to indicate
the successive periods at which the various nations were admitted
to the Church of Christ.

about the eleventh hour, they received every man a penny.
10 And when the first came, they supposed that they would
receive more; and they likewise received every man a
11 penny.   And when they received it, they murmured
12 against the householder, saying, These last have spent
but one hour, and thou hast made them equal unto us,
which have borne the burden of the day and the scorching
13 heat.   But he answered and said to one of them, Friend,
I do thee no wrong : didst not thou agree with me for a
14 penny ? Take up that which is thine, and go thy way ; it
15 is my will to give unto this last, even as unto thee.   Is it
not lawful for me to do what I will with mine own ? or is
16 thine eye evil, because I am good ?   So the last shall be
first, and the first last.

17-19. Jesus going up to Jerusalem foretells His Passion for
the third time.   This prediction is more definite and detailed
than those which precede.   See chs. xvi. 21, xvii. 22, 23;
and Mark x. 32-34; Luke xviii. 31-34.   St Mark and
St Luke add 'shall spit upon him' (Mark), 'shall be spit
upon' (Luke); St Matthew alone names crucifixion; St Luke,
by omitting all mention of the chief priests and scribes,
throws into prominence the share of the Gentiles in the
Passion: an instance of the manner in which the Evangelists

---

12. **hour.** 'During the residence in Babylon the Hebrews
adopted the division of the day into twelve hours, whose duration
varied with the length of the day.' Edersheim, *Temple, &c.,
in the Time of our Lord* (p. 174).   **borne the burden.** This
may be regarded as man's estimate of his own merits; which
is not the divine estimate.   The words echo the tone of 'What
shall we have?' ch. xix. 27.   Man does not here acquiesce in the
judge's decision, as in the parable of the Debtors, ch. xviii.
What is just does not at first *seem* just, but, as in science many
things that seemed untrue are proved to be true, what seems
unjust will be proved just when we know all.   **the burden
of the day and the scorching heat.**   The labourers hired in the
cool evening hours would escape the long toil, and what is more
the scorching sirocco or hot wind which blows from the desert at
sunrise.
15. **is thine eye evil.** The sense is: Art thou envious
because I am just?
16. **the first.** Not only, as primarily in the parable, the
first called, but the first in position, knowledge and influence.

adapted their narrative to their special readers. For
distinctive points in the several predictions of the Passion
see notes ch. xvii. 22, 23.

And as Jesus was going up to Jerusalem, he took the 17
twelve disciples apart, and in the way he said unto them,
Behold, we go up to Jerusalem; and the Son of man shall 18
be delivered unto the chief priests and scribes; and they
shall condemn him to death, and shall deliver him unto 19
the Gentiles to mock, and to scourge, and to crucify: and
the third day he shall be raised up.

20–28. Salome's prayer for her sons, and the answer of Jesus.
Mark x. 35–45. St Mark begins 'And there come near unto
him James and John, the sons of Zebedee, saying, &c.' For
once St Matthew is more graphic and true to detail than St Mark.

Then came to him the mother of the sons of Zebedee 20
with her sons, worshipping *him*, and asking a certain
thing of him. And he said unto her, What wouldest 21
thou? She saith unto him, Command that these my two
sons may sit, one on thy right hand, and one on thy left 22
hand, in thy kingdom. But Jesus answered and said, Ye
know not what ye ask. Are ye able to drink the cup that
I am about to drink? They say unto him, We are able.
He saith unto them, My cup indeed ye shall drink: but 23
to sit on my right hand, and on *my* left hand, is not mine

18, 19. Observe the exactness of the prediction; the Sanhedrin
shall condemn but not kill, the Gentiles shall scourge and crucify.

20. the mother of the sons of Zebedee. Her name was
Salome, as we learn by comparing Matthew xxvii. 56 with
Mark xv. 40.

22. Ye know not. Observe, Jesus addresses the sons, not
the mother. **the cup that I am about to drink,** i.e. the
destiny in store for me. Cp. among other passages, Is. li. 17,
'Thou hast drunken the bowl of the cup of staggering, and
drained it,' and Ps. lxxv. 8.

23. My cup indeed ye shall drink. James was slain by
the sword of Herod Agrippa I. (Acts xii. 2). John suffered
many persecutions, but died a natural death. The rebuke of
Jesus is very gentle; His soul knew what suffering was in store
or the two brothers.

to give, but *it is for them* for whom it hath been prepared
24 of my Father. And when the ten heard it, they were
moved with indignation concerning the two brethren.
25 But Jesus called them unto him, and said, Ye know that
the rulers of the Gentiles lord it over them, and their
26 great ones exercise authority over them. Not so shall it
be among you: but whosoever would become great among
27 you shall be your minister; and whosoever would be first
28 among you shall be your servant: even as the Son of
man came not to be ministered unto, but to minister, and
to give his life a ransom for many.

> 29-34. Two men cured of blindness. Mark x. 46-52; Luke
> xviii. 35-43. There are remarkable divergences in the
> Synoptic accounts of this miracle. Some indeed have
> supposed that different miracles are related by the Evan-
> gelists. St Mark speaks of one man, 'the son of Timæus,
> Bartimæus, a blind beggar.' St Luke also mentions one only,
> but describes the incident as taking place 'as he drew nigh
> unto Jericho,' whereas St Matthew and St Mark state that
> the miracle was wrought 'as they went out from Jericho.'
> It is of course possible that St Luke narrates a separate
> miracle. The only other solution is to suppose an inaccuracy
> in an unimportant detail.

29   And as they went out from Jericho, a great multitude

---

24. they were moved with indignation. The indignation
of the 'Ten' displayed the same spirit and motive as the request
of the sons of Zebedee. It seemed as if the jealousies and
intrigues of an earthly court were breaking out among the
disciples of Jesus.

28. ransom. Only here and Mark x. 45 in the N.T., a price
paid for the redemption of a captive from slavery. For the
thought cp. Rom. iii. 24; 1 Cor. vi. 20; 1 Pet. i. 19.

29. a great multitude. The caravan of Galilæans and
others going up to Jerusalem for the Passover. Their numbers
would protect them from attack in the dangerous mountain
defiles leading to the capital. Jericho was at this time a
flourishing city. It was opulent even in the days of Joshua
from the fertility of the surrounding plain, its extensive commerce,
and from the metals found in the neighbourhood. Levelled to
the ground and laid under a curse by Joshua, it was afterwards
rebuilt by Hiel the Bethelite, and regained a portion of its former

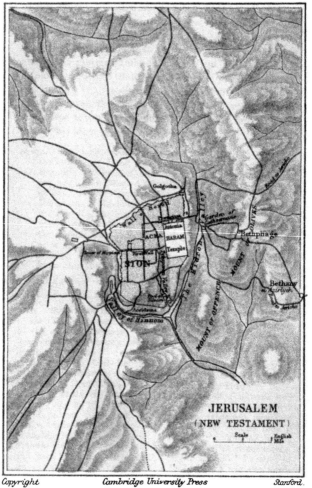

JERUSALEM
(NEW TESTAMENT)

Scale

English Mile

followed him. And behold, two blind men sitting by the 30
way side, when they heard that Jesus was passing by,
cried out, saying, Lord, have mercy on us, thou son of
David. And the multitude rebuked them, that they 31
should hold their peace: but they cried out the more,
saying, Lord, have mercy on us, thou son of David. And 32
Jesus stood still, and called them, and said, What will ye
that I should do unto you? They say unto him, Lord, 33
that our eyes may be opened. And Jesus, being moved 34
with compassion, touched their eyes : and straightway
they received their sight, and followed him.

21 1–11. The Royal Entry into Jerusalem. Mark xi. 1–11 ;
Luke xix. 29–40 ; John xii. 12–19. St Luke alone places
here the incident of Christ weeping over Jerusalem (xix.
40–44).

And when they drew nigh unto Jerusalem, and came **21**
unto Bethphage, unto the mount of Olives, then Jesus sent
two disciples, saying unto them, Go into the village that 2
is over against you, and straightway ye shall find an ass
tied, and a colt with her: loose *them*, and bring *them* unto

---

prosperity. At this period the balsam trade was a principal
source of its wealth.

Herod the Great beautified the city with palaces and public
buildings, and here he died. After Herod's death Jericho was
sacked and burnt, but restored by his son Archelaus.

34. followed him. It is probable that very many of those
who had received sight and soundness of limb by the word or
touch of Jesus followed Him to Jerusalem.

Nisan 9 (*Palm Sunday*).

1. Here there is the great interest of a fourfold comparison.
In the Synoptics the same sequence is observed, and the points
of contact are numerous ; yet each Evangelist has characteristic
points of separate description. St John connects the joyous
recognition of the crowd with the raising of Lazarus.   **unto
Bethphage, unto the mount of Olives.** No remains have been
discovered of Bethphage ('place of green or winter figs') and
its exact position is unknown. It was probably west of Bethany,
and so near to Jerusalem as to be reckoned part of the Holy
City.

2. an ass tied, and a colt with her. 'A colt tied, whereon

3 me. And if any one say aught unto you, ye shall say, The
   Lord hath need of them; and straightway he will send
4 them. Now this is come to pass, that it might be fulfilled
   which was spoken by the prophet, saying,

5   Tell ye the daughter of Zion,
        Behold, thy King cometh unto thee,
        Meek, and riding upon an ass,
6   And upon a colt the foal of an ass.

   And the disciples went, and did even as Jesus appointed
7 them, and brought the ass, and the colt, and put on them
8 their garments; and he sat thereon. And the most part
   of the multitude spread their garments in the way; and
   others cut branches from the trees, and spread them in
9 the way. And the multitudes that went before him, and
   that followed, cried, saying, Hosanna to the son of David:
   Blessed *is* he that cometh in the name of the Lord;

---

no man ever yet sat' (Mark and Luke). St Matthew notes the
close correspondence with the words of the prophecy; see *v.* 5.
Oriental travellers describe the high estimation in which the ass
is held in the East. The variety of Hebrew names for these
animals indicates the many uses to which they are put. The
prophecy from Zechariah quoted *v.* 4 contains three distinct
Hebrew words for an 'ass.' 'Riding upon an ass (*chamôr*, from
a root meaning *red*) and upon a colt (*ayir*, 'a young male ass')
the foal (lit. 'the son') of an ass (*athôn* = 'a she-ass,' from a root
meaning 'slow').'

3. The account leads to the inference that the owner of the
ass was an adherent of Jesus who had perhaps not yet declared
himself. The number of such secret followers was perhaps very
large.

5. Tell ye the daughter of Zion. The quotation is abbre-
viated from Zech. ix. 9.

8. their garments, i.e. their upper garments, the *abbas* of
modern Arabs. Cp. with this the throne extemporised for Jehu,
2 Kings ix. 13.

9. Hosanna. Hebr. '*hoshiah-na*,' 'save now,' 'save, I pray.
Na is a particle of entreaty added to imperatives. They are the
first words of Ps. cxviii. 25. **Blessed is he that cometh** (Ps.
cxviii. 26). *He that cometh* (Hebr. Habba) was a recognized
Messianic title.

Hosanna in the highest. And when he was come into 10
Jerusalem, all the city was stirred, saying, Who is this?
And the multitudes said, This is the prophet, Jesus, from 11
Nazareth of Galilee.

12–14. The second Cleansing of the Temple. Mark xi. 15–18;
Luke xix. 45, 46. It is clear from the other Synoptists that
the Cleansing of the Temple took place on Nisan 10, not
on the day of the entry. St Mark says (xi. 11) that 'when
he had looked round about upon all things, it being now
eventide, he went out unto Bethany.' In point of time
'the Cursing of the Fig-tree' should precede the 'Cleansing
of the Temple.' St Mark adds to this account 'would not
suffer that any man should carry a vessel through the
temple.' St Matthew alone mentions the healing of the
lame and the blind, and omits the incident of 'the widow's
mite,' recorded by the other Synoptists. The first 'Cleansing
of the Temple,' at the commencement of our Lord's ministry,
is recorded John ii. 13–17.

And Jesus entered into the temple of God, and cast out 12
all them that sold and bought in the temple, and overthrew
the tables of the money-changers, and the seats of them
that sold the doves; and he saith unto them, It is written, 13
My house shall be called a house of prayer: but ye make

---

10. From two passages of Josephus (*B. J.* II. 14. 3 and
VI. 9. 3) it is calculated that 2,700,000, or even a greater number,
were present at the passover, numbers encamping in the vicinity
of the holy city.

Monday, Nisan 10.

The events of this day extend to *v.* 23 of this Chapter.

12. them that sold and bought. The traffic consisted in the
sale of oxen and sheep, and such requisites for sacrifice as wine,
salt, and oil. The merchandise took place in the Court of the
Gentiles.

13. My house. The passage is quoted from Is. lvi. 7, but
with the omission of the words 'for all peoples': these are included
in the quotation by St Mark but not by St Luke. The context
in Isaiah treats of the admission of the Gentiles: 'Yet will I
gather *others* to him, beside his own that are gathered.'
(*v.* 8). **ye make it a den of robbers,** cp. Jer. vii. 11, 'Is this
house which is called by my name become a den of robbers in
your eyes?' Thus two separate passages of the O.T. are com-
bined in a contrasted or parallel form. The caves of Palestine

14 it a den of robbers. And the blind and the lame came to
him in the temple: and he healed them.

15-17. The children's praise. Peculiar to St Matthew.

15 But when the chief priests and the scribes saw the
wonderful things that he did, and the children that were
crying in the temple and saying, Hosanna to the son of

16 David; they were moved with indignation, and said unto
him, Hearest thou what these are saying? And Jesus
saith unto them, Yea: did ye never read, Out of the
mouth of babes and sucklings thou hast perfected praise?

17 And he left them, and went forth out of the city to Bethany,
and lodged there.

18-22. The cursing of the Fig-tree. Mark xi. 12-14, and
20-24. St Mark places this incident before the 'Cleansing
of the Temple,' see note *vv.* 12-14. It is an interesting
and leading instance of miracle and parable in one. The
miracle is an acted parable.

18 Now in the morning as he returned to the city, he

---

had always been refuges for the lawless, and in the reign of Herod
the Great the robbers dwelling in caves had rebelled against him
and resisted his power, Jos. *Ant.* I. 12.

15. the chief priests. (1) The high-priest, (2) those who
had served that office, (3) the priests who were members of the
high-priest's family, and (4) perhaps, the heads of the twenty-
four priestly courses. See note ch. xxvi. 3. **the children that
were crying.** Children were taught at an early age to join in
the Temple services. These caught the familiar feast-day strain
from the Galilæan pilgrims, and unconscious of all that their
words meant, saluted Jesus.

16. Out of the mouth of babes. The LXX. version is
followed, the rendering of the Hebrew is: 'out of (or by) the
mouth of babes and sucklings hast thou established strength.'
Ps. viii. 2. The ruling thought of the opening verses is the
glory of God set forth in His works. The 'scarcely articulate'
cry of an infant proves, like the heaven and the stars, the power
and providence of God. So also the children in the Temple
attest the truth of God.

17. Bethany. *House of dates,* or according to Caspari, *Place
of shops, or merchant tents,* on the S.E. of the Mount of Olives.
Here Jesus lodged with Lazarus and his sisters.

hungered. And seeing a fig tree by the way side, he 19
came to it, and found nothing thereon, but leaves only;
and he saith unto it, Let there be no fruit from thee
henceforward for ever. And immediately the fig tree
withered away. And when the disciples saw it, they 20
marvelled, saying, How did the fig tree immediately
wither away? And Jesus answered and said unto them, 21
Verily I say unto you, If ye have faith, and doubt not, ye
shall not only do what is done to the fig tree, but even if
ye shall say unto this mountain, Be thou taken up and
cast into the sea, it shall be done. And all things, 22
whatsoever ye shall ask in prayer, believing, ye shall
receive.

23–27. The authority of Christ is questioned. Mark xi. 27–33;
Luke xx. 1–8.

And when he was come into the temple, the chief 23
priests and the elders of the people came unto him as
he was teaching, and said, By what authority doest
thou these things? and who gave thee this authority?

---

19. a fig tree. Lit. *a single fig tree*, standing alone, and so
conspicuous. **but leaves only.** The fig tree loses its leaves in
the winter: but one species (see Shaw's *Travels*, p. 370, and
Land and Book, p. 23), if favoured by the season and in a good
position, puts forth fruit and leaves in the very early spring, the
fruit appearing before the leaves. The teaching of the incident
depends on this circumstance (cp. Luke xiii. 6–9). The early
fig tree, conspicuous among its leafless brethren, seemed alone to
make a show of fruit and to invite inspection. So Israel, alone
among the nations of the world, held forth a promise. From
Israel alone could fruit be expected; but none was found, and
their harvest-time was past. Therefore Israel perished as a nation,
while the Gentile races, barren hitherto, but now on the verge
of their spring-time, were ready to burst into blossom and bear
fruit.

Tuesday, Nisan 11.

**23. By what authority doest thou these things? and who
gave thee this authority?** The second question is not a mere
repetition of the first. Jesus is asked (1) what kind of authority
He possesses—human or divine? (2) By whose agency this

24 And Jesus answered and said unto them, I also will ask you one question, which if ye tell me, I likewise
25 will tell you by what authority I do these things. The baptism of John, whence was it? from heaven or from men? And they reasoned with themselves, saying, If we shall say, From heaven; he will say unto us, Why
26 then did ye not believe him? But if we shall say, From men; we fear the multitude; for all hold John as a prophet.
27 And they answered Jesus, and said, We know not. He also said unto them, Neither tell I you by what authority I do these things.

28-32. The parable of the Two Sons, and the explanation of it. Peculiar to St Matthew. St Luke omits the parable, perhaps as referring especially to Israel. The parable follows in close connexion with the question as to the teaching of John. The parables and discourses that follow deal no longer with the distant future of the Church, but with an immediate present. The subjects illustrated are—(1) The rejection of the Messiah. (2) The rejection of the Jews as a nation. (3) The Judgment, (a) which has already begun; (b) which will be enacted terribly at the siege of Jerusalem; and (c) finally fulfilled at the end of the world.

28 But what think ye? A man had two sons; and he came

authority was bestowed? No one had a right to teach unless 'authority' had been conferred upon him by the scribes.

24. I also will ask you one question. This form of argument was usual. The question of the chief priests was really an attack. Jesus meets that attack by a counter-question which presented equal difficulties in three ways—whether they said from heaven, or of men, or left it unanswered. To say from heaven was equivalent to acknowledging Jesus as Christ, to say from men was to incur the hostility of the people, to be silent was to resign their pretensions as spiritual chiefs of the nation.

25. Why then did ye not believe him? A clear proof (1) that the priests had kept aloof from John though he was of the priestly caste; and (2) that John pointed to Jesus as the Messiah.

28. two sons, representing (1) the sinners who first refused to do God's will, but repented at the preaching of John; and (2) the Pharisees who, having 'the righteousness which is of

to the first, and said, Son, go work to-day in the vineyard.
And he answered and said, I will not : but afterward he 29
repented himself, and went.   And he came to the second, 30
and said likewise.   And he answered and said, I *go*, sir :
and went not.   Whether of the twain did the will of his 31
father?   They say, The first.   Jesus saith unto them,
Verily I say unto you, that the publicans and the harlots
go into the kingdom of God before you.   For John came 32
unto you in the way of righteousness, and ye believed
him not : but the publicans and the harlots believed him :
and ye, when ye saw it, did not even repent yourselves
afterward, that ye might believe him.

33-46.   The Wicked Husbandmen.   Mark xii. 1-12 ; Luke xx.
    9-19.   No parable interprets itself more clearly than this.
    Israel is represented by an image which the prophets had
    made familiar and unmistakable—the Vineyard of the Lord.
    The householder who planted the Vineyard and fenced it
    round signifies God the Father, who created the nation for
    Himself—a peculiar and separate people.   The husbandmen
    are the Jews, and especially the Pharisees, the spiritual
    leaders of the Jews.   The servants are the prophets of God,
    the Son is the Lord Jesus Christ.

Hear another parable : There was a man that was a 33
householder, which planted a vineyard, and set a hedge

the law' (Phil. iii. 9), professed to do God's will but did it
not.
    32.   John.   The mention of John points to the connexion
between this parable and the preceding incident.   **the way of
righteousness.**   A Hebrew expression.   Cp. 'the way of God,'
ch. xxii. 16; 'the way of salvation,' Acts xvi. 17.   The Christian
doctrine was called in a special sense 'the way' (Acts xix. 9, 23).
did not even repent yourselves.   Did not even change your
mind (see above, *v*. 29), much less repented in the deeper
sense.
    33.   planted a vineyard.   Cp. the parable in Isaiah v. 1-7,
where the description is very similar to this.   See also Ps. lxxx.
8-16; Jer. ii. 21; Ezek. xv. 1-6.   The vine was adopted as a
national emblem on the Maccabean coins.   **set a hedge about it.**
Defended it with a stone wall or with a fence of prickly pears.
Israel was separated throughout her history politically, and even

about it, and digged a winepress in it, and built a tower,
and let it out to husbandmen, and went into another
34 country.   And when the season of the fruits drew near,
he sent his servants to the husbandmen, to receive his
35 fruits.   And the husbandmen took his servants, and beat
36 one, and killed another, and stoned another.   Again, he
sent other servants more than the first: and they did unto
37 them in like manner.   But afterward he sent unto them
38 his son, saying, They will reverence my son.   But the
husbandmen, when they saw the son, said among themselves, This is the heir; come, let us kill him, and take
39 his inheritance.   And they took him, and cast him forth
40 out of the vineyard, and killed him.   When therefore the
lord of the vineyard shall come, what will he do unto
41 those husbandmen?   They say unto him, He will miserably
destroy those miserable men, and will let out the vineyard
unto other husbandmen, which shall render him the fruits
42 in their seasons.   Jesus saith unto them, Did ye never
read in the scriptures,

---

physically, by the natural position of Palestine.   **digged a winepress.** The winepress was often dug or hewn out of the limestone
rock in Palestine.   There were two receptacles or vats.   The
upper one was strictly the press, the lower one the vinevat into
which the expressed juice of the grape passed.   The two vats
are mentioned together only in Joel iii. 13.   **a tower.** Probably
a wooden booth raised on a high platform, in which a watcher
was stationed to guard the grapes.   Neither the winepress nor
the tower seems to have any special significance in the interpretation of the parable.   **let it out to husbandmen.** It was usual
for the tenant to hold the land on condition of paying part of the
produce as rent.   See the parable of the Unjust Steward, St Luke
xvi. 1–8.

    35.   beat one, and killed another. See ch. xxiii. 35.

    39.   cast him forth out of the vineyard. Words that recall
the crucifixion of Jesus outside the city of Jerusalem.

    41.   They say unto him. An interruption from the listening
crowd, which marks the intense interest with which these parables
were heard.   The indignation of the bystanders is aroused as if
it were a tale of actual life.

    42.   in the scriptures. Ps. cxviii. 22.   The original reference

The stone which the builders rejected,

The same was made the head of the corner:

This was from the Lord,

And it is marvellous in our eyes?

Therefore say I unto you, The kingdom of God shall be 43
taken away from you, and shall be given to a nation
bringing forth the fruits thereof. And he that falleth on 44
this stone shall be broken to pieces: but on whomsoever
it shall fall, it will scatter him as dust. And when the 45
chief priests and the Pharisees heard his parables, they
perceived that he spake of them. And when they sought 46
to lay hold on him, they feared the multitudes, because
they took him for a prophet.

22 1–14. The parable of the Royal Marriage Feast. Peculiar
to St Matthew. The parable recorded by St Luke (xiv.
16–24), though similar to this in some respects, differs in its
context and special teaching and in many details. As of the
other parables of the Passion, the primary intention of this
regards the present and the immediate future. The parable
falls into two divisions, (1) *vv.* 1–7; (2) *vv.* 8–14. In the
first (1) the servants are John Baptist and the first disciples
of Christ; the feast is the Kingdom of God, or the Christian

---

was to a stone used in the erection of the second Temple. The
'corner stone' is the Jewish nation rejected at first, afterwards
restored from captivity. Christ transfers this image to His
Church, formed of Jew and Gentile alike, which, though
despised at first, was destined to become great.   **the head
of the corner**. The stone that connects the two walls at the top
and supports the roof.

44. he that falleth on this stone &c. An earthenware
vessel falling on a mass of rock would be shattered, but if the
mass of rock fell upon it, it would be reduced to dust and
scattered.

46. when they sought to lay hold on him. The Sanhedrin
aimed at two things: (1) to seize Jesus quickly, for the Passover
(during which no hostile measures could be taken) was close at
hand; and because Jesus might be expected to quit Jerusalem
after the feast. (2) To seize Him apart from the people; for
the Galilæans would suffer no one to lay hands on their King
and Prophet. Treachery alone enabled the Jews to secure their
end.

Church; the invited guests, who refuse to come, are the
Jews; the vengeance taken was literally fulfilled at the siege
of Jerusalem, A.D. 70. (2) This division relates to the
preaching of the Gospel to the Gentiles. As in the Net
(ch. xiii. 47) or in the Corn-field (ch. xiii. 24), worthy and
unworthy are mingled until the King separates.

22 And Jesus answered and spake again in parables unto
2 them, saying, The kingdom of heaven is likened unto a
certain king, which made a marriage feast for his son,
3 and sent forth his servants to call them that were bidden
4 to the marriage feast: and they would not come. Again
he sent forth other servants, saying, Tell them that are
bidden, Behold, I have made ready my dinner: my oxen
and my fatlings are killed, and all things are ready: come
5 to the marriage feast. But they made light of it, and
went their ways, one to his own farm, another to his
6 merchandise: and the rest laid hold on his servants, and
7 entreated them shamefully, and killed them. But the
king was wroth; and he sent his armies, and destroyed
8 those murderers, and burned their city. Then saith he to
his servants, The wedding is ready, but they that were
9 bidden were not worthy. Go ye therefore unto the partings
of the highways, and as many as ye shall find, bid to the
10 marriage feast. And those servants went out into the
highways, and gathered together all as many as they
found, both bad and good: and the wedding was filled
11 with guests. But when the king came in to behold the
guests, he saw there a man which had not on a wedding-
12 garment: and he saith unto him, Friend, how camest

---

3. sent forth his servants or *slaves*. This was in accordance
with Eastern custom. Cp. Esther v. 8, and vi. 14.
7. the king was wroth. For a subject to scorn the summons
to the royal feast implied disloyalty and rebellion.
10. those servants went out. The 'servants' are the
earliest Christian missionaries, St Paul, Silas, Barnabas and
others.
11. a wedding-garment. The festive robe which in this
instance it is supposed the master of the feast himself provided,

thou in hither not having a wedding-garment? And he
was speechless. Then the king said to the servants, Bind 13
him hand and foot, and cast him out into the outer darkness; there shall be the weeping and gnashing of teeth.
For many are called, but few chosen.   14

15-22. The temptation of the Herodians. The tribute money.
    Mark xii. 13-17; Luke xx. 20-26.

Then went the Pharisees, and took counsel how they 15
might ensnare him in *his* talk. And they send to him 16
their disciples, with the Herodians, saying, Master, we
know that thou art true, and teachest the way of God in
truth, and carest not for any one: for thou regardest not
the person of men. Tell us therefore, What thinkest 17
thou? Is it lawful to give tribute unto Cæsar, or not?
But Jesus perceived their wickedness, and said, Why 18

so that there was no excuse. In the East a special significance
is attached to garments. To give and still more to exchange
garments was a sign of a covenant and of conferring privilege
from remote antiquity. (See 1 Sam. xviii. 4, 2 Kings ii. 13 and
cp. Matt. ix. 20.)

13. the outer darkness. The dark, wild night, without
moon or stars, the cold and gloom of which would contrast
terribly with the warmth and light within; or perhaps the dark
dungeon outside the brightness of the banquet-hall.

15. how they might ensnare, as a fowler ensnares birds:
used here only in N.T. All the previous attempts had been to
discredit Jesus as a religious teacher; the present is an attempt
to expose Him to the hostility of the Roman government.

16. Herodians. Servants or supporters of Herod; as a rule
they were opposed to the Pharisees, who disliked the government
both of the Romans and of the Herodian dynasty.   **regardest
not the person of men,** i.e. 'Thou art not moved by external
appearance; neither wealth, power, nor prestige will influence
thy decision.' These men pretended to honour Jesus for justice
and impartiality.

17. Is it lawful to give tribute unto Cæsar. The question
was an attempt to see whether Jesus would adopt the watchword
of the Zealots—'there is no king but God.' This special tribute,
the poll-tax levied on each individual, was particularly offensive
to the patriotic party among the Jews. It was thought to be
forbidden in Deut. xvii. 15.

19 tempt ye me, ye hypocrites? Shew me the tribute money.
20 And they brought unto him a penny. And he saith unto
21 them, Whose is this image and superscription? They
say unto him, Cæsar's. Then saith he unto them, Render
therefore unto Cæsar the things that are Cæsar's; and
22 unto God the things that are God's. And when they
heard it, they marvelled, and left him, and went their
way.

23-33. The Sadducees tempt Jesus. The Condition of the
Future Life. Mark xii. 18-27; Luke xx. 27-39.

23   On that day there came to him Sadducees, which say
24 that there is no resurrection: and they asked him, saying,
Master, Moses said, If a man die, having no children, his
brother shall marry his wife, and raise up seed unto his
25 brother. Now there were with us seven brethren: and
the first married and deceased, and having no seed left
26 his wife unto his brother; in like manner the second also,
27 and the third, unto the seventh. And after them all the
28 woman died. In the resurrection therefore whose wife
29 shall she be of the seven? for they all had her. But
Jesus answered and said unto them, Ye do err, not
30 knowing the scriptures, nor the power of God. For in

---

19. a penny. A *denarius*, bearing probably the image of
Tiberius. The Jewish coins were not impressed with the effigy
of their kings.

21. Render therefore unto Cæsar the things that are Cæsar's.
'Pay back *therefore*.' The Jewish teachers laid down the
principle that 'He is king whose coin passes current.' St Paul
expands this principle, which underlies our Lord's answer (Rom.
xiii. 1 foll.).

23. Sadducees. See note ch. iii. 7. This is the only direct
contact of the Sadducees with Jesus.

24. his brother shall marry his wife. This is sometimes
called the 'levirate law,' from Lat. *levir*, a brother-in-law; see
Deut. xxv. 5.

29. not knowing, i.e. 'because ye do not know' (1) **the
scriptures,** which affirm the doctrine; nor (2) **the power of
God,** which is able to effect the resurrection, and after the
resurrection to create a new order of things in the new world.

the resurrection they neither marry, nor are given in marriage, but are as angels in heaven. But as touching 31 the resurrection of the dead, have ye not read that which was spoken unto you by God, saying, I am the God of 32 Abraham, and the God of Isaac, and the God of Jacob? God is not *the God* of the dead, but of the living. And 33 when the multitudes heard it, they were astonished at his teaching.

34-40. **The Greatest Commandment.** Mark xii. 28-34; cp. Luke x. 25-28. In Luke the question is asked at an earlier period of the ministry, after the return of the Seventy; and the meaning of 'neighbour' is illustrated by the parable of the 'Good Samaritan.'

But the Pharisees, when they heard that he had put 34 the Sadducees to silence, gathered themselves together. And one of them, a lawyer, asked him a question, tempting 35 him, Master, which is the great commandment in the law? 36 And he said unto him, Thou shalt love the Lord thy God 37 with all thy heart, and with all thy soul, and with all thy mind. This is the great and first commandment. And 38 a second like *unto it* is this, Thou shalt love thy neighbour 39 as thyself. On these two commandments hangeth the 40 whole law, and the prophets.

41-46. **The Son of David.** Mark xii. 35-37; Luke xx. 41-44.

Now while the Pharisees were gathered together, Jesus 41 asked them a question, saying, What think ye of the 42

---

30. in the resurrection, i.e. in the life which begins with the resurrection. The argument of Jesus is: if God is a God of the living and if He is the God of Abraham, Abraham is living, and therefore there is a resurrection.

34. had put...to silence. Literally *gagged* or *muzzled*, hence silenced completely, not only for the moment.

35. a lawyer, i.e. an interpreter of the written law, as distinguished from the 'traditions' or unwritten law.

37. See Deut. vi. 5.

heart...soul...mind. St Mark and St Luke add 'strength.' The command is to love God with all the power of will, spirit, intellect, and physical strength.

Christ? whose son is he? They say unto him, *The son*
43 of David.   He saith unto them, How then doth David in
the Spirit call him Lord, saying,

44   The Lord said unto my Lord,
        Sit thou on my right hand,
        Till I put thine enemies underneath thy feet?

45
46 If David then calleth him Lord, how is he his son? And
no one was able to answer him a word, neither durst
any man from that day forth ask him any more questions.

23 1-36. A rebuke of the Pharisees and of religious hypocrisy.

1-7. Strength and weakness of the Pharisees. They are the
successors of Moses, *v.* 2; but they say and do not, 3-7.
Only a part of this discourse appears in the other Synoptics;
for this portion cp. Mark xii. 38-40; Luke xi. 43-46, xx.
46, 47.

23   Then spake Jesus to the multitudes and to his disciples,
2 saying, The scribes and the Pharisees sit on Moses' seat:
3 all things therefore whatsoever they bid you, *these* do and
observe: but do not ye after their works; for they say,
4 and do not.   Yea, they bind heavy burdens and grievous
to be borne, and lay them on men's shoulders; but they
5 themselves will not move them with their finger.   But all
their works they do for to be seen of men: for they make
broad their phylacteries, and enlarge the borders *of their*

---

44. The Lord said unto my Lord. Ps. cx. 1. According to
the Hebrew, *Jehovah said to Adoni*, i.e. to my sovereign Lord,
the Messiah, the Son of David.

46. The Jews always referred the words of this Psalm to the
Messiah.

2. sit on Moses' seat, i.e. succeed him as teachers. For
sitting as the posture of a teacher cp. ch. v. 1.

4. bind heavy burdens. The picture is of the merciless
camel- or ass-driver, who makes up burdens, not only heavy but
unwieldy and so difficult to carry, and then placing them on the
animals' shoulders stands by indifferently, raising no finger to
lighten or even adjust the burden.

5. phylacteries. Literally, *defences*, and in late Greek
'amulets' or 'charms.' The Hebrew name, *tephillin*, which is
still in use, signifies 'prayers.' They were slips of parchment

garments, and love the chief place at feasts, and the chief 6
seats in the synagogues, and the salutations in the market- 7
places, and to be called of men, Rabbi.

8-12. The contrast of Christian conduct.

But be not ye called Rabbi : for one is your teacher, and 8
all ye are brethren. And call no man your father on the 9
earth : for one is your Father, which is in heaven. Neither 10
be ye called masters : for one is your master, *even* the
Christ. But he that is greatest among you shall be your 11
servant. And whosoever shall exalt himself shall be 12
humbled ; and whosoever shall humble himself shall be
exalted.

13-33. Seven woes denounced against the Scribes and Pharisees.

But woe unto you, scribes and Pharisees, hypocrites ! 13
because ye shut the kingdom of heaven against men : for

---

inscribed with four portions of the Law (Ex. xii. 3-10, 11-17;
Deut. vi. 4-9; xi. 13-21) enclosed in little cases or boxes made
of calfskin, and fastened by leather straps to the left arm and
on the forehead, in accordance with a literal interpretation of
Ex. xiii. 16 and Deut. vi. 8. To make the phylacteries, or
rather the cases which contained them, broad and conspicuous
was to assume a character of superior piety, for the phylacteries
were symbols of devotion. Jesus does not prohibit the practice
of wearing phylacteries, but the ostentatious enlargement of
them. It is thought by many that our Saviour Himself wore
phylacteries. **enlarge the borders of their garments.** Strictly,
the fringe of the tallith, or cloak : another instance of ostentation ;
the blue threads in the fringe—the colour of the sky—were a type
of heavenly purity. Our Lord Himself wore the fringed tallith
(see ch. ix. 20); the offence of the Pharisees consisted in en-
larging the symbolical fringes.
  6. the chief place at feasts. The Jews like the Romans
reclined at their meals, and each seat on the different couches
had its special dignity.
  7. Rabbi. Literally, my great [one], lord. This title, with
which the great doctors of the law were saluted, was quite
modern in our Lord's day. The true teaching on this point is
found in the Talmud, 'Love the work but hate the title.'
  11. Cp. ch. xx. 26, 27.
  13. ye shut the kingdom of heaven. In allusion to the

ye enter not in yourselves, neither suffer ye them that are
entering in to enter.

15 Woe unto you, scribes and Pharisees, hypocrites! for
ye compass sea and land to make one proselyte; and
when he is become so, ye make him twofold more a son
of hell than yourselves.

16 Woe unto you, ye blind guides, which say, Whosoever
shall swear by the temple, it is nothing; but whosoever
17 shall swear by the gold of the temple, he is a debtor. Ye
fools and blind: for whether is greater, the gold, or the
18 temple that hath sanctified the gold? And, Whosoever
shall swear by the altar, it is nothing; but whosoever
19 shall swear by the gift that is upon it, he is a debtor. Ye
blind: for whether is greater, the gift, or the altar that
20 sanctifieth the gift? He therefore that sweareth by the
21 altar, sweareth by it, and by all things thereon. And he
that sweareth by the temple, sweareth by it, and by him
22 that dwelleth therein. And he that sweareth by the
heaven, sweareth by the throne of God, and by him
that sitteth thereon.

23 Woe unto you, scribes and Pharisees, hypocrites! for

---

symbolic 'key of knowledge' given to the scribe on admission to
the order. They use their keys to shut rather than to open the
doors of the kingdom.

14. This verse, the words of which stand for certain in
Mark xii. 40, Luke xx. 47, is rejected on decisive evidence here.

15. **proselyte.** Literally, *one who approaches*, hence, 'a
worshipper' (cp. Heb. x. 1), a 'convert.' The word occurs in
three other passages, Acts ii. 11, vi. 5, xiii. 43. **twofold more
a son of hell.** In accordance with a tendency in new converts
to exaggerate the external points of the creed which they adopt,
Gentile proselytes strained to the utmost the worst features of
Pharisaism. **son of hell.** Lit. *son of Gehenna*, i.e. a criminal
worthy to be flung into the accursed valley of Hinnom, or
Gehenna.

16. **the gold of the temple,** i.e. the offerings made to the
Temple, called 'Corban,' or 'devoted'; the use of that word
made an oath binding, see ch. xv. 5.

ye tithe mint and anise and cummin, and have left undone
the weightier matters of the law, judgement, and mercy,
and faith: but these ye ought to have done, and not to
have left the other undone. Ye blind guides, which strain 24
out the gnat, and swallow the camel.

Woe unto you, scribes and Pharisees, hypocrites! for 25
ye cleanse the outside of the cup and of the platter, but
within they are full from extortion and excess. Thou 26
blind Pharisee, cleanse first the inside of the cup and
of the platter, that the outside thereof may become clean
also.

Woe unto you, scribes and Pharisees, hypocrites! for 27
ye are like unto whited sepulchres, which outwardly
appear beautiful, but inwardly are full of dead men's
bones, and of all uncleanness. Even so ye also outwardly 28
appear righteous unto men, but inwardly ye are full of
hypocrisy and iniquity.

Woe unto you, scribes and Pharisees, hypocrites! for 29
ye build the sepulchres of the prophets, and garnish the
tombs of the righteous, and say, If we had been in the 30
days of our fathers, we should not have been partakers
with them in the blood of the prophets. Wherefore ye 31
witness to yourselves, that ye are sons of them that slew

---

23. ye tithe &c. 'Mint and rue and every herb' (Luke xi.
42). Zeal in paying tithes was one of the results of the reform
under the Maccabees.

25. are full. The outside of the cup and platter is the
external behaviour and conduct of the Pharisee, the inside of the
cup is his heart and real life.   **from extortion and excess,** i.e.
'*from rapacity and incontinence.*'

27. whited sepulchres. In Luke the comparison is to
'tombs which appear not,' by walking over which men unconsciously defile themselves. To avoid this ceremonial defilement
the Jews carefully whitewashed the graves or marked them with
chalk on a fixed day every year—the fifteenth of Adar.

31. witness to yourselves. You call yourselves children,
and indeed you *are* children of those who slew the prophets.
You inherit their wickedness in compassing the death of the
Prophet of the Lord. See note ch. iii. 7.

32 the prophets. Fill ye up then the measure of your fathers.

33 Ye serpents, ye offspring of vipers, how shall ye escape the judgement of hell?

34-36. The martyrs of Christ.

34 Therefore, behold, I send unto you prophets, and wise men, and scribes: some of them shall ye kill and crucify; and some of them shall ye scourge in your synagogues,

35 and persecute from city to city: that upon you may come all the righteous blood shed on the earth, from the blood of Abel the righteous unto the blood of Zachariah son of Barachiah, whom ye slew between the sanctuary and the

36 altar. Verily I say unto you, All these things shall come upon this generation.

37-39. The fate of Jerusalem.

37   O Jerusalem, Jerusalem, which killeth the prophets, and stoneth them that are sent unto her! how often

---

33. offspring of vipers. See note ch. iii. 7.

34. I send unto you prophets, and wise men, and scribes. Marking the continuity of the Christian with the Jewish Church. **shall ye kill and crucify.** Kill, directly as Stephen (Acts vii. 59), indirectly as James (Acts xii. 2), and crucify, by means of the Roman power, as Symeon, second bishop of Jerusalem (Eus. *H. E.* III. 32).

from city to city. As Paul pursued Christians to Damascus; as he was himself driven from Antioch in Pisidia, from Iconium, from Philippi, and from Thessalonica.

35. Zachariah son of Barachiah. The Zechariah whose death is recorded 2 Chron. xxiv. 20–22 was the son of Jehoiada; Zechariah the prophet was a son of Berachiah, but of his death no mention is made. The allusion must be to the first-named Zechariah, and by an error, whether original or due to a later hand is uncertain, his father is named Barachiah instead of Jehoiada.   **between the sanctuary and the altar.** Even the priests were not allowed at all times to tread that sacred part of the Temple courts.

37. O Jerusalem, Jerusalem. From Luke xiii. 34 it appears that our Lord spoke these words in a different connexion at an earlier period of His ministry.   For the pathetic reiteration of the name, cp. ch. xxvii. 26.   **killeth...stoneth.** Recalling the precise expressions of ch. xxi. 35.

would I have gathered thy children together, even as a
hen gathereth her chickens under her wings, and ye
would not! Behold, your house is left unto you desolate. 38
For I say unto you, Ye shall not see me henceforth, till 39
ye shall say, Blessed *is* he that cometh in the name of the
Lord.

24 1-22. Prediction of the fall of Jerusalem. Mark xiii. 1-end;
Luke xxi. 5-36. This chapter opens with the great discourse
of Jesus, which is continued to the end of ch. xxv. That
discourse contains (1) a prediction of the fall of Jerusalem,
(2) a prediction of the end of the world, (3) Parables in
relation to these predictions. Since the fall of Jerusalem is
regarded throughout as a vivid type of the Last Judgment
it is difficult to determine the limits of (1) and (2). In some
parts however, especially to the end of *v.* 22, it will be clearly
seen that the primary and immediate reference is to the fall
of Jerusalem.

And Jesus went out from the temple, and was going on **24**
his way; and his disciples came to him to shew him the
buildings of the temple. But he answered and said unto 2
them, See ye not all these things? verily I say unto you,
There shall not be left here one stone upon another, that
shall not be thrown down.

And as he sat on the mount of Olives, the disciples 3
came unto him privately, saying, Tell us, when shall these

---

38. your house, i.e. Jerusalem, rather than the Temple.
till ye shall say. Till, like the children in these Temple courts,
ye recognize Me as the Messiah.

1. was going on his way. This gives a more exact picture
than 'went out' of A.V. As Jesus was crossing the valley of
Kidron His disciples came to Him and stopped Him, and prayed
Him to look at the buildings of the Temple where full in view
it rose with its colonnades of dazzling white marble, surmounted
with golden roof and pinnacles, and founded on a substructure
of huge stones.

2. There shall not be left here one stone upon another.
The Temple was destroyed by fire, notwithstanding every effort
made by Titus to save it.

3. the disciples. St Mark names the four, Peter and James,
and John and Andrew.

things be? and what *shall be* the sign of thy coming, and
4 of the end of the world? And Jesus answered and said
5 unto them, Take heed that no man lead you astray. For
many shall come in my name, saying, I am the Christ;
6 and shall lead many astray. And ye shall hear of wars
and rumours of wars: see that ye be not troubled: for
these things must needs come to pass; but the end is not
7 yet. For nation shall rise against nation, and kingdom
against kingdom: and there shall be famines and earth-
8 quakes in divers places. But all these things are the
9 beginning of travail. Then shall they deliver you up
unto tribulation, and shall kill you: and ye shall be hated
10 of all the nations for my name's sake. And then shall
many stumble, and shall deliver up one another, and shall
11 hate one another. And many false prophets shall arise,
12 and shall lead many astray. And because iniquity shall
13 be multiplied, the love of the many shall wax cold. But

---

thy coming. Lit. *thy presence*, used with the same special
meaning, 1 Thess. ii. 19; Jas. v. 7; 2 Pet. i. 16; 1 John ii. 28.
The precise word 'coming,' or 'advent,' which the Church has
adopted in reference to the second 'presence' of Christ, has no
exact equivalent in this prophecy. **end of the world.** See
ch. xiii. 39, 40.

5. I am the Christ. The appearance of false Messiahs shall
be the first sign. St John bears witness to the fulfilment of this
sign: 'Even now have there arisen many antichrists, whereby we
know that it is the last hour.' 1 John ii. 18.

6. wars and rumours of wars. The second sign. Philo
and Josephus describe the disturbed state of Judæa from this
date to the siege of Jerusalem. Massacres of the Jews were
perpetrated at Cæsarea, at Alexandria, in Babylonia and in
Syria.

10. shall many stumble. Shall fall, fail in loyalty, be
tempted to forsake the faith. Cp. ch. xiii. 21.

11. false prophets. At the siege of Jerusalem 'false prophets
suborned by the Zealots kept the people in a state of feverish
excitement, as though the appointed Deliverer would still
appear.'

12. the love of the many, i.e. of the majority. Love or
'charity' (1 Cor. xiii.) became the chief distinguishing grace or.
virtue of the Christian life. If love grows cold Christianity

he that endureth to the end, the same shall be saved.
And this gospel of the kingdom shall be preached in the 14
whole world for a testimony unto all the nations; and
then shall the end come.

When therefore ye see the abomination of desolation, 15
which was spoken of by Daniel the prophet, standing in
the holy place (let him that readeth understand), then let 16
them that are in Judæa flee unto the mountains : let him 17
that is on the housetop not go down to take out the things
that are in his house : and let him that is in the field not 18
return back to take his cloke. But woe unto them that 19
are with child and to them that give suck in those days !
And pray ye that your flight be not in the winter, neither 20

---

itself fails. In the Synoptic Gospels the word is used only here
and St Luke xi. 42.

13. he that endureth. In St Luke the expression of this
thought is : ' In your patience ye shall win your souls,' i.e. *your
higher lives.* Ch. xxi. 19, R.V.

15. the abomination of desolation, i.e. *the abomination
that maketh desolate,* the act of sacrilege which is a sign and a
cause of desolation. In the time of the Maccabees when ·the
statue of Jupiter was placed within the Temple it was called
the 'abomination (or idol) of desolation' (1 Macc. i. 54).
Our Lord refers to some similar profanity in the capture of
Jerusalem. **let him that readeth understand.** These
words are almost beyond a doubt an insertion of the Evangelist,
and not part of our Lord's discourse.

16. flee unto the mountains. Many Christians, warned by
this prediction, took refuge at Pella in Peræa during the siege of
Jerusalem.

17. not go down, i.e. either (1) pass from the roof to the
entrance, and thence to the street, without entering any apart-
ments, or (2) escape along the flat roofs from house to house.

18. return back to take his cloke, i.e. the outer garment,
which the field labourer would throw off while at work, wearing
the tunic only.

20. in the winter. When swollen streams, bitterly cold and
long nights would increase the misery and danger of the fugitives.
on a sabbath. When religious scruples might delay the flight.
The extent of a Sabbath-day's journey was 2,000 cubits. Here,
however, the question meets us, how far Jewish observances would
affect the Christians. Probably the early Christians observed

21 on a sabbath : for then shall be great tribulation, such as
hath not been from the beginning of the world until now,
22 no, nor ever shall be.   And except those days had been
shortened, no flesh would have been saved : but for the
elect's sake those days shall be shortened.

> 23-31. The Second Coming of Christ. Mark xiii. 21-27 ;
> Luke xxi. 24-28.

23 Then if any man shall say unto you, Lo, here is the
24 Christ, or, Here ; believe *it* not.   For there shall arise
false Christs, and false prophets, and shall shew great
signs and wonders ; so as to lead astray, if possible, even
25 the elect.   Behold, I have told you beforehand.   If there-
26 fore they shall say unto you, Behold, he is in the wilderness ;
go not forth : Behold, he is in the inner chambers ; believe

---

both the Sabbath and the Lord's day. But in any case many
impediments would arise against flight on the Sabbath-day.
St Matthew alone records these words of warning.

21. great tribulation. No words can describe the unequalled
horrors of this siege. It was the Passover season, and Jews from
all parts were crowded within the walls. Three factions, at
desperate feud with each other, were posted on the heights of
Sion and on the Temple Mount. These only united to fling
themselves at intervals upon the Roman entrenchments, and
then resumed their hate. The Temple courts swam with the
blood of civil discord, which was literally mingled with the blood
of the sacrifices. Jewish prisoners were crucified by hundreds
in view of their friends, while within the city the wretched
inhabitants were reduced by famine to the most loathsome of food
and to deeds of unspeakable cruelty. Jerusalem was taken on
the 10th August, A.D. 70. 1,100,000 Jews perished in the siege,
100,000 were sold into slavery. With the fall of Jerusalem,
Israel ceased to exist as a nation. It was truly 'a last day,' a
day of judgment.

22. those days had been shortened. Several circumstances
concurred to shorten the duration of the siege, such as the scanty
supply of provisions, the crowded state of the city, the internal
dissensions, and the abandonment of important defences.

23. Then. According to Chrysostom, Jerome and others,
who make the division at *v.* 22, 'then' marks a transition, and
the description which follows is applicable to the end of the
world, not to the fall of Jerusalem.

26. in the inner chambers. Here probably 'the lecture rooms'

it not. For as the lightning cometh forth from the east, 27
and is seen even unto the west; so shall be the coming
of the Son of man. Wheresoever the carcase is, there 28
will the eagles be gathered together.

But immediately, after the tribulation of those days, 29
the sun shall be darkened, and the moon shall not give
her light, and the stars shall fall from heaven, and the
powers of the heavens shall be shaken: and then shall 30
appear the sign of the Son of man in heaven: and then
shall all the tribes of the earth mourn, and they shall see
the Son of man coming on the clouds of heaven with
power and great glory. And he shall send forth his 31
angels with a great sound of a trumpet, and they shall
gather together his elect from the four winds, from one
end of heaven to the other.

---

of the synagogue, so that the meaning of the verse would be,
'whether the false Christ come like John the Baptist in the
desert, or like a great Rabbi in the schools of the synagogue, be
not deceived.'

27. is seen. The flash is instantly visible in the opposite
quarter of the heaven. Like lightning all-pervading, swift,
sudden and of dazzling brightness, shall be the coming of the
Son of man.

28. Wheresoever the carcase is. The spiritual perception
will discern wherever the Lord comes, by a subtle sense
like that by which the vulture is cognisant of his distant
prey.

29. the sun shall be darkened. Such figurative language
is frequent with the Hebrew prophets; it implies (1) the
perplexity and confusion of a sudden revolution, a great change;
the very sources of light become darkness, cp. Isaiah xiii. 10,
and (2) the darkness of distress, as Ezek. xxxii. 7, 8.

30. the sign of the Son of man. What this shall be it is
vain to conjecture, but when it appears its import will be instantly
recognized by the faithful.

31. with a great sound of a trumpet. The image would
be suggestive to the Jews, who were called together in the camp
by silver trumpets (Numb. x. 2 foll.). Moreover, the great
festivals, the commencement of the year, and other celebrations
were announced by trumpets. There will be once again a
marshalling of the host of Jehovah, of God's Church.

32-35. The parable of the Fig Tree. Mark xiii. 28-31 ; Luke
   xxi. 29-33.

32 Now from the fig tree learn her parable : when her
   branch is now become tender, and putteth forth its leaves,
33 ye know that the summer is nigh ; even so ye also, when
   ye see all these things, know ye that he is nigh, *even* at
34 the doors. Verily I say unto you, This generation shall
   not pass away, till all these things be accomplished.
35 Heaven and earth shall pass away, but my words shall
   not pass away.

36-End of 25. Parables and teachings concerning the Second
   Advent.

36-51. The Coming of Christ; the need of watchfulness. More
   briefly reported in Mark xiii. 32-37 ; Luke xxi. 34-36.

36 But of that day and hour knoweth no one, not even the
   angels of heaven, neither the Son, but the Father only.
37 And as *were* the days of Noah, so shall be the coming of
38 the Son of man. For as in those days which were before
   the flood they were eating and drinking, marrying and
   giving in marriage, until the day that Noah entered into
39 the ark, and they knew not until the flood came, and took

32. from the fig tree learn her parable. The lesson that
the fig tree teaches. The parable relates to the siege of Jerusalem and the ruin of the Jewish nationality, illustrating *vv.* 4-
22. It was springtime, and the fig tree was putting forth its
leaf-buds; not more certainly does that natural sign foretell the
coming harvest than the signs of Christ shall foretell the fall of
the Holy City. **tender,** i.e. ready to sprout.
33. he is nigh, at the harvest-time of God—the end of this
æon or period at the fall of Jerusalem.
37. the days of Noah. As at other critical times in history
—the days before the Flood—the eve of the destruction of Sodom
and Gomorrah—so before the 'presence' of Christ the world will
be given up to enjoyment ('eating and drinking'), it will rest its
hopes in the present, and plan for the continuance of the existing
order ('marrying and giving in marriage'), it will be immersed
in business ('bought, sold, planted, builded,' Luke xvii. 28), all
which things are the perils of the religious life—the cares, riches,
pleasures, that choke the good seed (Luke viii. 14).

them all away; so shall be the coming of the Son of man.
Then shall two men be in the field; one is taken, and one 40
is left: two women *shall be* grinding at the mill; one is 41
taken, and one is left. Watch therefore: for ye know not 42
on what day your Lord cometh.

43, 44. The Lord cometh as a thief in the night. Luke xii.
39, 40.

But know this, that if the master of the house had known 43
in what watch the thief was coming, he would have
watched, and would not have suffered his house to be
broken through. Therefore be ye also ready: for in an 44
hour that ye think not the Son of man cometh.

45-51. The stewards of God. Luke xii. 41-48, where this
parable is joined on to the preceding one by a question of
St Peter, 'Lord, speakest thou this parable unto us, or even
unto all?' Mark xiii. 37 has 'What I say unto you, I say
unto all, Watch.' Here, and throughout the discourse, the
disciples are specially addressed.

Who then is the faithful and wise servant, whom his lord 45
hath set over his household, to give them their food in
due season? Blessed is that servant, whom his lord when 46
he cometh shall find so doing. Verily I say unto you, 47

---

41. two women shall be grinding at the mill. In southern
Palestine, where there are no mill-streams, hand-mills are to be
seen and heard in every village. 'Two women sit at the mill
facing each other; both having hold of the handle by which the
upper is turned round on the nether mill-stone.' *Land and Book*,
p. 526.

43. the master of the house. 'Goodman' of A.V. is probably a corruption for A.S. *gumman*, a prominent man, or *guma*,
a man. **to be broken through.** Rather *dug through*. See
ch. vi. 19, 20.

45. faithful and wise servant. The steward was generally
a slave whom his master had chosen on account of his trust-
worthiness and intelligence to be steward of his estate. From
this short parable springs the conception of the stewardship of
the Christian ministry expanded in the Epistles and indelibly
fixed in religious thought. And from the Latin version of this
and parallel passages such expressions as *'the present dispensation,'*
'the Christian dispensation,' are derived.

48 that he will set him over all that he hath.   But if that evil
49 servant shall say in his heart, My lord tarrieth ; and shall
begin to beat his fellow-servants, and shall eat and drink
50 with the drunken ; the lord of that servant shall come in
a day when he expecteth not, and in an hour when he
51 knoweth not, and shall cut him asunder, and appoint his
portion with the hypocrites : there shall be the weeping
and gnashing of teeth.

25 1-13.   The parable of the Ten Virgins.   In St Matthew
only.

25   Then shall the kingdom of heaven be likened unto ten
virgins, which took their lamps, and went forth to meet
2 the bridegroom.   And five of them were foolish, and five
3 were wise.   For the foolish, when they took their lamps,
4 took no oil with them : but the wise took oil in their
5 vessels with their lamps.   Now while the bridegroom

----

1. Then. In the Last Day—the time just spoken of.   This
parable is another warning for the disciples of Christ ' to watch.'
Like the rest of the discourse it is primarily addressed to the
Apostles, and after them to the pastors of the Church, who are
posted as sentinels for the coming of Christ ; lastly, to all
Christians.   Whatever interpretation may be put on the lesser
incidents they must be subordinated to the lesson of the parable
—vigilance, and the reason for vigilance—the certainty of the
event, and the uncertainty as to the time of its occurrence.
lamps.   Better *torches*, R.V. *marg*.   **to meet the bridegroom.**
The usual Jewish custom was for the 'friends of the bridegroom'
to conduct the bride to her husband's home ; and when the
procession arrived, the bridegroom went forth to lead the bride
across the threshold.   The imagery of the parable, however,
implies that the bridegroom himself went to fetch his bride,
perhaps from a great distance, while a group of maidens awaited
his return ready to welcome him in Oriental fashion with lamps
and flambeaux.

3. foolish.   All watch for their Lord, but some only—'the
wise'—with true intensity and with due provision for the watch.
The foolish virgins have sufficient oil if the Lord come quickly ;
not sufficient for long and patient expectation.   It is a rebuke to
shallow religion that dies away when the excitement passes.
The oil seems to mean generally the spiritual life or preparedness
for the Lord's coming.

tarried, they all slumbered and slept. But at midnight 6
there is a cry, Behold, the bridegroom! Come ye forth
to meet him. Then all those virgins arose, and trimmed 7
their lamps. And the foolish said unto the wise, Give us 8
of your oil; for our lamps are going out. But the wise 9
answered, saying, Peradventure there will not be enough
for us and you: go ye rather to them that sell, and buy
for yourselves. And while they went away to buy, the 10
bridegroom came; and they that were ready went in with
him to the marriage feast: and the door was shut.
Afterward come also the other virgins, saying, Lord, 11
Lord, open to us. But he answered and said, Verily 12
I say unto you, I know you not. Watch therefore, for ye 13
know not the day nor the hour.

14–30. The parable of the Talents, in this Gospel only. The
parable of the Pounds, Luke xix. 12–27, is similar, but there
are important points of distinction; (1) in regard to the
occasions on which the two parables are given; (2) in the
special incidents of each. The lesson is still partly of
watchfulness, it is still in the first instance for the Apostles,
and mainly always for those who bear office in the Church.
But fresh thoughts enter into this parable: (1) There is
work to be done in the time of waiting: the watching must
not be idle or unemployed; (2) Even the least talented is
responsible.

---

5. they all slumbered and slept. Sleep represents the
ignorance as to the time of Christ's coming; it is not to be
interpreted of unwatchfulness, it is not a guilty or imprudent
sleep, as in the parable of the thief coming by night (ch. xxiv.
43).

7. trimmed. By addition of oil, and by clearing the fibres
with a needle.

8. are going out. This rendering is a great improvement
both in correctness and vividness on 'are gone out' of A.V.

9. Peradventure there will not be enough for us and you.
The bridal procession, in which there would be need of burning
torches, was still to be made. The wise cannot impart their oil:
—an incident necessary to the leading idea of the parable:—
nothing can make up for unreadiness at the last moment.

13. Watch therefore. Our Lord's explanation of the parable,
showing the true purport of it.

14 For *it is* as *when* a man, going into another country,
called his own servants, and delivered unto them his
15 goods. And unto one he gave five talents, to another
two, to another one; to each according to his several
16 ability; and he went on his journey. Straightway he
that received the five talents went and traded with them,
17 and made other five talents. In like manner he also that
18 *received* the two gained other two. But he that received
the one went away and digged in the earth, and hid his
19 lord's money. Now after a long time the lord of those
servants cometh, and maketh a reckoning with them.
20 And he that received the five talents came and brought
other five talents, saying, Lord, thou deliveredst unto me
21 five talents : lo, I have gained other five talents. His
lord said unto him, Well done, good and faithful servant :
thou hast been faithful over a few things, I will set thee
over many things : enter thou into the joy of thy lord.
22 And he also that *received* the two talents came and said,
Lord, thou deliveredst unto me two talents : lo, I have
23 gained other two talents. His lord said unto him, Well

---

14. delivered unto them his goods. Cp. Mark xiii. 34.
Christ in His absence gives to each a portion of His own
authority and of His own work on earth. A great deal of the
commerce of antiquity was managed by slaves, who were thus
often entrusted with responsible functions (cp. ch. xxiv. 45). In
this case they are expected to use their master's money in trade
or in cultivation of the soil, and to make as large an increase as
possible.

15. unto one he gave five talents. In the parable of the
Pounds or 'minæ' (Luke xix.), each subject receives one pound.
Here the truth is indicated that there is variety in the services
wrought for God in respect of dignity and of difficulty. More
will be required of the influential and enlightened than of the
ignorant and poor. **talents.** See ch. xviii. 24. It is from
this parable that the word 'talents' has passed into modern
languages in the sense of 'abilities,' or 'mental gifts.'

19. after a long time. Another hint that the second coming
of Christ would be long deferred.

21. the joy of thy lord. The life of happiness which thy
lord enjoys, and which he imparts to thee.

done, good and faithful servant ; thou hast been faithful over a few things, I will set thee over many things : enter thou into the joy of thy lord.   And he also that had 24 received the one talent came and said, Lord, I knew thee that thou art a hard man, reaping where thou didst not sow, and gathering where thou didst not scatter : and 25 I was afraid, and went away and hid thy talent in the earth : lo, thou hast thine own.   But his lord answered 26 and said unto him, Thou wicked and slothful servant, thou knewest that I reap where I sowed not, and gather where I did not scatter ; thou oughtest therefore to have 27 put my money to the bankers, and at my coming I should have received back mine own with interest.   Take ye 28 away therefore the talent from him, and give it unto him that hath the ten talents.   For unto every one that hath 29 shall be given, and he shall have abundance : but from him that hath not, even that which he hath shall be taken away.   And cast ye out the unprofitable servant into the 30 outer darkness : there shall be the weeping and gnashing of teeth.

31-46. The Day of Judgment.

But when the Son of man shall come in his glory, and 31 all the angels with him, then shall he sit on the throne of his glory : and before him shall be gathered all the 32

---

24.   gathering where thou didst not scatter, i.e. 'gathering into the garner from another's threshing-floor where thou hast not winnowed' (Meyer) ; so, 'exacting interest where thou hast invested no money.' The accusation was false, but the lord takes his slave at his word, 'thou oughtest *therefore*,' for that very reason.

27.   my money. It was not thine own.   **with interest**. This was the very least the slave could have done : to make money in this way required no personal exertion.

29.   The thought conveyed by this verse is true, even in worldly matters : talents not used pass away from their possessor : and the hard worker seems to gather to himself what is lost by the idle.

nations : and he shall separate them one from another, as
33 the shepherd separateth the sheep from the goats : and
he shall set the sheep on his right hand, but the goats on
34 the left.   Then shall the King say unto them on his
right hand, Come, ye blessed of my Father, inherit the
kingdom prepared for you from the foundation of the
35 world : for I was an hungred, and ye gave me meat : I
was thirsty, and ye gave me drink : I was a stranger, and
36 ye took me in ; naked, and ye clothed me : I was sick,
and ye visited me : I was in prison, and ye came unto
37 me.   Then shall the righteous answer him, saying, Lord,
when saw we thee an hungred, and fed thee ? or athirst,
38 and gave thee drink ? And when saw we thee a stranger,
39 and took thee in ? or naked, and clothed thee ? And when
40 saw we thee sick, or in prison, and came unto thee ? And
the King shall answer and say unto them, Verily I say
unto you, Inasmuch as ye did it unto one of these my
41 brethren, *even* these least, ye did it unto me.   Then shall

---

32. all the nations. Both Jews and Gentiles. The reference
is to a time when the distinction between Jew and Gentile will
have vanished.

34. The righteous as sons of the Father inherit of right the
Kingdom that has been prepared for *them*, whereas the dis-
inherited children pass into the fire of the ages, prepared not for
them but for the devil and his angels.

35, 36. There is a climax in this enumeration. The first three
are recognized duties, the last three are voluntary acts of self-
forgetting love.   Common humanity would move a man to
relieve his bitterest foe when perishing by hunger or by thirst
(see Rom. xii. 20).   Oriental custom required at least a bare
hospitality.   But to clothe the naked implies a liberal and loving
spirit, to visit the sick is an act of spontaneous self-sacrifice, to go
to the wretched outcasts in prison was perhaps an unheard-of act
of charity in those days.   The words of the Lord were long in
bearing fruit.

40. ye did it unto me. This unconscious personal service of
Christ may be contrasted with the conscious but unreal knowledge
of Christ assumed by false prophets ; see Luke xiii. 26.   Christ
identifies Himself with His Church, as in His words to Saul
(Acts ix. 4).

he say also unto them on the left hand, Depart from me,
ye cursed, into the eternal fire which. is prepared for the
devil and his angels : for I was an hungred, and ye gave 42
me no meat : I was thirsty, and ye gave me no drink : I 43
was a stranger, and ye took me not in ; naked, and ye
clothed me not ; sick, and in prison, and ye visited me
not. Then shall they also answer, saying, Lord, when 44
saw we thee an hungred, or athirst, or a stranger, or
naked, or sick, or in prison, and did not minister unto
thee? Then shall he answer them, saying, Verily I say 45
unto you, Inasmuch as ye did it not unto one of these
least, ye did it not unto me. And these shall go away in- 46
to eternal punishment: but the righteous into eternal life.

26. 1–5. The approach of the Passover. Jesus again foretells His Death. The Sanhedrin meet. Mark xiv. 1, 2;
Luke xxii. 1, 2. Cp. John xi. 55–57, where we read that
'the chief priests and the Pharisees had given commandment, that, if any man knew where he was, he should
shew it, that they might take him.' That Jesus should be
able for so many days to 'speak openly in the Temple,'
and show Himself to the people without fear of capture,
is a proof of the deep hold He had taken on the enthusiasm
and affection of His fellow-countrymen.

And it came to pass, when Jesus had finished all these **26**
words, he said unto his disciples, Ye know that after two 2
days the passover cometh, and the Son of man is delivered

---

44. unto thee. The position of the personal pronouns
throughout is emphatic.

45. Inasmuch as ye did it not. Men will be judged not
only for evil done, but for good left undone. In this view sins
are regarded as debts unpaid.

46. punishment. The Greek word means punishment which
corrects or reforms. The only other passage in the N.T. where
the word is used is 1 John iv. 18.

Wednesday, Nisan 12.

2. the passover commemorated the deliverance of Israel
from the Egyptian bondage. The ordinances of the first
Passover are narrated Exod. xii. 1–14, but some of those were
modified in later times. It was no longer necessary to choose
the lamb on the 10th of Nisan. The blood was sprinkled on

3 up to be crucified. Then were gathered together the
chief priests, and the elders of the people, unto the court
4 of the high priest, who was called Caiaphas; and they
took counsel together that they might take Jesus by
5 subtilty, and kill him. But they said, Not during the
feast, lest a tumult arise among the people.

> 6-13. The Feast in the house of Simon the Leper. Mark xiv.
> 3-9; John xii. 1-8. St John's narrative places this incident
> on the evening of the Sabbath—the last Sabbath spent by
> Jesus on earth—before the triumphal entry. St Matthew
> has here disregarded the strictly chronological order. A
> comparison with St Mark will show how accurately the
> words of Jesus are remembered; the rest of the incident is
> told in somewhat different language.

6 Now when Jesus was in Bethany, in the house of
7 Simon the leper, there came unto him a woman having

---

the altar, not on the door-post; those who partook of the
paschal meal no longer 'stood with loins girded, with shoes
on their feet, with staff in hand,' but reclined on couches, as at
an ordinary meal; it was no longer unlawful to leave the house
before morning (Exod. xii. 22).

3. **the chief priests, and the elders of the people** &c., i.e. the
Sanhedrin, the supreme council, of the Jewish people. It was
both a deliberative assembly and a court of justice. The president
or *Nasi* (prince) was generally, though not always, the high-priest.
The number of members was seventy-one. The powers of this
Court did not extend to the infliction of capital punishment; see
John xviii. 31. **Caiaphas.** Joseph Caiaphas, the son-in-law
of Annas, was appointed high-priest A.D. 26, and was deposed
A.D. 38. The high priesthood had long ceased to be held for
life and to descend from father to son; appointments were made
at the caprice of the Roman government. Annas, who had been
high-priest, was still regarded as such by popular opinion, which
did not recognize his deposition.

4. **by subtilty.** It was no longer possible (1) to entrap Him
by argument (xxii. 46); (2) to discredit Him with the Roman
government (xxii. 22); or (3) to take Him by force.

5. **during the feast.** Including the Passover and the seven
days of unleavened bread. **lest a tumult arise.** The great
danger at the time of the Passover, when the people, numbering
hundreds of thousands, filled the city and encamped in tents outside the walls like a vast army.

6. **the leper**, i.e. he had been a leper.

an alabaster cruse of exceeding precious ointment, and
she poured it upon his head, as he sat at meat. But 8
when the disciples saw it, they had indignation, saying,
To what purpose is this waste? For this *ointment* might 9
have been sold for much, and given to the poor. But 10
Jesus perceiving it said unto them, Why trouble ye the
woman? for she hath wrought a good work upon me.
For ye have the poor always with you; but me ye have 11
not always. For in that she poured this ointment upon 12
my body, she did it to prepare me for burial. Verily 13
I say unto you, Wheresoever this gospel shall be
preached in the whole world, that also which this woman
hath done shall be spoken of for a memorial of her.

14-16. The treachery of Judas. Mark xiv. 10, 11; Luke xxii.
3-6. St Mark, like St Matthew, connects the treachery of
Judas with the scene in Simon's house. His worldly hopes
fell altogether at the thought of 'burial.' It is a striking
juxtaposition: as Mary's is the highest deed of loving and
clear-sighted faith, Judas' is the darkest act of treacherous
and misguided hate.

Then one of the twelve, who was called Judas Iscariot, 14
went unto the chief priests, and said, What are ye willing 15
to give me, and I will deliver him unto you? And they
weighed unto him thirty pieces of silver. And from that 16
time he sought opportunity to deliver him *unto them*.

---

7. These *alabaster boxes* or *unguent-flasks* were usually made
of the Oriental or onyx alabaster, with long narrow necks, which
let the oil escape drop by drop, and could easily be broken
(Mark xiv. 3). But the shape and material varied.

8. **they had indignation.** 'There were some that had indignation' (Mark); 'But Judas Iscariot, one of his disciples,...saith'
(John).

10. **a good work.** The Lord passes a higher commendation
on this than on any other act recorded in the N.T.; it implied a
faith that enabled Mary to see, as no one else then did, the truth
of the Kingdom. She saw that Jesus was still a King, though
destined to die. The same thought—the certainty of the death
of Jesus—that estranged Judas made her devotion more intense.

15. **thirty pieces of silver,** *thirty silver shekels.* St Matthew
alone names the sum, which = 120 denarii. Thirty shekels was
the price of a slave (Ex. xxi. 32); a fact which gives force to our

17–19. Preparations for the Last Supper. Mark xiv. 12–16;
Luke xxii. 7–13. Nisan 13—from the sunset of Wednesday
to the sunset of Thursday—Jesus seems to have passed in
retirement ; no events are recorded.

17 Now on the first *day* of unleavened bread the disciples
came to Jesus, saying, Where wilt thou that we make
18 ready for thee to eat the passover ? And he said, Go into
the city to such a man, and say unto him, The Master
saith, My time is at hand ; I keep the passover at thy

Lord's words, ch. xx. 28, and to 'took upon him the form of a
servant,' Phil. ii. 7, 8.

Friday, Nisan 14.

17. Now on the first day &c. This was the 14th of Nisan,
which commenced after sunset on the 13th; it was also called
the preparation of the Passover. The feast of unleavened bread
followed the Passover, and lasted seven days, from the 15th to
the 21st of Nisan. Hence the two feasts are sometimes included
in the term 'Passover,' sometimes in that of 'unleavened bread.'
On the evening of 13th of Nisan every head of the family carefully searched for and collected by the light of a candle all the
leaven, which was kept and destroyed before midday on the 14th.
The offering of the lamb took place on the 14th at the evening
sacrifice, which on this day commenced at 1.30; or if the *preparation* fell on a Friday, at 12.30. The paschal meal was
celebrated after sunset on the 14th, i.e. strictly on the 15th of
Nisan. The events of the Passover are full of difficulty for the
harmonist. It is however almost certain that the 'Last Supper'
was not the paschal meal, but was partaken of on the 14th, that
is, after sunset on the 13th of Nisan. The order of events in the
'Passion' was as follows: When the 14th commenced, at sunset,
Jesus sent two disciples to prepare the feast for that evening,
instead of for the following evening. The supper succeeds,
which bears a paschal character, and follows the paschal ceremonial. Early in the morning of the 14th of Nisan the irregular
sitting of the Sanhedrin took place. Then followed the formal
sitting of the Sanhedrin, and the trial before Pilate, the 'remission' to Herod, and, finally, the Crucifixion. During the very
hours when our Great High-Priest was offering Himself as a
sacrifice for our sins upon the Cross, the Jewish people were
engaged in slaying thousands of lambs in view of the paschal
feast about to commence.

18. to such a man. *To a certain man* (one who is known,
but not named), with whom the arrangements had been pre-
viously made. He was doubtless a follower of Jesus. It was
usual for the inhabitants of Jerusalem to lend guest-chambers to

house with my disciples. And the disciples did as Jesus 19
appointed them ; and they made ready the passover.

20-30. **The Last Supper.** Mark xiv. 17–26; Luke xxii. 14–38.
In this deeply important parallel St Matthew and St Mark
are in close, almost identical, correspondence. In Luke the
dispute as to who should be the greatest is recorded, and the
warning to Peter related as happening before Jesus departed
for the Mount of Olives. St John omits the institution of the
Eucharist, but relates the washing of the disciples' feet by our
Lord, and has preserved the discourses of Jesus, chh. xiii.–
xvii. end. 1 Cor. xi. 23–26 ; where the institution of the
Eucharist is narrated nearly in St Luke's words.

Now when even was come, he was sitting at meat with 20
the twelve disciples ; and as they were eating, he said, 21
Verily I say unto you, that one of you shall betray me.

---

the strangers who came to the feast, and no other payment was
accepted save the skin of the paschal lamb.

20. he was sitting at meat with the twelve. The paschal
ceremonial, so far as it bears on the Gospel narrative, may be
described as follows : (a) The meal began with a cup of red
wine mixed with water : this is the *first* cup mentioned, Luke
xxii. 17. After this the guests washed their hands. (b) The
bitter herbs, symbolic of the bitter bondage in Egypt, were then
brought in together with unleavened cakes, and a sauce called
charoseth, made of fruits and vinegar, into which the unleavened
bread and bitter herbs were dipped. This explains, 'he it is, to
whom I shall give a *sop*,' John xiii. 26. (c) The *second* cup was
then mixed and blessed like the first. The father then explained
the meaning of the rite (Exod. xiii. 8). The first part of the
'*hallel*' (Psalms cxiii. and cxiv.) was then chanted by the
company. (d) After this the paschal lamb was placed before
the guests. This is called in a special sense 'the supper.' But
at the Last Supper there was no paschal lamb. Christ Himself
was our Passover 'sacrificed for us' (1 Cor. v. 7). He was there
being slain for us—His body was being given, His blood being
shed. At this point, when according to the ordinary ritual the
company partook of the paschal lamb, Jesus 'took bread and
blessed it, and he gave to the disciples' (*v.* 26). (e) The *third*
cup, or 'cup of blessing,' so called because a special blessing
was pronounced upon it, followed : 'after *supper* he took the
cup' (Luke). 'He took the cup *when he had supped*' (Paul).
This is the 'cup' named in *v.* 27. (f) After a *fourth* cup the
company chanted (see *v.* 30) the second part of the '*hallel*'
(Psalms cxv.—cxviii.).

22 And they were exceeding sorrowful, and began to say
23 unto him every one, Is it I, Lord? And he answered and
    said, He that dipped his hand with me in the dish, the
24 same shall betray me. The Son of man goeth, even as it
    is written of him : but woe unto that man through whom
    the Son of man is betrayed ! good were it for that man if
25 he had not been born. And Judas, which betrayed him,
    answered and said, Is it I, Rabbi? He saith unto him,
26 Thou hast said. And as they were eating, Jesus took
    bread, and blessed, and brake it ; and he gave to the
27 disciples, and said, Take, eat ; this is my body. And he
    took a cup, and gave thanks, and gave to them, saying,
28 Drink ye all of it ; for this is my blood of the covenant,
29 which is shed for many unto remission of sins. But I say
    unto you, I will not drink henceforth of this fruit of the
    vine, until that day when I drink it new with you in my
    Father's kingdom.

---

23. He that dipped his hand with me, i.e. in the *charoseth*,
see above, *v.* 20 (*b*).

25. Thou hast said. This is a formula of assent both in
Hebrew and Greek, and is still used in Palestine in that sense.
These words seem to have been spoken in a low voice inaudible
to the rest.

27. a cup. See note *v.* 20 (*e*).

28. this is my blood. The blood of the sacrifice was the
seal and assurance of the old covenant; so wine, which is the
blood of Christ once shed, is the seal of the new covenant. The
thought of shedding of blood would certainly connect itself with
the ratification of a covenant in the minds of the Apostles. From
a covenant ratified by the victim's blood (Gen. xv. 18) began the
divine and glorious history of the Jewish race. By sprinkling of
blood the covenant was confirmed in the wilderness : see Ex.
xxiv. 8, where the very expression occurs 'the blood of the
covenant'; and now a new covenant (cp. Jer. xxxi. 33) confirmed by the victim's blood is destined to be the starting-point
of a still more divine and glorious history. **shed,** i.e. *now
being shed*. The sacrifice has already begun.   **unto remission of sins** ; 'unto' here marks the intention, 'in order that
there may be remission of sins.' St Matthew alone records these
words in this connexion.

29. when I drink it new with you. The reference is to the

And when they had sung a hymn, they went out unto 30
the mount of Olives.

31-35. All shall be offended. Mark xiv. 27-31; Luke xxii.
    31-34. Cp. John xiii. 36-38 and xvi. 32.

Then saith Jesus unto them, All ye shall be offended in 31
me this night: for it is written, I will smite the shepherd,
and the sheep of the flock shall be scattered abroad.
But after I am raised up, I will go before you into Galilee. 32
But Peter answered and said unto him, If all shall be 33
offended in thee, I will never be offended. Jesus said 34
unto him, Verily I say unto thee, that this night, before
the cock crow, thou shalt deny me thrice. Peter saith 35
unto him, Even if I must die with thee, *yet* will I not deny
thee. Likewise also said all the disciples.

36-46. The Agony in the Garden of Gethsemane. Mark xiv.
    32-42; Luke xxii. 39-46; John xviii. 1. In St Luke's
    account verses 43, 44 are peculiar to his Gospel; but their
    genuineness is questioned. The use of the word 'agony' by
    the same Evangelist has given the title to this passage.

Then cometh Jesus with them unto a place called 36
Gethsemane, and saith unto his disciples, Sit ye here,
while I go yonder and pray. And he took with him 37
Peter and the two sons of Zebedee, and began to be

---

feast, which is a symbol of the glorified life, cp. Luke xxii. 30.
The new wine signifies the new higher existence (ch. ix. 17),
which Christ would share with His Saints. The expression may
also symbolize the Christian as distinguished from the Jewish
dispensation, and be referred specially to the celebration of the
Eucharist, in which Christ joins with the faithful in the feast of
the Kingdom of God on earth.

30. when they had sung a hymn. 'Having chanted' the
second part of the *hallel*. See note on *v.* 20 (*f*).

31. I will smite &c. Zech. xiii. 7. The context describes
the purification of Jerusalem in the last days—'in that day there
shall be a fountain opened to the house of David and to the
inhabitants of Jerusalem'—the discomfiture of the false prophets,
and the victory of Jehovah on the Mount of Olives.

36. Gethsemane = *the oil-press.*

37. Peter and the two sons of Zebedee. See ch. xvii. 1 and

C.   10

38 sorrowful and sore troubled. Then saith he unto them,
My soul is exceeding sorrowful, even unto death : abide
39 ye here, and watch with me. And he went forward
a little, and fell on his face, and prayed, saying, O my
Father, if it be possible, let this cup pass away from me :
40 nevertheless, not as I will, but as thou wilt. And he
cometh unto the disciples, and findeth them sleeping, and
saith unto Peter, What, could ye not watch with me one
41 hour? Watch and pray, that ye enter not into temptation :
42 the spirit indeed is willing, but the flesh is weak. Again
a second time he went away, and prayed, saying, O my
Father, if this cannot pass away, except I drink it, thy
43 will be done. And he came again and found them
44 sleeping, for their eyes were heavy. And he left them
again, and went away, and prayed a third time, saying
45 again the same words. Then cometh he to the disciples,
and saith unto them, Sleep on now, and take your rest :
behold, the hour is at hand, and the Son of man is
46 betrayed into the hands of sinners. Arise, let us be
going : behold, he is at hand that betrayeth me.

Mark v. 37. The Evangelist St John was thus a witness of
this scene ; hence, as we should expect, his narrative of the
arrest of Jesus is very full of particulars.   **sore troubled.** The
Greek word conveys the idea both of maddening grief, and of
weariness after toil.

38. watch with me. The Son of man in this dark hour asks
for human sympathy.

39. this cup. See note, ch. xx. 22. Were these words
overheard by the sons of Zebedee? Christ was probably praying
aloud, according to the usual custom. If so, the thought of their
ambition and of their Master's answer would surely recur to them
(ch. xx. 20–23).   **not as I will.** In the 'Agony,' as in the
Temptation, the Son submits Himself to His Father's will.

40. could ye not watch...? *had you not strength* to watch ?
This was an instance of failing to serve God with their strength
(Mark xii. 30).

41. the spirit indeed is willing. The touch of clemency
mingled with the rebuke is characteristic of the gentleness' of
Jesus.

45, 46. Sleep on...Arise. The sudden transition may be

47-56. The arrest of Jesus. St Mark xiv. 43-50; St Luke xxii. 47-53; St John xviii. 3-11.

And while he yet spake, lo, Judas, one of the twelve, 47 came, and with him a great multitude with swords and staves, from the chief priests and elders of the people. Now he that betrayed him gave them a sign, saying, 48 Whomsoever I shall kiss, that is he: take him. And 49 straightway he came to Jesus, and said, Hail, Rabbi; and kissed him. And Jesus said unto him, Friend, *do* that 50 for which thou art come. Then they came and laid hands on Jesus, and took him. And behold, one of them 51 that were with Jesus stretched out his hand, and drew his sword, and smote the servant of the high priest, and struck off his ear. Then saith Jesus unto him, Put up 52

---

explained by supposing that at that very moment Judas appeared, and the time for action had come. The short, quick sentences, especially as reported by St Mark, favour this suggestion.

47. a great multitude with swords and staves. By comparing the different accounts it appears that the body guided by Judas consisted of (1) a company of Roman soldiers; (2) a detachment of the Levitical temple-guard (Luke); (3) certain members of the Sanhedrin and Pharisees.

49. kissed him. Lit. *kissed him with fervour, or repeatedly.* Notwithstanding a long tradition it may be doubted whether Judas kissed our Lord on the face. At the present day the Armenian scholar kisses his master's *hand* with the utmost reverence.

50. do that for which thou art come. An important emendation of 'wherefore art thou come?' A.V. **laid hands on Jesus, and took him.** St John, who does not mention the kiss of Judas, sets the self-surrender of Jesus in a clear light: 'I told you that I am he: if therefore ye seek me, let these go their way.'

51. one of them. This was St Peter, named by St John, but not by the earlier Evangelists, probably from motives of prudence. **the servant.** Or, rather, *slave.* St John gives his name, Malchus. St Luke alone records the cure of Malchus.

52-54. These verses are peculiar to St Matthew; each Evangelist has recorded sayings unnoticed by the others. It is easy to understand that in these exciting moments each by-stander would perceive a part only of what was said or done.

again thy sword into its place : for all they that take the
53 sword shall perish with the sword. Or thinkest thou
that I cannot beseech my Father, and he shall even now
54 send me more than twelve legions of angels? How then
55 should the scriptures be fulfilled, that thus it must be? In
that hour said Jesus to the multitudes, Are ye come out
as against a robber with swords and staves to seize me?
I sat daily in the temple teaching, and ye took me not.
56 But all this is come to pass, that the scriptures of the
prophets might be fulfilled. Then all the disciples left
him, and fled.

57-68. Jesus is brought before Caiaphas. The first and in-
formal meeting of the Sanhedrin. St Mark xiv. 53-65;
St Luke xxii. 54 and 63-65. St Luke reports this first
irregular trial with less detail than the other synoptists, but
gives the account of the second *formal* sitting at greater
length.

57   And they that had taken Jesus led him away to *the
house of* Caiaphas the high priest, where the scribes and

52. they that take the sword, i.e. against rightful authority.
The truth of this saying was exemplified by the slaughter of
nearly a million and a half of Jews, who 'took the sword'
against Rome A.D. 67-70.
53. twelve legions. It is characteristic of this Gospel that
the authority and kingly majesty of Jesus should be suggested at
a moment when every hope seemed to have perished.
55. a robber. See note, ch. xxi. 13.
56. all this is come to pass &c. These are probably the words
of Christ, and not a reflection by the Evangelist (cp. Mark xiv.
49); if so, they were, for most of the disciples, their Master's last
words.   **Then.**   Closely connected with the preceding words.
If *this* was the fulfilment of prophecy, *their* interpretation was
indeed mistaken.   It was the death-blow to temporal hopes.
57. Jesus was first taken to the house of Annas, whose great
influence (he was still high-priest in the eyes of the people)
would make it necessary to have his sanction for the subsequent
measures.   The subjoined order of events is certainly not free
from difficulties, but is the most probable solution of the question:
(1) From the garden of Gethsemane Jesus was taken to Annas;
thence, after brief questioning (St John xviii. 19-23), (2) to
Caiaphas, in another part of the sacerdotal palace, where some

the elders were gathered together. But Peter followed 58
him afar off, unto the court of the high priest, and entered
in, and sat with the officers, to see the end. Now the 59
chief priests and the whole council sought false witness
against Jesus, that they might put him to death ; and 60
they found it not, though many false witnesses came.
But afterward came two, and said, This man said, I am 61
able to destroy the temple of God, and to build it in three
days. And the high priest stood up, and said unto him, 62
Answerest thou nothing? what is it which these witness
against thee? But Jesus held his peace. And the high 63
priest said unto him, I adjure thee by the living God, that
thou tell us whether thou be the Christ, the Son of God.
Jesus saith unto him, Thou hast said : nevertheless I say 64
unto you, Henceforth ye shall see the Son of man sitting
at the right hand of power, and coming on the clouds of
heaven. Then the high priest rent his garments, saying, 65
He hath spoken blasphemy : what further need have we
of witnesses? behold, now ye have heard the blasphemy :
what think ye? They answered and said, He is worthy of 66

---

members of the Sanhedrin had hastily met, and the *first* irregular
trial of Jesus took place at night; Matt. xxvi. 57–68; Mark xiv.
52–65; Luke xxii. 54 and 63–65. (3) Early in the morning a
second and formal trial was held by the Sanhedrin. This is
related by St Luke, ch. xxii. 66–71: and is mentioned by
St Matthew, ch. xxvii. 1; and in St Mark xv. 1. (4) The trial
before Pontius Pilate, consisting of two parts : (*a*) a preliminary
examination (for which there is a technical legal phrase in
St Luke xxiii. 14); (*b*) a final trial and sentence to death.
(5) The *remission* to Herod, recorded by St Luke only, xxiii.
7–11; between the two Roman trials, (*a*) and (*b*).

59. sought false witness. To *seek* witnesses at all was
against the spirit of the Law.

61. I am able to destroy &c. See John ii. 19. The words
of Jesus are misquoted, and a false construction is put on them.

64. Thou hast said. See note *v.* 25.

65. the high priest rent his garments. This act was
enjoined by the Rabbinical rules. When the charge of blasphemy
was proved 'the judges standing on their feet rend their garments,
and do not sew them up again.'

67 death. Then did they spit in his face and buffet him :
and some smote him with the palms of their hands,
68 saying, Prophesy unto us, thou Christ : who is he that
struck thee ?

> 69–75. The denial of Peter. St Mark xiv. 66–72 ; Luke xxii.
> 54–62 ; John xviii. 15–18, and 25–27. The accounts differ
> slightly, and exactly in such a way as the evidence of
> honest witnesses might be expected to differ in describing
> the minor details (which at the time would appear un-
> important) in a scene full of stir and momentous incidents.

69   Now Peter was sitting without in the court : and a
maid came unto him, saying, Thou also wast with Jesus
70 the Galilæan. But he denied before them all, saying,
71 I know not what thou sayest. And when he was gone
out into the porch, another *maid* saw him, and saith unto
them that were there, This man also was with Jesus the
72 Nazarene. And again he denied with an oath, I know
73 not the man. And after a little while they that stood by
came and said to Peter, Of a truth thou also art *one* of
74 them ; for thy speech bewrayeth thee. Then began he to
curse and to swear, I know not the man. And straight-
75 way the cock crew. And Peter remembered the word
which Jesus had said, Before the cock crow, thou shalt
deny me thrice. And he went out, and wept bitterly.

---

68. Prophesy unto us. Observe the coarse, popular idea of
prophecy breaking out, according to which prophecy is a
meaningless exhibition of miraculous power. A similar vein of
thought shows itself in the second temptation (ch. iv. 6).
69. in the court. In Oriental houses the street door opens
into an entrance hall or passage : this is the 'porch' of *v.* 71 ;
beyond this is a central court open to the sky and surrounded by
pillars. The reception rooms are usually on the ground-floor,
and are built round the central court. Probably the hall or
room in which Jesus was being tried opened upon the court.
Thus Jesus was able to look upon Peter.
73. bewrayeth. *manifests thee, is evidence against thee.*
Bewray is a strengthened form of the Anglo-Saxon *wrégan* to
accuse.

27 1.   The second and formal meeting of the Sanhedrin.
St Mark xv. 1; St Luke xxii. 66–71; not mentioned by
St John.

Now when morning was come, all the chief priests **27**
and the elders of the people took counsel against Jesus to
put him to death :

2.   The delivery to Pontius Pilate.   St Mark xv. 1; St Luke
xxiii. 1; St John xviii. 28; 'they lead Jesus therefore from
Caiaphas into the palace (or *Prætorium*): and it was
early.'

and they bound him, and led him away, and delivered 2
him up to Pilate the governor.

3–10.   The Remorse of Judas.   He returns the thirty shekels.
The use made of them.   Peculiar to St Matthew.

Then Judas, which betrayed him, when he saw that he 3
was condemned, repented himself, and brought back the
thirty pieces of silver to the chief priests and elders,
saying, I have sinned in that I betrayed innocent blood. 4
But they said, What is that to us? see thou *to it*.   And 5
he cast down the pieces of silver into the sanctuary, and
departed; and he went away and hanged himself.   And 6

---

2.   Pontius Pilatus was the governor, or more accurately the
Procurator, of Judæa, which after the banishment of Archelaus
(see ch. ii. 22) had been placed under the direct government of
Rome, and attached as a dependency to Syria.   Pilate filled this
office during the last ten years of the reign of Tiberius, to whom
as Procurator in an imperial province he was directly responsible.
The wish of the Sanhedrin in delivering Jesus to Pilate was to
have their sentence confirmed without enquiry, see ch. xxvi. 66.
3.   **when he saw that he was condemned.**   It has been
argued from these words that Judas had not expected this result
of his treachery.   He had hoped that Jesus would by a mighty
manifestation of His divine power usher in at once the Kingdom
whose coming was too long delayed.   The whole tenour of the
narrative, however, contradicts such an inference.
5.   **into the sanctuary,** or *holy place*, which only the priests
could enter.   **went away and hanged himself.**   The account
given in Acts i. 18 of the end of Judas differs in some particulars
from the account given here.   A full knowledge of the facts
would probably enable us to reconcile the two statements.

the chief priests took the pieces of silver, and said, It is
not lawful to put them into the treasury, since it is the
7 price of blood. And they took counsel, and bought with
8 them the potter's field, to bury strangers in. Wherefore
that field was called, The field of blood, unto this day.
9 Then was fulfilled that which was spoken by Jeremiah
the prophet, saying, And they took the thirty pieces of
silver, the price of him that was priced, whom *certain* of
10 the children of Israel did price; and they gave them for
the potter's field, as the Lord appointed me.

> 11–26. The trial before Pontius Pilate. St Mark xv. 2–15;
> St Luke xxiii. 2–5 and 13–24; St John xviii. 29–xix. 16.
> St Luke states the threefold charge most clearly: 'We found
> this [fellow] (1) perverting our nation; (2) and forbidding to
> give tribute to Cæsar; (3) saying that He Himself is Christ
> a King.' Pilate, true to the Roman sense of justice, refused
> merely to confirm the sentence of the Sanhedrin. He
> asked, 'What accusation bring ye against this man?' (John
> xviii. 29), being determined to try the case. This accusation
> amounted to a charge of treason—the greatest crime known
> to Roman law. Of the three points of accusation, (2) was
> utterly false; (1) and (3) though *in a sense* true, were not
> true in the sense intended. The answer or defence of
> Jesus is that He is a King, but that His 'kingdom is not
> of this world,' therefore (it is inferred) the 'perversion of
> the people' was not a rebellion that threatened the Roman
> Government; see note *v.* 11. The defence was complete,
> as Pilate admits: 'I find no fault in him.'

11 Now Jesus stood before the governor: and the governor asked him, saying, Art thou the King of the Jews?
12 And Jesus said unto him, Thou sayest. And when
he was accused by the chief priests and elders, he

---

7. **the potter's field** &c. Tradition places *Aceldama* (Acts i.
19) in the valley of Hinnom, south of Jerusalem.

9. **spoken by Jeremiah the prophet.** The citation is from
Zech. xi. 12. For reasons to explain the ascription of the words
to Zechariah rather than to Jeremiah see *Cambridge Greek
Testament ad loc.*

11. **Art thou the King of the Jews?** The answer of
Jesus to this question, and His explanation to Pilate of the
Kingdom of God, are given at length, John xviii. 33–37.

answered nothing.   Then saith Pilate unto him, Hearest 13
thou not how many things they witness against thee?
And he gave him no answer, not even to one word: 14
insomuch that the governor marvelled greatly.   Now at 15
the feast the governor was wont to release unto the
multitude one prisoner, whom they would.   And they had 16
then a notable prisoner, called Barabbas.   When therefore 17
they were gathered together, Pilate said unto them,
Whom will ye that I release unto you?   Barabbas, or
Jesus which is called Christ?   For he knew that for envy 18
they had delivered him up.   And while he was sitting on 19
the judgement-seat, his wife sent unto him, saying, Have
thou nothing to do with that righteous man: for I have
suffered many things this day in a dream because of him.
Now the chief priests and the elders persuaded the 20
multitudes that they should ask for Barabbas, and destroy
Jesus.   But the governor answered and said unto them, 21

---

15. to release.   The origin of this custom is quite unknown:
St Mark says, 'as he was wont to do unto them,' as if the custom
originated with Pilate; St John has, 'Ye have a custom.'
(The words, Luke xxiii. 17, A.V., 'of necessity he must release'
are rejected in R.V.)   The release of prisoners was not unusual
at certain high festivals at Athens and Rome.

17. When therefore they were gathered together.   In accordance, probably, with the custom named *v.* 15, an appeal was made
to the *people*, not to the Sanhedrin.   Pilate was sitting on the
tribunal to ascertain the popular decision; at this point he was
interrupted by his wife's messengers, and while he was engaged
with them, the chief priests employed themselves in persuading
the people to demand Barabbas rather than Jesus.

19. the judgement-seat, or *tribunal,* was generally a raised
platform in the Basilica or court where the judges sat: here a
portable tribunal, from which the sentence was pronounced:
it was placed on a tessellated pavement called Gabbatha
(John xix. 13).

his wife.   Her name was Claudia Procula: tradition states
that she was a proselyte of the gate, which is by no means
unlikely, as many of the Jewish proselytes were women.
suffered many things.   Not 'suffered many things' in the
sense of suffering pain, but 'experienced many sensations,' i.e.
'*felt much.*'

Whether of the twain will ye that I release unto you?
22 And they said, Barabbas. Pilate saith unto them, What
then shall I do unto Jesus which is called Christ? They
23 all say, Let him be crucified. And he said, Why, what
evil hath he done? But they cried out exceedingly,
24 saying, Let him be crucified. So when Pilate saw that
he prevailed nothing, but rather that a tumult was arising,
he took water, and washed his hands before the multitude, saying, I am innocent of the blood of this righteous
25 man : see ye *to it*. And all the people answered and
26 said, His blood *be* on us, and on our children. Then
released he unto them Barabbas : but Jesus he scourged
and delivered to be crucified.

27–30. Jesus is mocked by the Roman soldiers. Mark xv. 16–
19 ; John xix. 1–3. St Luke; who records the mockery of

---

21. Whether of the twain &c. Once more the question
is put to the people (see *v.* 17). His wife's message had made
Pilate anxious to acquit Jesus. But the very form of the question
implied condemnation. Jesus was classed with Barabbas as a
condemned prisoner.

23. they cried out exceedingly, saying, Let him be crucified.
There is no further question even of a show of legality or justice :
the traditional clemency is quite forgotten ; the fanatical crowd,
pressing round the doors of the Prætorium, which they cannot
enter, join with excited gesticulations in one loud and furious cry
for the blood of Jesus.

24. when Pilate saw &c. St Luke relates a further attempt
on Pilate's part to release Jesus, 'I will therefore chastise him and
release him' (Luke xxiii. 22). Will not the cruel torture of a
Roman scourging melt their hearts? St John, at still greater
length, narrates the struggle in Pilate's mind between his sense
of justice and his respect for Jesus on the one hand, and on the
other his double fear of the Jews and of Cæsar.

25. His blood be on us. Peculiar to Matthew. St Peter
finds as the sole excuse for his fellow-countrymen, 'I wot
that in ignorance ye did it, as did also your rulers' (Acts iii.
17).

26. scourged. Scourging usually preceded crucifixion. It
was in itself a cruel and barbarous torture, under which the
victim often perished.

Herod's soldiers, makes no mention of these insults on the part of the Roman guard.

Then the soldiers of the governor took Jesus into the 27 palace, and gathered unto him the whole band. And 28 they stripped him, and put on him a scarlet robe. And 29 they plaited a crown of thorns and put it upon his head, and a reed in his right hand ; and they kneeled down before him, and mocked him, saying, Hail, King of the Jews ! And they spat upon him, and took the reed and 30 smote him on the head.

31, 32. Jesus is led to Crucifixion. Mark xv. 20, 21; Luke xxiii. 26–32 ; John xix. 16, 17. St Luke has several particulars of what happened on the way to Golgotha, omitted in the other Gospels. The great company of people and of women who followed Him ; the touching address of Jesus to the women; the last warning of the coming sorrows; the leading of two malefactors with Him.

And when they had mocked him, they took off from him 31 the robe, and put on him his garments, and led him away to crucify him.

And as they came out, they found a man of Cyrene, 32 Simon by name : him they compelled to go *with them*, that he might bear his cross.

---

27. the palace, or '*prætorium*' (Mark), the official residence of the governor, in which there would be a court of justice.
28. a scarlet robe. A soldier's scarf ; it was generally worn by superior officers, but its use was not confined to them. This may have been a worn-out scarf belonging to Pilate ; it is different from the 'gorgeous apparel' (Luke xxiii. 11) which Herod's soldiers put on Jesus.
32. a man of Cyrene, Simon by name. (1) 'coming from the country ' (Mark and Luke), (2) the father of Alexander and Rufus (Mark). Nothing further is known of Simon. But there is perhaps a reference to his son Rufus in Rom. xvi. 13. For Cyrene see Acts vi. 9, xi. 20, and xiii. 1. **compelled.** See note ch. v. 41, where the same word is used, and the custom referred to of which this is an instance. If, as was probable, Simon became a Christian, it would be his pride to have been ' pressed into the service' of the Great King.

33-50. The Crucifixion and Death of Jesus. Mark xv. 22-37;
Luke xxiii. 33-46; John xix. 18-30. St Mark's account
differs little from St Matthew's. St Luke names the
mockery of the soldiers and the words of the robbers
to one another and to Jesus. Three of the sayings on
the Cross are related by St Luke only: 'Father, forgive
them; for they know not what they do';—'Verily I say
unto thee, To-day shalt thou be with me in Paradise';—
'Father, into thy hands I commend my spirit.' Among
other particulars recorded by St John alone are the attempt
to alter the superscription—the commendation of His mother
to John—the breaking of the malefactors' legs—the piercing
of Jesus—three sayings from the Cross: 'Woman, behold
thy son!' and to the disciple, 'Behold thy mother!'—'I
thirst'—'It is finished.' St Matthew and St Mark alone
record the cry of loneliness: 'Eli, Eli, lama sabachthani?'

33 And when they were come unto a place called Golgotha,
34 that is to say, The place of a skull, they gave him wine to
drink mingled with gall: and when he had tasted it, he
35 would not drink. And when they had crucified him, they
36 parted his garments among them, casting lots: and they
37 sat and watched him there. And they set up over his

---

33. Golgotha. The site of Golgotha is not known for
certain; it was outside the walls, but 'nigh to the city' (John
xix. 20), probably near the public road where people passed by
(*v.* 39); it contained a garden (John xix. 41). The name, which
='place of a skull,' is generally thought to be derived from the
shape and appearance of the hillock or mound on which the
crosses were reared. A green hill outside the Damascus gate
answers this description, and for this and other stronger reasons
is by many authorities identified with Golgotha. Pictures often
mislead by representing the Crucifixion as taking place on a lofty
hill at a considerable distance from the city.

34. wine. 'Wine mingled with myrrh' (Mark). This was
the *sour wine*, or *posca*, ordinarily drunk by the Roman soldiers,
mingled with myrrh, and given as a stupefying draught to deaden
the sense of pain.

35. parted his garments. St John describes the division
more accurately; they divided His outer garments, but cast
lots for the seamless tunic.

36. watched him. Fearing lest a rescue should be attempted
by the friends of Jesus.

head his accusation written, THIS IS JESUS THE KING OF
THE JEWS.   Then are there crucified with him two 38
robbers, one on the right hand, and one on the left.   And 39
they that passed by railed on him, wagging their heads,
and saying, Thou that destroyest the temple, and buildest 40
it in three days, save thyself: if thou art the Son of God,
come down from the cross.   In like manner also the 41
chief priests mocking *him*, with the scribes and elders,
said, He saved others ; himself he cannot save.   He is 42
the King of Israel ; let him now come down from the
cross, and we will believe on him.   He trusteth on God ; 43
let him deliver him now, if he desireth him : for he said,
I am the Son of God.   And the robbers also that were 44
crucified with him cast upon him the same reproach.

---

37. his accusation.   It was the Roman custom to place on
the cross over the criminal's head a *titulus*, or placard, stating
the crime for which he suffered.   St John records Pilate's
refusal to alter the inscription, and mentions that the title
was written in Hebrew and Greek and Latin.

38. two robbers ; in all probability partners in the crime of
Barabbas.   The mountain robbers, or banditti, were always
ready to take part in such desperate risings against the Roman
power.   In the eyes of the Jews they would be patriots.

39.   See Ps. xxii. 7.   This was not a Psalm of David, but
was probably composed by one of the exiles during the Babylonish Captivity.

40. Thou that destroyest &c.   This is the mockery of the
Jewish populace, who have caught up the charges brought
against Jesus before the Sanhedrin.   The taunts of the soldiers
are named by St Luke alone: 'If thou art the King of the Jews,
save thyself' (xxiii. 37).

42. He saved others.   These words in the original would
recall the 'hosannas' in the Temple which had enraged the chief
priests ; see note, ch. xxi. 9.   They also connect themselves with
the name of Jesus.

43. He trusteth on God.   See Ps. xxii. 8.   The chief priests
unconsciously apply to the true Messiah the very words of a
Messianic psalm.

44. the robbers also &c.   They would naturally catch at the
thought that the deliverer failed to give deliverance.   St Luke
alone relates that 'one of the malefactors which were hanged
railed on him...the other answered,...rebuking him.'   It is by no

45 Now from the sixth hour there was darkness over all
46 the land until the ninth hour. And about the ninth hour
Jesus cried with a loud voice, saying, Eli, Eli, lama
sabachthani? that is, My God, my God, why hast thou
47 forsaken me? And some of them that stood there, when
48 they heard it, said, This man calleth Elijah. And
straightway one of them ran, and took a sponge, and
filled it with vinegar, and put it on a reed, and gave him
49 to drink. And the rest said, Let be; let us see whether
50 Elijah cometh to save him. And Jesus cried again with
a loud voice, and yielded up his spirit.

51-56. Events that followed the Crucifixion. (1) The veil of
the Temple rent; (2) the earthquake; (3) the saints arise;
(4) the centurion at the Cross; (5) the watching of the
women. Of these, (2) and (3) are peculiar to St Matthew.
Mark xv. 38-41; Luke xxiii. 45, 47-49, where the grief of
the spectators is an additional fact. St John omits these

means impossible that the penitent robber may have seen and
heard Jesus in Galilee.

45. from the sixth hour. From 12 to 3 o'clock in the after-
noon, the hours of the Paschal sacrifice. **there was darkness
over all the land.** Not the darkness of an eclipse, for it was
the time of the Paschal full moon, but a miraculous darkness
symbolic of that solemn hour, and veiling the agonies of the
Son of man, when human soul and body alike were enduring
the extremity of anguish and suffering for sin.

46. Eli, Eli &c. Ps. xxii. 1. This was probably the fourth
word from the Cross; the fifth, 'I thirst' (John); the sixth, 'It
is finished' (John); the seventh, 'Father, into thy hands I commend my spirit' (Luke). It is thought by some that after these
words the darkness, which had lasted to the ninth hour, rolled
away; others think that it lasted till the death of Jesus.

47. calleth Elijah. This was probably spoken in pure
mockery, not in a real belief that Jesus expected the personal
reappearance of Elijah.

48. took a sponge &c. The soldiers' sour wine (*posca*), the
reed, or hyssop stalk (John), and the sponge, were kept in
readiness to quench the sufferers' thirst.

50. cried again with a loud voice. Perhaps an inarticulate
cry is meant, or perhaps a sixth word from the Cross, 'It is
finished' (John xix. 30).

incidents, but records the breaking of the malefactors' legs and the piercing of Jesus' side.

And behold, the veil of the temple was rent in twain from 51 the top to the bottom ; and the earth did quake ; and the rocks were rent ; and the tombs were opened ; and many 52 bodies of the saints that had fallen asleep were raised ; and coming forth out of the tombs after his resurrection 53 they entered into the holy city and appeared unto many. Now the centurion, and they that were with him watching 54 Jesus, when they saw the earthquake, and the things that were done, feared exceedingly, saying, Truly this was the Son of God. And many women were there beholding 55 from afar, which had followed Jesus from Galilee, minis- tering unto him : among whom was Mary Magdalene, 56 and Mary the mother of James and Joses, and the mother of the sons of Zebedee.

---

51. the veil of the temple. The veil meant is that which separated the holy of holies from the holy place. The rending of the veil signifies that henceforth there is free access for man to God the Father through Jesus Christ. See Heb. x. 19, 20.

54. the centurion. The centurion in command of the guard of four soldiers who watched the execution. As the Roman centurions were not chosen so much for impetuous courage as for judgment, firmness and presence of mind, there were doubtless many noble and thoughtful characters among them.

55. ministering unto him. The beginning of the ministry of women—the female diaconate—in the Christian Church.

56. Mary Magdalene. Mentioned here for the first time by St Matthew. She was probably named from Magdala (*Mejdel*) on the Lake of Gennesaret. She had been a victim of demoniacal possession, but was cured by Jesus (Luke viii. 2), and then joined the company of faithful women who followed Him with the Twelve. Mary Magdalene is named by St John as standing by the cross of Jesus, together with 'his mother, and his mother's sister, Mary the wife of Clopas' (xix. 25). With these she watched the entombment of the Lord, and, after the Sabbath rest, early in the morning she was present at the sepulchre with sweet spices to anoint Him.

Mary the mother of James and Joses. Perhaps the same Mary who was the wife of Cleopas, Clopas, or Alphæus (different forms of one name), mentioned John xix. 25. If so, according

57-66. The Entombment. Mark xv. 42-47; Luke xxiii. 50-56; John xix. 38-42. *Vv.* 62-66 are peculiar to St Matthew. St Mark notes the wonder of Pilate that Jesus was already dead, and the evidence of the centurion to the fact. St John mentions the co-operation of Nicodemus—like Joseph, a member of the Sanhedrin, who 'consented not to the deed of them'—who brought 'a mixture of myrrh and aloes, about a hundred pound weight.'

57 And when even was come, there came a rich man from Arimathæa, named Joseph, who also himself was 58 Jesus' disciple : this man went to Pilate, and asked for the body of Jesus. Then Pilate commanded it to be 59 given up. And Joseph took the body, and wrapped it in 60 a clean linen cloth, and laid it in his own new tomb, which he had hewn out in the rock : and he rolled a great

---

to *one* interpretation of the passage in John, the sister of the Blessed Virgin.   **the mother of the sons of Zebedee.**   Salome. See ch. xx. 20.

57.   Arimathæa is generally identified with Ramathaim-zophim, on Mount Ephraim, the birth-place of Samuel (1 Sam. i. 1), the site of which is undetermined.   **Joseph.**   From the other two Synoptic Gospels we learn that he was 'an honourable (Mark) councillor (Mark and Luke),' i.e. a member of the Sanhedrin. Like Nicodemus, he was a secret disciple of Jesus, and must undoubtedly have absented himself from the meetings of the Sanhedrin when Jesus was condemned.   He 'had not consented to their counsel and deed' (Luke).

58.   **commanded it to be given up.**   After having ascertained from the centurion that Jesus was dead.   Usually those who suffered crucifixion lingered for days upon the cross.   By Roman law the corpse of a crucified person was not buried except by express permission of the emperor.   A concession was made in favour of the Jews, whose law did not suffer a man to hang all night upon a tree.

60.   **new tomb**, 'new,' in the sense of not having been used. St John mentions that the tomb was 'in a garden in the place where he was crucified' (xix. 41).   It was probably hewn out of the face of the rock near the ground (John xx. 11), and the body of Jesus would lie horizontally in it.   This was the first instance and a signal one of the power of the Cross of Christ to inspire enthusiasm and courage at the darkest hour.   Up to this time Joseph had been a secret disciple, now he braves everything for the *dead* Christ.

stone to the door of the tomb, and departed. And Mary 61
Magdalene was there, and the other Mary, sitting over
against the sepulchre.

Now on the morrow, which is *the day* after the 62
Preparation, the chief priests and the Pharisees were
gathered together unto Pilate, saying, Sir, we remember 63
that that deceiver said, while he was yet alive, After three
days I rise again. Command therefore that the sepulchre 64
be made sure until the third day, lest haply his disciples
come and steal him away, and say unto the people, He is
risen from the dead: and the last error will be worse than
the first. Pilate said unto them, Ye have a guard: go 65
your way, make it *as* sure as ye can. So they went, and 66
made the sepulchre sure, sealing the stone, the guard
being with them.

28 1–8. The Resurrection. Mark xvi. 1–8; Luke xxiv. 1–12;
John xx. 1–18. From a comparison of the different accounts
we gather that the order of events was as follows: First
Mary Magdalene and the other Mary, having come early to
the tomb, were addressed by the Angel and saw the empty
sepulchre; they hasten to inform Peter and the other disciples;
Peter and John visit the tomb and depart; Mary Magdalene,

---

61. the other Mary. See *v.* 56.
62. on the morrow. It was after sunset on Nisan 14. The
preparation was over, the Sabbath and the Paschal feast had
commenced. This explanation of the somewhat unusual phrase
accords with the view already taken of the Last Supper and the
Passover. While Christ's enemies were busy this Sabbath-day,
His friends rested according to the commandment (Luke xxiii. 56).
63. that deceiver said &c. It appears from this that the
priests and Pharisees understood the true import of Christ's
words, 'Destroy this temple, and after three days I will raise it
up,' which they wilfully misinterpreted to the people.
65. Ye have a guard. The meaning is either (1) that Pilate
refuses the request; 'Ye have a guard of your own'—(a) the
Levitical temple guard, or more probably (b) a small body of
soldiers whom Pilate may have already placed at their disposal—
or (2) he grants it curtly and angrily, 'Take a watch; begone.'
66. sealing the stone. 'The sealing was by means of a
cord or string passing across the stone at the mouth of the
sepulchre and fastened at either end to the rock by sealing clay.'

left alone, beholds her Lord, whom at first she does not recognize; soon afterwards the Lord appears a second time to Mary Magdalene, now in the company of other women.

28 Now late on the sabbath day, as it began to dawn toward the first *day* of the week, came Mary Magdalene 2 and the other Mary to see the sepulchre. And behold, there was a great earthquake ; for an angel of the Lord descended from heaven, and came and rolled away the 3 stone, and sat upon it. His appearance was as lightning, 4 and his raiment white as snow : and for fear of him the 5 watchers did quake, and became as dead men. And the angel answered and said unto the women, Fear not ye : for I know that ye seek Jesus, which hath been crucified. 6 He is not here ; for he is risen, even as he said. Come, 7 see the place where the Lord lay. And go quickly, and tell his disciples, He is risen from the dead ; and lo, he goeth before you into Galilee; there shall ye see him : lo, 8 I have told you. And they departed quickly from the tomb with fear and great joy, and ran to bring his disciples word.

9, 10. The appearance of Jesus to Mary Magdalene and the other Mary. Recorded by St Matthew only.

9 And behold, Jesus met them, saying, All hail. And they came and took hold of his feet, and worshipped him. 10 Then saith Jesus unto them, Fear not : go tell my brethren that they depart into Galilee, and there shall they see me.

---

1. **to see the sepulchre.** Both St Mark and St Luke mention that they brought spices and ointments.

3. **His appearance,** not the thing itself but the thing as beholden (Trench, *N. T. Syn.* 2nd series, p. 93).

6. **see the place where the Lord lay.** In order that they might be convinced of the fact.

9, 10. Jesus had already appeared to Mary Magdalene *alone*. We must suppose that she was now joined by the other Mary, and perhaps by Salome, Joanna, and others; and while these were going to announce the great news to the rest of the disciples

11–15. **The** Roman guards are bribed. This important testimony is given by St Matthew only.

Now while they were going, behold, some of the 11 guard came into the city, and told unto the chief priests all the things that were come to pass. And when they 12 were assembled with the elders, and had taken counsel, they gave large money unto the soldiers, saying, Say ye, 13 His disciples came by night, and stole him away while we slept. And if this come to the governor's ears, we will 14 persuade him, and rid you of care. So they took the 15 money, and did as they were taught: and this saying was spread abroad among the Jews, *and continueth* until this day.

16, 17. Jesus appears to the Eleven in Galilee. Peculiar to St Matthew.

But the eleven disciples went into Galilee, unto the 16

[Peter and John already knew] the Lord Jesus met them. The following is a list of the different recorded appearances of Jesus during the forty days :—(1) To Mary Magdalene alone (John xx. 14 foll.; Mark xvi. 9). (2) To Mary Magdalene, the other Mary, and perhaps other women (Matthew xxviii. 9, 10). (3) To Peter (Luke xxiv. 34; 1 Cor. xv. 5). (4) To Cleopas and another on the way to Emmaus (Luke xxiv. 13–35). (5) To the Apostles, in the absence of Thomas, at Jerusalem (Mark xvi. 14; Luke xxiv. 36; John xx. 19). (6) To the eleven Apostles at Jerusalem (John xx. 26). (7) To seven disciples at the Sea of Tiberias (John xxi. 1–24). (8) To the Eleven on the highland of Galilee (Matthew xxviii. 16). (9) To five hundred brethren at once—possibly the same appearance as (8) (1 Cor. xv. 6). (10) To James, the Lord's brother (1 Cor. xv. 7). (11) To the Eleven in the neighbourhood of the Holy City (Mark xvi. 19, 20; Luke xxiv. 50; Acts i. 3–12; 1 Cor. xv. 7).

9. All hail. The Greek salutation, both on meeting and on parting. **took hold of his feet.** The immemorial usage in the East in obeisance to a sovereign prince. In the interesting clay cylinder of Cyrus he says of the subject kings: 'they brought me their full tribute and kissed my feet.'

12. large money. Lit. *many pieces of silver*, a *largess*.

13. while we slept. The penalty for which would be death.

14. persuade (by bribes). **rid you of care,** i.e. free you from fear of punishment.

17 mountain where Jesus had appointed them. And when they saw him, they worshipped *him* : but some doubted.

18–20. The Last Charge to the Apostles.

18 And Jesus came to them and spake unto them, saying, All authority hath been given unto me in heaven and on
19 earth. Go ye therefore, and make disciples of all the nations, baptizing them into the name of the Father
20 and of the Son and of the Holy Ghost : teaching them to observe all things whatsoever I commanded you : and lo, I am with you alway, even unto the end of the world.

---

16. the mountain. Perhaps the highland behind Tell Hûm or Capernaum, the scene of their earliest intercourse with Christ, and the very spot where the New Law was first proclaimed. There the brethren, possibly five hundred in number [see *vv.* 9, 10 (8) (9)], besides the Eleven, awaited the coming of the Great Shepherd (*v.* 7).

18. hath been given. Strictly *was given* from eternity. These words, in which the infallible King Himself announces His eternal possession of the Kingdom, St Matthew, who is essentially the historian of the Kingdom, alone records.

19. make disciples of: cp. Acts xiv. 21, and see ch. xiii. 52, xxvii. 57, where the same word is used. **into the name.** Jewish proselytes were baptized into the name of the Father; Jesus adds the name of the Son and of the Holy Ghost. In the instances of baptism recorded in the Acts, ii. 38, viii. 16, x. 48, xix. 5, the name of Jesus Christ (or the Lord Jesus) alone occurs in the baptismal formula, but the promise of the Holy Ghost is given (ii. 38), or the gift of the Holy Ghost follows the rite (viii. 17, xix. 6), or precedes it (x. 44, 47).

20. with you alway. The Lord Jesus had already taught His disciples during the forty days how He could be present with them and yet be unseen by them. They could then the more easily believe this promise. **unto the end of the world.** See note ch. xiii. 39.

INDEX TO NOTES.

For EU product safety concerns, contact us at Calle de José Abascal, 56–1°, 28003 Madrid, Spain or eugpsr@cambridge.org.

www.ingramcontent.com/pod-product-compliance
Ingram Content Group UK Ltd.
Pitfield, Milton Keynes, MK11 3LW, UK
UKHW020310140625
459647UK00018B/1819